True to
Her Nature

THE BOOK GALLERY WEST, INC.
Buy - Sell - Trade
4121 N.W. 16th Blvd.
Gainesville, FL 32605
352-371-1234

True to Her Nature

CHANGING ADVICE TO AMERICAN WOMEN

MAXINE L. MARGOLIS

University of Florida

WAVELAND
PRESS, INC.

Prospect Heights, Illinois

For information about this book, write or call:
Waveland Press, Inc.
P.O. Box 400
Prospect Heights, Illinois 60070
(847) 634-0081

Cover Painting: *True to Her Nature*, by Sharon McGinley. Collection of M. L. Margolis and J. T. Milanich.

Printed in the United States of America

7 6 5 4 3 2 1

For Nara
With much love and great admiration
Mamãe Coruja

CONTENTS

PREFACE AND ACKNOWLEDGEMENTS

This book had its inception as an updated edition of *Mothers and Such: Views of American Women and Why They Changed* (University of California Press), a book published more than fifteen years ago, that went out of print in 1998. Sometime after Waveland Press agreed to publish a new, revised edition, I decided much more was needed than my original plans for a second edition had called for: simply a brief updating of women's employment patterns and a survey of recent advice to American women on good mothering and good housekeeping.

Over the intervening years my writing had improved in crispness and clarity and I found a lot of awkard academese and needless stylistic wordiness in the original. Even though it was published as a trade book meant for a general audience, I now marveled at its redundancy and theoretical thickets. In the end I wound up rewriting the entire book, eliminating repetitive examples of prescriptive literature and highlighting and expanding the analysis of the historical contexts in which the advice was offered. I also provide new employment figures and updated advice as planned.

With so many academics gorging on excess verbiage, publishing pieces that only a select group of fellow academics could hope to understand, I sought to do otherwise. Clear language and clear analysis were my goals and the current volume is the result.

Some well deserved thanks are in order for the help I received. My son-in-law Nicola Cetorelli and his colleague Dan Aaronson, economists at the Federal Reserve Bank in Chicago, supplied the Current Population Survey data on women's occupational distribution. As always, my husband Jerry Milanich saw to my care and feeding during the writing of this book and helped me in innumerable ways preparing it for publication. And I thank my daughter, Nara Milanich, to whom this volume is so lovingly dedicated, for her very insightful comments, and for the delight of being her mother!

M.L.M.
Gainesville, Florida
February 2000

THE ANTHROPOLOGICAL
PERSPECTIVE

Genuine research seeks explanations, not just examples, its goal is understanding, not reassurance.
                    Robert Asahina, "Social Science Fiction," 1981

This is a book about women in the United States written by an anthropologist. Why an anthropologist? Given the outpouring of scholarship on American women over the past three decades, why would an anthropologist, often
erroneously stereotyped as a person interested only in "exotic" peoples in
remote jungles, write a book on women's roles in the United States? What
can anthropology contribute to our understanding of changes in women's
roles over the course of American history? A good deal, I believe.

Anthropologists, because of their broad cross-cultural perspective, take
little in the way of human behavior for granted. For most generalizations
about the way people live, anthropologists can cite exceptions to the rule.
This does not mean that there are no regularities in human behavior and culture but only that anthropologists are usually more careful than most people
about making generalizations that people "everywhere" behave in this way or
that. For example, the claim that women are the primary caretakers of children all over the world is readily disputed by anthropologists who can provide
examples of cultures in which older children have principal caretaking
responsibility. The assertion that women are universally "domestic," that in
all cultures they keep the home fires burning while men go out to "make a liv-

1

ing," also is easily challenged. Anthropologists can point to dozens of foraging and horticultural societies in which there is no distinct domestic realm and
in which women as well as men contribute to the work of earning a living.

Anthropologists recognize that women's roles and beliefs about women's
"natural" propensities differ from one culture to another. They recognize
that women's roles in Western industrial societies and their supporting ideologies are simply variants of a diverse human picture. Moreover, anthropologists insist that their own culture's beliefs about the roles and aptitudes of
women are neither more natural nor more rational than the practices and
beliefs of other cultures.

But how do we explain the various roles that women play in societies
around the world and their accompanying ideologies about women's "true
nature" and "proper place"? Why is it that at some times and in some places
women are viewed as naturally domestic and nurturing and are thought to be
the only ones who can properly care for children, while at other times and in
other places this belief is attenuated or absent? Why is it that in some societies and some social classes women carry heavy loads of water and firewood
and engage in the back-breaking activities of planting and harvesting crops,
while in other societies and other social classes women are said to be too "delicate" for such heavy work? Why is it that tasks labeled "women's work" in
some cultures are assigned exclusively to men in others?

Although no one has the final and definitive answers to these and myriad
other questions, some anthropologists have made considerable headway
toward explaining them. I believe that those who have been most successful
have adopted a theoretical approach and research strategy called cultural
materialism, which assumes that explanations for cultural similarities and differences lie in the material conditions of human life: how people make a living, how they relate to their environments, and how they reproduce themselves. These conditions are termed the infrastructure of a society. In the
words of anthropologist Marvin Harris (1979:ix), cultural materialism is
"based on the simple premise that human social life is a response to the practical problems of human existence."

Cultural materialism rejects the time-worn adage that "ideas change the
world." Instead, it holds that over time changes in a society's material base
will lead to functionally compatible changes in its social and political structures along with modifications in its secular and religious ideologies, all of
which enhance the continuity and stability of the system as a whole (Harris
1999). The ultimate goal of this approach is to explain, not simply describe,
cultural variations in the way people live.

This type of analysis has been fruitful in explaining certain aspects of
human gender roles. Previous studies employing a cultural materialist paradigm have shown that variations in men's and women's roles are related to
environmental, technological, and demographic factors, to a people's way of
making a living, and to social and political arrangements. An important
assumption of cultural materialism is that biology is not destiny. On the con-

trary, the diverse roles that women play in different cultures, along with varying ideologies about women's nature, are linked to and molded by such mundane factors as subsistence strategies and population pressure. From a materialist point of view women's roles are neither grounded in biology nor indeterminate in nature, fluctuating through time for no apparent reason. Ideas about women's capabilities and proper place do not change at random—they are ultimately shaped by a society's sexual division of labor, which in turn is causally related to its productive and reproductive imperatives.

A word of caution is in order here. While cultural materialism looks to the productive and reproductive modes in a given society in order to account for its structural and ideological components, it does not postulate a simplistic, mechanistic correspondence between material conditions and structural and ideological phenomena. There may be a time lag before an ideology evolves that is compatible with changed material conditions. A relevant example of such a lag is the case of the "feminine mystique," an ideology celebrating the joys of domesticity (Friedan 1974). The feminine mystique flourished during the 1950s, a time when married women were taking jobs in record numbers, but belated recognition of women's large-scale employment did not come until the feminist resurgence more than a decade later. Still, from the perspective of cultural materialism, the women's movement was ultimately a *result*, rather than a *cause* of women's massive entry into the labor force. Women did not take jobs because a feminist ideology "liberated" them to do so. As we will see in chapter 6, the reason that so many married women sought employment lies in such material factors as high rates of inflation, falling male wages, and an increase in demand for female labor.

The advantages of cultural materialism—combined with an anthropological perspective—become clear when we contrast it with an ideological approach to women's roles. According to sociologist William Goode (1963:56), changes in ideas altered the position of women in Western society:

> I believe that the crucial crystallizing variable—i.e., the necessary but not sufficient cause of the betterment of Western woman's position—was ideological: the gradual, logical, philosophical extension to women of originally Protestant notions about the rights and responsibilities of the individual undermined the traditional idea of "woman's proper place."

This statement presents two problems. The "traditional idea of woman's proper place" refers to the common misconception that women in pre-industrial societies do not work outside the home because cultural values deem such work inappropriate. Goode claims that this ideology changed in Western society and a new value system emerged that permitted women to engage in work outside the home. But his facts are wrong. In many pre-industrial societies women not only work outside the household, but make important contributions to subsistence. Goode assumes that women's traditional role is one of economic dependence and total confinement to the domestic realm. In fact, female economic dependence and the very existence of a separate "feminine" domestic sphere are relatively recent phenomena. In Western society they are artifacts of industrialization; they date only from the nineteenth century, and even then were strongly tied to social class.

Aside from Goode's inaccurate information, there is also a basic flaw in his analysis. He fails to explain why and under what conditions Protestant values of individual rights and responsibilities were extended to women. He claims that this ideology spelled the end of traditional beliefs about women's proper place, but he does not explain *under what conditions* this momentous ideological change took place—why it occurred when and where it did, and what other changes made these new ideas appropriate.

One might raise similar questions about the revival of American feminism in the late 1960s and early 1970s. What caused it? Why did it occur when it did rather than ten or twenty years earlier? Common wisdom has it that the resurgence of feminism had essentially ideological roots, that the women's movement grew out of the Civil Rights movement of the 1960s. Women were sick and tired of being the "gofers" of the Left and began to demand the same rights as men. While it is true that the Civil Rights movement in challenging racial hierarchies may have paved the way for women to question gender hierarchies, this analysis overlooks the fact that relatively few women were active in the Civil Rights movement, nor does it explain why untold numbers of women were dissatisfied with the status quo.

Others point to Betty Friedan's *The Feminine Mystique* (1974) as the first contemporary statement of female discontent and the founding document of the women's movement. To be sure, Friedan's book, first published in 1963, did strike a responsive chord and became a much discussed best-seller. But why the reaction to it? Why didn't Simone de Beauvoir's feminist tome *The Second Sex*, published in 1952 in the United States, also become an immediate best-seller? Although de Beauvoir's book has been widely read in this country and elsewhere, its popularity postdated its publication by at least a decade. I conclude that when *The Second Sex* was first published, it did not have a wide impact because conditions were not ripe for a feminist revival. By the time *The Feminine Mystique* appeared, however, conditions were very different.

The suggestion that women were suddenly prompted to action by the Civil Rights movement or by a best-selling book ignores the conditions of millions of women's lives in the late 1950s and 1960s. More married, middle-class women than ever before held jobs, but these jobs were usually low-paying and dead-end. At the same time such women continued to bear primary responsibility for child care and housework. Surely these conditions explain the roots of female discontent, discontent that led to the rebirth of feminism and the popularity of books that decried the contemporary version of women's "proper place."

Here we can see the value of a materialist conception of history. Seemingly indeterminate and inexplicable fluctuations in women's roles and their attendant ideologies become intelligible in light of their material causes. Cultural materialism provides no ready-made explanation for changes in any particular set of roles or in any particular system of beliefs. Instead, it analyzes the larger context in which these changes took place and then tries to answer the vital question: Why here and now?

Middle-class American women as mothers, housewives, and workers are the focus of these pages. These different roles and the prescriptions about them, although treated separately in this volume, are closely related. It is impossible, for example, to understand changes in the perception of the role of mother over the course of American history without also looking at women's work both within and outside the home. It is no coincidence that as the life-sustaining productive activities of middle-class women dwindled in the nineteenth century, their maternal and housekeeping duties were thrown into sharp relief and became the subject of numerous prescriptive treatises. The definitions and duties of motherhood and homemaking are not the fixed and inevitable consequence of childbearing and housekeeping. Rather they are social constructs that vary over time.

Changes in roles and in their accompanying ideologies can be explained only within a larger material context. They cannot be understood apart from the productive and reproductive imperatives that prevailed at the time the changes occurred. For this reason I will intersperse a variety of data with my primary discussion of the roles of middle-class women. At one time or another a number of material factors impinged on the definition of the roles of middle-class American women, and I will focus on these factors in the pages to follow. Just which factors were important? They include such basic variables as household versus industrial production, a manufacturing versus a service-oriented economy, the demand or lack of demand for middle-class women's labor outside the home, the infant mortality rate and middle-class women's average completed fertility rate, the needs of business and industry for quality employees, and the changing costs and benefits of rearing the middle-class children who would become those employees. This brief list will suffice; the actual explanation of how these and other material factors affected women's roles at different points in American history is the subject of this book.

A FEW CAVEATS

Before addressing substantive issues, I would like to make it clear what this book is and is not about. Following the warnings of historians Mary Beth Norton and Carol Ruth Berkin (1979), I do not deal with the question of the relative status of middle-class women at any given period in American history. I do not claim that middle-class women were better or worse off during any particular era. I certainly have my own opinions on the matter, but this book does not make such determinations. The assertion that women played a central role in the household economy of colonial days, for example, is not meant to suggest that women enjoyed equality with men as a result of their productive activities or that they had more power than mid-nineteenth-century housewives whose domestic production had been greatly curtailed. What I am concerned with is determining why women's roles changed and how these changes were reflected in contemporary perceptions of "woman's nature" and "proper place."

To describe the ideological component of the roles of middle-class women I have used prescriptive history—historical and contemporary books, manuals, and other popular writings that have advised women how to act, thus informing them what their roles are or ought to be. I reviewed all of the most popular manuals published in any given period, including twentieth-century best-sellers or those known to have had large sales in the nineteenth century. In addition, I randomly selected other, apparently minor, prescriptive writings for each of the periods covered. I also surveyed articles from nineteenth-century ladies' magazines and twentieth-century mass circulation monthlies like the *Ladies' Home Journal* and *Good Housekeeping* in an attempt to recreate their assumptions about the proper roles for middle-class women.

As a number of historians have pointed out, employing prescriptive writings in historical research is problematic (Mechling 1975; Zuckerman 1975). It raises a number of unanswered, perhaps unanswerable, questions: Who bought these manuals and magazines? Were they actually read? And, if they were read, how seriously was their advice taken? Did such advice affect the way middle-class women saw themselves? Did it influence their behavior? As a social scientist I am well aware of the complex relationship between ideology and behavior, including the obvious limitations of prescriptive literature as a guide to such behavior.

Prescriptive literature as a source for beliefs about American women is also suspect because of the strong class bias of the majority of this literature. Most child-care manuals and household guides were written by and intended for the white, urban middle class. The dictum "cleanliness is next to godliness," which appeared in so many late nineteenth-century housekeeping manuals, took a middle-class standard of living for granted. And the directives of John B. Watson (1928), the dean of American child-rearing experts in the 1920s, certainly assumed an affluent lifestyle; Watson insisted that every child have a room of his or her own. These and other prescriptive writings were indeed addressed to the white middle-class woman, and as such they do not and cannot provide us with a guide to contemporary views of poor, non-white, or immigrant women.

Some of the manuals also display a regional bias. During the nineteenth century, in particular, most domestic advisors were writers living in the older, more settled, eastern regions of the country. This bias is reflected in the housekeeping guides dating from the late 1800s; some took it for granted that all households had certain domestic equipment that was too costly or simply unavailable to poor women or women in rural areas of the country.

On the other hand, the middle-class limitations of prescriptive data should not be exaggerated because the ideals inherent in the injunctions may have filtered down to working-class and immigrant groups. I agree with historian Carl Degler (1980:82–83), who argues that the "downward projection" of middle-class values was likely "in a society like that of the United States, where class consciousness was weak, and widespread literacy permitted a large majority of women to inform themselves of the standards of the middle and upper classes." Not only were a majority of nineteenth-century Americans literate, but a majority belonged to the middle class. Degler estimates that if commercial farm families are included in that designation, up to 60 percent of the nineteenth-century American population was middle class. Then, too, we know that working-class and immigrant women did read such "middle-class" founts of advice as the early twentieth-century publications of the Children's Bureau and that women from a variety of backgrounds wrote letters to the Bureau (Ladd-Taylor 1986, 1995). It is still a moot question, of course, whether the dicta contained therein affected the behavior of these women any more or less than it affected the behavior of their middle-class counterparts.

Prescriptive literature, then, tells us little about how women actually lived or what they thought. Moreover, it is difficult to know how such advice was received by the white, middle-class female audience at whom it was primarily aimed. At no point, therefore, am I suggesting that what the advice givers were saying, women were actually doing. I am not analyzing how the advice given during different historical periods was translated into actual behavior by the women who lived during those times; the influence of prescriptive writings on the lives of women is not the subject of this book.

But despite these limitations, prescriptive literature serves a crucial purpose: it tells us much about ideological trends during different eras of American history. Both the tone and content of books and articles on motherhood, housekeeping, and women as workers changed over time. Why did a cult of motherhood emerge in the manuals after 1830? Why were late-nineteenth-century housewives advised of the difficulty and high purpose of their domestic duties when such tasks were barely mentioned in the writings of an earlier day? Why, during the 1950s, were married woman told that it was all right to take a part-time job but not to pursue a full-time career? In other words, *how and why did the advice itself change over time*? Again, by adopting a cultural materialist paradigm, we know that these and other variations in the directives aimed at middle-class American women are not free-floating and random; rather they are related to and shaped by the productive and reproductive conditions that prevailed at the time the advice was proffered.

Examining such sources raises an obvious question. Who were the advice givers, and why did they shore up the interests of American business and industry? Were they mere puppets who did the bidding of certain elements in American society? Was there collusion between prescriptive writers and powerful elites whose interests lay in teaching women their proper place? I am not suggesting any conspiracy between women's advisors and groups that stood to benefit from the advice women were given. This implies a level of conscious and deliberate behavior that is unnecessary to my argument that at most times in American history, there was a certain consistency—a mesh or fit—between the general dicta of the prescriptive writers and basic economic and social requirements of society.

Some of the advice givers were best-selling authors of their day, while others filled the pages of the *Ladies' Home Journal, Good Housekeeping,* and other women's magazines. But the identity of these writers and their specific relationships to other elements in American society are not important to this analysis. What is important is that they wrote books and articles that were published and widely disseminated, books and articles expounding ideologies that helped perpetuate the current order by explaining and rationalizing the status quo and women's position it. Moreover, the directives at any one time reveal a rather remarkable consensus that is difficult to attribute to chance. The mission of the prescriptive writers is clear: they provided ideologies about women's place in the scheme of things, a place that varied over time according the exigencies of the material order.

A brief word about chronology. In terms of major productive changes and their effects on women's roles, the time span I call the nineteenth century did not really get under way until the 1830s. That decade was a watershed, and its significance is reflected in the arrangement of the chapters on the mother role and on housework. The same is true of the period I term the twentieth century. If we are interested in the transformation of the home by modern conveniences and concomitant changes in standards of good house-keeping, the twentieth century actually began after World War I. This too is reflected in the organization of the chapters on housework.

PUTTING MOTHERS ON THE PEDESTAL

Motherhood as we know it today is a surprisingly new institution. It is also
a unique one, the product of an affluent society. In most of human history
and in most parts of the world even today, adult, able-bodied women have
been, and still are, too valuable in their productive capacity to be spared
for the exclusive care of children.

Jessie Bernard, *The Future of Motherhood*, 1974

Debates about the conflict between motherhood and work have lessened
in intensity over the last two decades as millions of middle-class wives and
mothers have taken jobs and as employment for such women has become the
norm rather than the exception. But these developments have not met with
unanimous approval. Just think of the demand by groups like the Christian
Coalition for a return to "traditional family values," code words for the presence of a full-time housewife-mother in the home. Still, biting denunciations
of working mothers—so common during much of the twentieth century—are
far less frequent today. Many women are pleased to be living at a time when
they feel free to take a job or pursue a career. They feel more comfortable
working because it is no longer an article of faith that Mom's employment is
harmful to her children. But what is often overlooked is that this is not the
first time in American history when work and motherhood were thought compatible and when a woman's productive activities were seen as essential to her
family's well-being.

Ideas about the proper maternal role have changed over the past 250 years in the United States. Not until the nineteenth century were children's development and well-being viewed as the major, if not the sole responsibility of their mothers who were urged to devote themselves full-time to their parental duties. During the eighteenth century, in contrast, child rearing was neither a discrete nor an exclusively female task. There was little emphasis on motherhood per se, and both parents were advised to "raise up" their children together.

Such changes in ideas about motherhood are not isolated cultural artifacts resulting from random ideological fashions. These shifts in values are molded by changes in the nature of the family and in the American economy. As we will see, motherhood as a full-time career for middle-class women first arose as women's role in the domestic economy diminished, productive labor was removed from the household, the family became more isolated from the larger community, the need for educated children increased, and the birthrate declined. As a result of these developments, beginning in the 1830s the exclusivity of the mother–child dyad and the incessant duties of motherhood emerged as givens in American child-rearing manuals and other prescriptive writings aimed at the middle class.

One of the principal factors influencing the middle-class mother's role and the ideology surrounding it was the decline of domestic production. During the colonial period when women were responsible for the manufacture and use of a wide variety of household products essential to daily living, women could not devote themselves full-time to motherhood. But in the early nineteenth century, as manufacturing left the home for the factory, middle-class women found themselves freed up to spend more time on child care. And before long they were told that such full-time care was essential. In essence, the emphasis on maternity was one way of solving what became known as the "woman question." Once a woman's productive skills were no longer needed, what was to occupy her time? The answer was summarized in a single word: motherhood.

The daily presence or absence of men in the home also shaped the American definition of motherhood. During colonial times when men, women, and children all worked together in or near the household, there were no firm distinctions in parental responsibilities. It was the duty of both parents to rear their children, and fathers were thought to be especially important to a proper religious education. But when men's work began to take them away from home for most of the day—an arrangement that began with the onset of industrialization nearly two hundred years ago—child-rearing responsibilities fell more heavily on mothers. And, once again, middle-class mothers were told that this was in the nature of things.

Household size and contacts with the outside world also influenced the mother role. Prior to the nineteenth century when most households were larger than the nuclear family, when they consisted of more people than just a married couple and their children, the presence of other adults who could take a hand in child care diluted maternal responsibility. Because the household was the site of both life and work, because there was a constant coming and going of people, the mother–child tie was but one of many relationships. But as the country industrialized in the nineteenth century, the home and the place of work became separate. Women were now the only adults who spent most of their time at home, and the mother–child relationship was thrown into sharp relief. Mothers took on all the burdens of child care, and their performance of these tasks became a major concern. Soon the middle-class mother was advised that she and she alone had the weighty mission of transforming her children into the model citizens of the day.

Fertility rates also shape the mother role, but not always in the way one might expect. It seems logical that the more children a woman has, the more she will be defined by her maternal role; after all, the care and feeding of a large brood demand so much time. But this was not always the case. The emphasis on motherhood in the nineteenth century actually *increased* as fertility among the middle class *decreased*. One explanation of this anomaly lies in what has been called the "procreative imperative" (Harris 1981:84). This refers to the promotion of cheap population growth by powerful elements in society that benefit from the rearing of high-quality children. As industrialization continued, the need for skilled labor correspondingly increased. Thus, the reification of maternity during the nineteenth century reflects a dual attempt to stem the falling birthrate of the middle class and increase the quality of children—the nation's future workers—through long-term mother care.

This preoccupation with motherhood and the corollary assumption that an exclusive mother–child relationship is both natural and inevitable is by no means universal. Ethnographic evidence suggests a good deal of variation in child-care arrangements and the ideologies that rationalize them. One study of 186 societies from around the world, for example, found that in less than half—46 percent—mothers were the primary or exclusive caretakers of infants. In another 40 percent of the societies primary care of infants was the responsibility of others, usually older siblings. More striking still is the finding that in less than 20 percent of the societies are mothers the primary or exclusive caretakers *after* infancy. The authors of this study conclude that "in the majority of these societies mothers are not the principal caretakers or companions of young children" (Weisner and Gallimore 1977:170).

How can we explain this conclusion, which contradicts the deeply held American belief in the central role of the mother in child care? A number of factors are involved, but one clue is that the living arrangement we take so much for granted—the married woman's residence in a nuclear family household made up exclusively of parents and children—is extremely rare cross-culturally. Such households are found in only about 6 percent of the societies listed in the massive Human Relations Area Files, the largest compilation of cross-cultural data in the world (Weisner and Gallimore 1977:170). So in most societies other kin who live in the household relieve mothers of some of the burden of child care.

Another factor influencing the degree of maternal responsibility is the nature and location of women's productive activities. In societies with economies based on foraging or cultivation, young children typically are taken care of by older siblings or by their mothers or other female relatives while these women are gathering or gardening. But in industrial societies where the workplace and the household are separate, production and child care are incompatible. It is in these same societies—ones in which women's activities typically are limited to the domestic sphere—that we find the duties of parenting weighing most heavily or exclusively on mothers (Brown 1970).

A study of mothers in six cultures points up the relative rarity of Western industrial child-care patterns. In the American community represented in the study 92 percent of the mothers said that they usually or always took care of their babies and children by themselves. The other five societies displayed considerably less maternal responsibility for child care. In the words of the authors: "The mothers in the U.S. sample have a significantly heavier burden (or joy) of baby care than the mothers in any other society." They explain: "Living in nuclear families isolated from their relatives and with all their older children in school most of the day the [American] mother spends more time in charge of both babies and older children than any other group" (Minturn and Lambert 1964:95–101, 112–113).

These studies suggest that the preoccupation of American experts with the mother–child relationship almost certainly is a result of social and economic developments in the United States and Western industrialized societies in general, societies that are characterized more than most by exclusive mother–child care arrangements. What we have come to think of as inevitable and biologically necessary is in great measure a consequence of our society's particular social and economic structure. We are certainly not unique in believing that our brand of mother–child relationship is natural and normal. People in every culture firmly believe that their own child-rearing practices stem from nature itself.

What is the evidence that American perceptions of the mother role did, in fact, change with industrialization? Sermons, child-care manuals, magazine articles, and other forms of popular literature are rich sources for contemporary images of the mother role. The maternal role, however, cannot be understood apart from other facets of child rearing. For example, the role prescribed for fathers during various periods in American history affected the role prescribed for mothers. Then, too, perceptions of the nature of children necessarily had an impact on definitions of proper mothering. And, finally, the varying child-care methods recommended by prescriptive writers influenced the writers' views of the maternal role since it was mothers, for the most part, who were expected to carry out their recommendations. For these reasons the prescriptive literature on mothering must be seen within the context of general child-rearing advice.

As discussed in chapter 1, using child-care manuals and other sources of advice to trace social attitudes is not without pitfalls. This literature records prescriptive dicta, not actual practice, and is subject to rationalizations and selective emphasis. Moreover, evidence suggests that child-care advice may have the least effect on just those women most likely to be aware of it. One scholar has questioned whether child-rearing manuals are evidence of either child-rearing values or child-rearing behavior, claiming that all the manuals tell us about are child-rearing manual writers' values (Mechling 1975).

Despite these caveats I believe prescriptive writings have an important place in a study of the changing perceptions of the middle-class mother in the United States. Even though child-rearing advice may not have influenced actual behavior, prescriptive writings emerge as cultural documents, as ideological constructs that are products of the social and economic milieu of their day. The extent to which this is so is reflected in the fact that, first, the advice itself changed over time and second, there was remarkable consensus among the advice givers of any given era as to what the "correct" maternal role should be. The main focus of these pages, then, is to analyze the larger social and economic forces that influenced the advice being offered and the conditions under which it changed.

This chapter covers the advice proffered to middle-class American women on their motherly duties from colonial times to 1940. A discussion of the maternal role after World War II, including its dramatic redefinition by child-care experts over the last three decades, appears in chapter 3.

RAISE UP YOUR CHILDREN TOGETHER: THE COLONIAL PERIOD TO 1785

Children in their first days, have greater benefit of good mothers. . . . But afterwards, when they come to riper years, good fathers are more behoveful of their forming in virtue and good manners.

John Robinson, Pastor & Founder, Plymouth Colony
(quoted in Bloch 1978b)

In the colonial era a distinct maternal role would have been incompatible with the realities of life since the mother–child relationship was enmeshed in the myriad daily tasks women performed for their families' survival. They kept house, tended gardens, raised poultry and cattle, churned milk into butter and cream, butchered livestock, tanned skins, pickled and preserved food, made candles, buttons, soap, beer, and cider, gathered and processed medicinal herbs, and spun and wove wool and cotton for family clothes. The wives of farmers, merchants, and artisans were busy with these duties, and the wives of merchants and artisans also often helped in their husbands' businesses. Child rearing, therefore, centered on teaching children the skills needed to keep the domestic economy going. It was not a separate task, but something that simply took place within the daily round of activities. This is why a New England mother could write in 1790 that her two children "had grown out of the way" and are "very little troble [*sic*]" when the younger of the two was still nursing (quoted in Cott 1977:58).

The agrarian economy of the seventeenth and eighteenth centuries had no clear-cut separation between the home and the world of work; the boundary between the pre-industrial family and society was permeable. Male and female spheres were contiguous and often overlapped, and the demands of the domestic economy ensured that neither sex was excluded from productive labor. Fathers took an active role in child rearing because they worked near the household. Craftsmen and tradesmen usually had their shops at home and farmers spent the long winter months there. The prescriptive literature of the day rarely or imprecisely distinguished between female or domestic themes and the masculine world of work, as later authors would. The few colonial domestic guides addressed both men and women under the assumption that they worked together in the household (Aries 1965; Sklar 1977).

Scholars now agree that the colonial family was not, as once thought, an extended one. Estimates suggest that at least 80 percent of colonial families were nuclear. But these were not the small insular nuclear families associated with the industrial era. The colonial family was nuclear only in the formal sense; parents and children formed its core, but mothers and fathers usually were not the only adults in the household. Some families took in maiden aunts or an aged parent; others had apprentices or journeymen, while domestic servants were common in the households of the well-to-do. Moreover, because the typical colonial couple had six to eight offspring, children ranging from infancy to adolescence often lived together in the same household. The practice of apprenticing children out and taking others in meant that at least some children were not brought up exclusively by their parents. Of most salience is that during the colonial period children's relationships were not nearly as mother centered as they later came to be in the encapsulated industrial variant of the nuclear family. Given the composition of the colonial American household, children received support from and were disciplined by a number of adults—their parents, apprentices or servants, older siblings, and perhaps other relatives (Degler 1980; Greven 1973b; Demos 1970; Bloch 1978b).

Indeed, children themselves were barely recognized as a separate human category in the American colonies. "There was little sense that children might somehow be a special group with their own needs and interests and capacities," writes historian John Demos (1970:57–58). Virtually all of the child-rearing advice of the day emphasized that children were "meer Loans from God, which He may call for when He pleases" (Mather 1978:108–09). Parents were told to bring up their children as good Christians, and discipline was emphasized, but no mention was made of developing the child's personality or individuality. Quite to the contrary, most sermons dwelt on the importance of breaking the child's will (Wadsworth 1972).

Since infant mortality rates were high, parents expected to lose some of their children. Infant mortality in the seventeenth century, for example, ranged from 10 to 30 percent in different parts of the colonies, a rate that was acknowledged in the sermons of the day. Cotton Mather (1978:108) counseled women how to behave on the death of a child: "She does not roar like a Beast, and howl, I cannot bear it; but She rather says, I can take anything at the Hands of God."

In the seventeenth and eighteenth centuries few child-care manuals were of American origin (most were English), but we can glean some indication of parental duties in the American colonies from the sermons of the day. In a 1712 sermon, Benjamin Wadsworth, pastor of the Church of Christ in Boston, distinguished mothers' responsibilities from fathers' when he urged the former to "suckle their children." But he then went on to say: "Having given these hints about Mothers, I may say of Parents (Comprehending both Father and Mother) they should provide for the outward supply and comfort of their Children. They should nourish and bring them up." In the discussion of religious instruction and the teaching of good manners and discipline that followed, all of Wadsworth's injunctions were addressed to "parents."

Colonial clergymen's sermons were consistent in their treatment of parental duties. Fathers were to supervise the secular and religious education of their children, teaching them to fear and respect God, but mothers also were advised of their responsibilities in this training. Both parents were admonished to set good examples for their children, and both were held responsible for their children's general well-being. Except for the greater authority bestowed on the father as head of the family, the prescribed roles for parents made no important distinctions on the basis of sex (Ulrich 1979; Bloch 1978a).

To be sure, women were thought to have special ties to their children during infancy, and infants were described as "hers" by both men and women. The realities of reproduction were certainly recognized, and here we find special advice to mothers. A number of clergy inveighed against wet nursing (the hiring of a new mother to breast-feed one's child), a practice that was, in fact, quite rare in the American colonies. In describing the duties of a righteous woman Cotton Mather (1978:105) admonished: "Her care for the Bodies of her Children shows itself in the nursing of them herself . . . She is not a Dame that shall scorn to nourish in the World, the Children whom she has already nourished in her Womb." Wet nursing was condemned because it was thought contrary to God's will and dangerous to the physical health of the child, not because it was believed to interfere with the development of a bond between mother and child (Bloch 1978a).

Once children reached the age of one or two, when their survival was more certain, all directives regarding child rearing were addressed to both parents. Fathers were expected to take a larger role once children reached an educable age. This was particularly true among the Puritans, who believed that the masculine qualities of religious understanding and self-discipline were essential in child rearing. One of the few distinctions made in the sermons of the day was in vocational training; this was the responsibility of the parent of the same sex as the child, although sometimes responsibility was removed from the family entirely. Children, particularly boys, often were sent out at age nine or ten to apprentice in other households, while children from other families were taken in to serve as apprentices (Ryan 1975; Bloch 1978a, 1978b).

A cult of motherhood did not exist because it would have been incongruous in this setting. Women were far too busy to devote long hours to purely maternal duties, and fathers, older siblings, and other adults were also on hand to see to children's needs and discipline. Moreover, because of high mortality rates, a woman was not likely to become obsessive about her children, some of whom would not survive to adulthood. It is little wonder that, as one scholar has remarked of the colonial period, "motherhood was singularly unidealized, usually disregarded as a subject, and even at times actually denigrated" (Bloch 1978a:101). Although women bore infants and cared for very young children, this role received less emphasis in the prescriptive literature than nearly any other aspect of women's lives. Motherhood, when it was discussed at all, was merged with the parental, domestic, and religious obligations of both sexes.

SOMETHING OLD, SOMETHING NEW: 1785–1820

Much depends upon your maternal care in the first stage of life; it is a pleasing duty, to which you are honorably called, both by nature and the custom of all nations.

Hugh Smith, *Letters to Married Women on Nursing and the Management of Children*, 1796

The cult of motherhood is usually associated with the middle and late nineteenth century, but it has roots in the prescriptive literature of an earlier era. During the late eighteenth and early nineteenth centuries the first indications of a special and distinct maternal role appeared in sermons, domestic guides, medical tomes, and child-rearing manuals. For the first time writers began stressing the critical importance of maternal care in early childhood (Cott 1977).

Significantly, these years also marked the onset of the industrial revolution in the United States. Markets slowly expanded, agricultural efficiency increased, transportation costs declined—all developments that led to greater specialization in the economic division of labor. Home manufacture for family use slowly was replaced by standardized factory production for the wider market.

The first industry that moved from the home to the factory was textile manufacture, one of women's traditional household tasks. As early as 1807 there were a dozen large textile mills in New England, and by 1810 farm families could buy cloth in village shops and from itinerant peddlers. The replacement of homespun by manufactured goods was a gradual process. In 1810 Secretary of the Treasury Albert Gallatin estimated that "about two-thirds of the clothing, including . . . house and table linen used by the inhabitants of the

United States, who do not reside in cities, is the product of family manufactures" (quoted in Degler 1980:361). Class membership and place of residence were primary factors in the reduction of home manufacture; more prosperous families, urban dwellers, and those living in the older settled areas of the East were the first to replace homemade goods with store-bought ones.

As women's role in the domestic economy gradually diminished, important changes also were taking place in the family. By the late eighteenth century the domestic sphere had begun to contract; the number of servants declined, the practice of taking in apprentices and journeymen had all but ceased and, with the expansion of economic opportunities, fathers were spending less time at home. But while fewer adults remained in the household, children were now living in it until they reached adolescence. Middle-class children were no longer apprenticed to other families and, by 1820, they generally lived at home until around the age of fifteen. The nuclear family itself became smaller as the birthrate declined, particularly in the more densely populated eastern regions of the country. For example, by the late eighteenth century in Andover, Massachusetts, women typically had five or six children while their grandmothers had averaged seven or eight (Degler 1980; Greven 1970).

Not only was the middle-class household smaller in size but, with the onset of industrialization, it was no longer a self-contained unit whose members were bound by common tasks. For the first time the place, scope, and pace of men's and women's work began to diverge sharply. As a distinct division of labor gradually arose between the home and the world of work, the household's contacts with the outside decreased. By the first decades of the nineteenth century the term "home" had come to be synonymous with place of retirement or retreat (Cott 1977).

Ideologies about the nature of children also started to shift. By 1800 the Calvinist belief in infant damnation had begun to give way to the Lockian doctrine of *tabula rasa*, which stressed the lack of innate evil (or good) and the importance of experience in molding the child (Frost 1973). In 1796 one physician wrote, "that any children are born with vicious inclinations, I would not willingly believe" (Smith 1796:108). Children, at least middle-class children, began to be seen as individuals. They were no longer viewed as miniature adults whose natural inclinations toward evil had to be broken; childhood was becoming a distinct period in the life cycle. The dictum that children should be treated as individuals with special needs and vast potential requiring focused nurturing placed a new and heavy responsibility on parents; failure in child rearing could no longer be blamed on "native corruption" (Slater 1977:148).

The prescriptive literature on child care in those years was in many ways transitional between the stark dicta of the colonial clergy and the effusive writings of the later nineteenth century advice givers. Prior to about 1830 such literature did not enjoy mass circulation but appeared in periodical articles, printed sermons, and occasional treatises. All of it came under the rubric "domestic education," primarily written by ministers and physicians for a white middle- and upper-middle-class audience. Most pertinent here was the transitional image of the role of the middle-class mother. Simply put, motherhood was being revamped. Duties that had once belonged to both mothers and fathers or to fathers alone were now becoming the sole province of mothers. One historian of the period notes that "fathers began to recede into the background in writings about the domestic education of children" (Slater 1977:93–94). Treatises on the treatment of childhood diseases, diet, and hygiene now were addressed to mothers alone. Some of the medical texts also offered advice on the psychological management of young children, stressing for the first time the importance of a mother's influence during the early impressionable years (Bloch 1978a).

Arguments against wet nursing also took on a new cast. Whereas earlier commentators condemned the practice for its ill effects on a child's health, writers now claimed that wet nursing also tainted a child's character. One of the earliest references to a special relationship between mother and child appears in this context. A 1798 tract printed in England (but read in America) urged women to nurse their children so as to avoid "the destruction, or at least the diminution of the sympathy between mother and child" (quoted in Frost 1973:72). Nursing was no longer simply a woman's religious duty but the key to her future happiness. "Those children who are neglected by their mothers during their infant years," wrote Dr. Hugh Smith in 1796, "forget all duty and affection towards them, when such mothers are in the decline of life." The good doctor exalted in the joys of breast feeding: "Tell me you who know the rapturous delight, how complete is the bliss of enfolding in your longing arms the dear, dear fruits of all your pains?"

Jane West's *Letters to a Young Lady*, published in London in 1806 but widely read in America, illustrates the transitional tone of much of the advice literature of the period. Like Puritan clergymen of earlier years, West warned her readers that "excessive affection is one of the most common faults of mothers" (West 1974:190). But allusions to fathers were few, and their child-rearing duties were not delineated as they had been in earlier tracts. Still, while the advice is addressed to mothers, West did not contend that every maternal mood and action indelibly marked the future character of her child, as would later authors.

One of the first child-rearing manuals published in the United States, *The Maternal Physician* (1811), was written by "an anonymous American matron." The author discussed the treatment of childhood diseases and suggested ways to ensure an infant's well-being, but she also foreshadowed the overwrought celebration of the joys of motherhood to come: "What can equal a mother's ecstasy when she catches the first emanation of mind in the . . . smile of her babe? Ten thousand raptures thrill her bosom before a tooth is formed." The author strongly favored breast feeding and decried the fashionable "tyranny" of putting a child out to wet nurse: "How dead to the finest feelings of our nature must that mother be, who can voluntarily banish her infant from her bosom." (An American Matron 1972:8, 17).

Another early guide is Dr. William Buchan's *Advice to Mothers*, published in Boston in 1809. The burgeoning scope of the maternal role is evident here. "The more I reflect on the situation of a mother, the more I am struck by the extent of her powers," Dr. Buchan wrote. And not all mothers are equal: "By a mother I do not mean the woman who merely brings a child into the world, but her who faithfully discharges the duties of a parent—whose chief concern is the well-being of her infant." But mothers walked a narrow line between neglect and overindulgence. "The obvious paths of nature are alike forsaken by the woman who gives up the care of her infant to a hireling . . . and by her who carries these duties to excess, who makes an idol of her child" (Buchan 1972:3, 77). This is an early instance of a recurrent theme in the prescriptive writings of the nineteenth and much of the twentieth centuries: Mothers, you must be ever on guard to do your job properly. Lurking in the shadows of these prescriptions were the pitiful figures of mothers who had failed, mothers who had not taken their duties seriously, or mothers who had performed them with excessive zeal.

Emphasis on the mother role was not limited to advice manuals. Between 1800 and 1820 a new theme appeared in many New England sermons: mothers are more important than fathers in molding the sensibilities and habits of children. One New Hampshire minister proclaimed in 1806: "Weighty beyond expression is the charge devolved to the female parent. It is not within the province of human wisdom to calculate all the happy consequences resulting from the persevering assiduity of mothers" (quoted in Cott 1977:86). While sermons of the day did not deny all paternal responsibility, they made clear that raising children was a specialized domestic activity that was largely the province of mothers. As historian Nancy Cott (1977:86) points out, this "emphasis departed from (and undermined) the patriarchal family ideal in which the mother, while entrusted with the physical care of her children, left their religious, moral, and intellectual guidance to her husband."

Although little is known about actual child-rearing practices in the early nineteenth century, the aim of the manual and sermon writers was to increase the amount of time and attention mothers devoted to infants and small children. For the first time in American history the care of young children was viewed as a full-time task, as a distinct profession requiring special knowledge. What had once been done according to tradition now demanded proper study. Even arguments favoring women's education were couched in terms of their role as mothers; women were to be educated because the formation of the future citizens of the republic lay in their hands (Sicherman 1975). It is ironic but by no means coincidental that, as their sphere narrowed and grew more insular, middle-class women were told that their importance to the future of the new nation was boundless.

Historian Ruth H. Bloch (1978b) notes that economic factors exercised a "push-pull" effect on child-rearing responsibilities. As the domestic production of middle-class mothers waned, and their domestic work lost its commercial value, fathers were spending more and more time outside the home, as did other adults who had once been part of the household. Women, left alone at home with their children—who were now remaining there until adolescence— began to assume almost complete responsibility for child care. The prescriptive literature, with its newly expanded definition of motherhood, was a response to these societal changes. In essence, as the female role in domestic production declined, the middle-class woman was told to focus on reproduction.

MOTHERHOOD, A FEARFUL RESPONSIBILITY: 1820–1870

> Mothers have as powerful an influence over the welfare of future gener-
> ations, as all other early causes combined.
>   Reverend John S. C. Abbott, *The Mother at Home*, 1833

The concept of the mother role that prevailed from the late eighteenth cen-tury to about 1820 was, in the words of historian Mary Ryan, "a rare and subdued hint of the extravagant celebration of motherhood to come" (1975:126). Begin-ning in the 1820s and gaining momentum in the 1830s and 1840s, a flood of man-uals and magazine articles gave advice on the maternal role, exulted in the joys of motherhood, and told women that good mothering was not only key to their own and their children's happiness, but crucial to the nation's destiny as well.

The era between 1820 and 1860 was one of rapid industrialization; indus-trial production doubled every decade. Although most Americans were still working in agriculture rather than in manufacturing—about 80 percent at the start of the period and 65 percent forty years later—it was an increasingly commercial agriculture that produced more for the market than for home consumption. The U.S. population also was becoming more urbanized. In 1820 only 7 percent of Americans lived in cities, but by 1860, 20 percent of Americans were residing in urban areas (Ryan 1979; Brownlee 1974).

The most salient change occurring during these years was the eventual demise of the self-sufficient household. The growth of industry, technological advances, improvements in transportation, and increased agricultural spe-cialization made more goods available, and the household became ever more reliant on the market to meet its basic needs. In short, the period between 1820 and 1860 witnessed the substitution of store-bought goods for home-made goods, and this shift had a profound impact on women's work. As early as the 1820s women's domestic production had diminished in scope and vari-ety to such an extent that they were left with only a residue of their former household tasks. In New England by 1830 home spinning and weaving were largely replaced by manufactured textiles and by mid-century women's pro-ductive skills had become even more superfluous: butter, candles, soap, med-icines, buttons, and cloth were widely available in stores. As early as 1838, the noted feminist and abolitionist Sarah Grimké remarked on the decline of home manufacture: "When all manufactures were domestic, then the domestic function might well consume all the time of a very able-bodied woman. But nowadays . . . when so much of woman's work is done by the butcher and the baker, by the tailor and the cook . . . you see how much of woman's time is left for other functions" (quoted in Degler 1980:376).

The removal of production from the home to the factory led to the demise of the once close relationship between the household and the business of society. For the first time "life"—the home—was divided from "work." Not only had the two spheres become separate, they were now viewed as incompatible. The home was a retreat from the competitive world of commerce and industry, a place of warmth and moral respite.

The home as retreat was also considerably smaller than it had been in earlier years. The middle-class American household declined in size throughout the nineteenth century and by mid-century its ancillary members had moved out—an unmarried sister might be teaching school in town and domestic servants were leaving to take better-paying factory jobs. Philip Greven's (1972) study of census data from eleven states illustrates this point. In 1790 the average number of freepersons per household was 5.8, in 1850 it was 5.5, and by 1890 it had declined to 4.9.

Part of the decrease in household size resulted from a falling birthrate. Population growth from reproduction declined steadily as the birthrate fell throughout the nineteenth century. By 1850 the average white woman was bearing only half as many children as her grandmother had. More striking still is the 50 percent decline in the average completed fertility rate for the century as a whole; it fell from 7.04 children per woman in 1800 to 3.56 in 1900 (Degler 1980).

The key question is: Why did women bear fewer children? Anthropologist Marvin Harris suggests that in industrializing, urbanizing societies children "tend to cost more and to be economically less valuable to their parents than children on farms" (1981:81). Children in agrarian societies cost relatively little to raise and can do a variety of simple tasks even when very young. But in cities the expense of rearing children increases, as does the length of their dependence. Nearly all of the items children need must be purchased, and schooling is required before they can become economically self-sufficient. In essence, urban children contribute less and cost more.

As the nineteenth century progressed the costs and benefits of having children shifted, particularly for the middle class, whose children required longer periods of socialization before they could make it on their own. The rearing of "quality" children—children who enjoyed a long period of dependency while they were educated to take their "rightful" position in society— was ever more costly. Perhaps this explains why the average middle-class family had fewer children.

But though fewer in number, children were gradually seen as requiring more care as ideas about their nature continued to evolve. The neutral tabula rasa of the first decades of the nineteenth century was supplanted by the "sweet angels" of the Romantic era. After 1830 children were routinely depicted as beings of great purity and innocence. They were naturally close to God, and their virtuous proclivities had only to be gently molded to ensure eternal salvation. Closely allied with this idealized image of the young was the conviction that only mothers had the power to transform malleable infants into moral, productive adults. For this reason many warned about the dangers of hiring nurses, for even the best nurse was never an adequate substitute for mother herself. Only a mother's care and influence, not that of fathers, older siblings, relatives or servants, could fulfill the special physical and spiritual needs of the growing child. Motherhood had become a careerlike obligation. And by the mid-nineteenth century, because middle-class children remained at home until well into adolescence, women were obliged to spend more years raising them (Slater 1977; Wishy 1968).

Some scholars claim that the nineteenth-century concern with the child as an individual and with proper child-rearing methods was the result of a decline in infant mortality. Parents, they argue, became more certain that their children would grow to adulthood and were thus willing to invest more time and energy in their offspring. But historian Carl Degler (1980) takes issue with this theory, citing data suggesting infant mortality did not, in fact, decline. Infant mortality might have been even higher than indicated in official statistics because of a high mortality rate among unreported births. Moreover, the argument could be reversed; perhaps growing concern for the child stemmed from the fact that infant mortality rates *did* remain so high. Indeed, Catherine Beecher (orig. 1841) and other manual writers contended that proper child care could help prevent the deaths of infants and young children.

The outpouring of advice manuals and other prescriptive writings after 1830 cannot be entirely explained either by continued high levels of infant mortality or by the fact that women were having fewer children and had the time to make a greater investment in each one. Another spur to the advice-giving boom was the nation's slowly growing need for children groomed to become professionals or to fill the administrative and management positions created by industrialization. What better and cheaper way to accomplish this than by urging middle-class women to devote many years and large amounts of (unpaid) time and energy to nurturing the future captains of business and industry?

The growing demand for a well-educated citizenry was tied to concern about the falling fertility rate among the middle class, a concern that also helps explain the era's luxuriant paeans to motherhood. But the relationship is not a simple one. It seems logical that if women had been taking these paeans seriously, they would have had more, rather than fewer children. And it certainly would be naive to assume that fertility decisions are made on the basis of advice books! I believe the link between the celebration of motherhood and the decline in fertility is as follows: as white middle-class families had fewer and fewer children, there was increasing alarm in certain quarters (Gordon 1977). Where would the future business leaders come from? Who was going to manage the nation's burgeoning industries? At a time when the fertility of nonwhites and immigrants was higher than that of native-born whites, the country's elite feared that the "backbone" of the nation was being diluted by "lesser types." The glorification of maternity that was directed at potential mothers of the "backbone" was an attempt, albeit an unsuccessful one, to encourage their reproductive activity.

Just how people in the nineteenth century controlled their fertility is not entirely understood, but evidence suggests that after 1840 American women began having more frequent abortions. An historian of the subject estimates one abortion for every twenty-five or thirty live births during the first decades of the century, a proportion that rose to about one in every five or six live births during the 1850s and 1860s (Mohr 1978). Most contemporary physicians agreed that the primary motive for abortion was control of family size, citing evidence that the majority of abortions were performed on married women. It is telling that prior to the nineteenth century there were no laws prohibiting abortion during the first months of pregnancy. The procedure was not illegal until "quickening," that is, until the movements of the fetus are felt by the mother at about four months. Laws banning abortion were first passed between 1821 and 1841, when ten states and one territory outlawed its practice. And by the Civil War nearly every state had laws prohibiting abortion at all stages of fetal development (Gordon 1977).

I do not think it mere chance that concern about falling birthrates, laws banning abortion, and the proliferation of child-care manuals lauding the maternal role all appeared at about the same time. The outpourings of the advice givers reflected the wider anxiety about middle-class women's declining fertility and sought to counteract it by dwelling on the joys of motherhood for their white, middle-class audience.

The contraction of women's productive activities in the smaller, more encapsulated nuclear household provided the necessary setting for this expanding emphasis on the mother role. There was now a sizable, literate audience of homebound women who were told of the importance of motherhood and given suggestions of time-consuming methods for its proper discharge. As the domestic sphere contracted and middle-class women found their lives increasingly centered around their husbands and children, they were advised of the gravity of their redefined role.

MATERNAL IDEALS

Maternity! Ecstatic sound! So twined round our heart, that it must cease
to throb ere we forget it, it is our first love, it is part of our religion.
The Ladies' Museum, 1825

A number of themes in nineteenth-century child-rearing manuals and magazine articles were weakly developed or entirely absent from the prescriptive writings of an earlier era. Foremost among these are that child care is the exclusive province of women, that motherhood is their primary function, and that mothers alone are responsible for their children's character development and future success or failure. By the 1830s motherhood had been transformed into a mission, putting "the entire burden of the child's well-being in this life and the next" in his or her mother's hands (Sunley 1963:152). These themes were not limited to child-rearing literature. Popular novels, poems, and biographies of famous men all stressed the important role of mothers in shaping their children's fate. Middle-class women were told that they had the power to produce misery or joy, depending on how they performed their parental duties.

Motherhood, as depicted in the prescriptive writings of the mid-nineteenth century, was a full-time occupation. "It truly requires all the affection of even a fond mother to administer dutifully to the numerous wants of a young child," wrote William Dewees (1847:64–65). Mrs. Lydia Sigourney in *Letters to Mothers* (1838:28, 87) agreed. A mother is "a sentinel who should never sleep at her post," she wrote. Women were urged to keep careful records of their children's behavior and development and to "study night and day the science that promotes the welfare of our infant."

Mothers, according to the advice givers, were perfectly suited to care for their children; no one else could do the job as well. As much as a mother's duties permitted, she was to "take the entire care of her own child," advised the popular domestic writer, Lydia Maria Child (orig. 1831). During the first "sacred" year, concurred Mrs. Sigourney, "trust not your treasure too much to the charge of hirelings. Have it under your superintendence night and day" (1838:16). Children whose mothers did not "take the entire care of them," opined the author of an 1841 *Parents* magazine article, faced real danger; a mother "cannot be long relieved without hazard or exchanged without loss."

Many writers stressed the sentimental benefits of an activity that received no material rewards. "How entire and perfect is the dominion over the unformed character of your infant. Write what you will, upon the printless tablet, with your wand of love," Mrs. Sigourney exulted (1838:10, 2). "My friends," she continued, "if in becoming a mother, you have reached the climax of your happiness, you have also taken a higher place on the scale of being." The love of children, proclaimed an editorial in *Godey's Ladies Book* (1860:272), "is as necessary to a woman's perfect development, as the sunshine and the rain are to the health and beauty of the flowers." Not only was a woman's happiness dependent on her civilizing task, her very identity was derived from it. "A woman is nobody. A wife is everything . . . and a mother is, next to God, all powerful," trumpeted a writer in a Philadelphia newspaper at mid-century (quoted in Calhoun 1960:84-85).

A corollary of the focus on mothers was the disappearance of fathers from the child-rearing manuals of the era. While some earlier tracts were addressed exclusively to mothers, most were written for "parents," and there was even an occasional "advice to fathers" manual. The shift from *parental* to *maternal* responsibility is evident in Philip Greven's (1973a) collection of sermons, treatises, and other sources of advice on child rearing dating from 1628 to 1861. The first eight excerpts, originally published between 1628 and 1814, are all addressed to "parents." It is not until John Abbott's 1833 essay "On the

Mother's Role in Education" that the maternal role is highlighted, and mothers are given primary responsibility for child care. By mid-century advice books assumed that children spent most of their time with their mothers, not their fathers, even though by law and custom final authority was in male hands.

The occasional references to fathers in the prescriptive writings of the day either remarked on their sovereignty in the home or noted that their real responsibilities lay outside of it. A father's duties, advised the *Ladies' Companion*, are "the acquisition of wealth, the advancement of his children in worldly honor—these are his self-imposed tasks" (quoted in Welter 1973:240). But some writers did lament the absence of fathers from the home. In an article entitled "Paternal Neglect" in an 1842 issue of *Parents* magazine, Reverend Abbott averred that the father's absence was an abundant source of domestic sorrow. "The father," he wrote, "eager in the pursuit of business, toils early and late, and finds no time to fulfill . . . duties to his children."

By mid-century good mothering was not only essential to the well-being and future of the child, but the lack of such devoted care was considered a threat to the moral fiber of the nation as well. "The destiny of a nation is shaped by its character," Reverend Beckwith proclaimed, "and that character . . . will ever be found to be molded chiefly by maternal hands" (1850:4). As part of the effort to convince middle-class women of their crucial role in the "nation's destiny," moral educators frequently cited the mothers of famous men. Just look at the glorious results of good mothering, women were told. George Washington's mother was a particular paragon of virtue. "The mother of Washington is entitled to the nation's gratitude," wrote Reverend Abbott. "She, in great measure formed the character of the hero and the statesman. We are indebted to God for the gift of Washington; but we are no less indebted to him for the gift of his inestimable mother" (1833:ii). Women were urged to take their nurturing seriously, for they never knew what the future held. "The mother may, in the unconscious child before her, behold some future Washington or Franklin" exulted a writer in *Ladies' Magazine* (1840). One book of this genre, *Mothers of the Wise and Good* (Burns 1851), went through four editions, while a host of magazine articles recounted the lives of famous men and their mothers' beneficial influence on them.

But a mother's influence could take a different turn. To put it colloquially, good mothers produced good boys, and bad mothers produced bad boys. Many advice writers dwelt long and graphically on the evils that sprang from poor mothering. An 1841 issue of *Parents* magazine contained a case study of a convict whose life of crime was analyzed in the following terms: "His mother, although hopefully pious, never prayed with him in private" Then a warning: "Reader, are you a parent? . . . Train up a child in the way he should go!" (quoted in Kuhn 1947:67). Mrs. Elizabeth Hall (1849), writing in *The Mother's Assistant*, made the point succinctly: "Perhaps there is no proposition that is so hackneyed, and at the same time so little understood, as that women are the prime cause of all the good and evil in human actions. . . . Yes, mothers, in a certain sense the destiny of a redeemed world is put into your hands."

Many authors noted that while women could not participate in the political realm, motherhood—because of its far-reaching influence—still gave women a lofty position in society. "Though she may not teach from the portico nor thunder from the forum . . . she may form and send forth the sages that shall govern and renovate the world," wrote Catherine Beecher (1829:54), the popular domestic educator. And, argued some advice givers, it was sensible to educate women because of their influence on the next generation. But it was *maternal* education they sought. In an 1845 tome, Edward Mansfield (1845:105) cited three reasons for educating women: "That they should as mothers be the fit teachers of infant men. That they should be the fit teachers of American men. That they should be the fit teachers of Christian men."

This preoccupation with motherhood is perplexing if not analyzed within the milieu that gave rise to it. The demise of the self-contained household economy, the isolation of a much reduced living unit, the separation of the home from the workplace, and the resultant segregation of daily life into male and female spheres were all elements that set the stage for this ideology. These factors, rather than any innate domestic propensity in women, explain the overweening emphasis on the mother role. On this point I take issue with historian Carl Degler, who writes that because only women bore and could feed children in the early years, it is not surprising that "the ideology of domesticity stressed that women's destiny was motherhood" (1980:84). But women had *always* borne and nursed children. Why does this ideology appear in full bloom only after 1820? In the words of another historian, Mary Ryan, why, for the first time, was "childhood socialization, and not merely the physical care of infants . . . subsumed under the category of motherhood?" (1975:84). Why, if there had always been mothers, had motherhood as a sacred calling only then been invented? The answer lies in the structural changes occurring in nineteenth-century society, changes that led to the increased seclusion of women and children in the home, the lessened burden of household manufacture, the need for "high-quality" children, and the growing concern with the declining birthrate of the white middle class. These changes more than adequately explain why motherhood, as never before, stood out as a discrete task.

CONSCIOUS MOTHERHOOD: 1870–1900

Woman of this age has to learn that to save man is to study man.
Emma Marwedel, *Conscious Motherhood*, 1887

From the 1870s on, guides to child care came increasingly under professional scrutiny and control. This was the era of "scientific" child study, when a number of works on child development were widely read by the general public. Whereas ministers and matrons once were regarded as authorities on child care, now specialists had the final word. The "scientizing" of child rearing was part of a general movement that viewed science as the key to solving social problems. The basic tenet of child study was that scientific child care could produce the type of adults essential to the nation's greatness while, at the same time, reducing or eliminating criminality and vice (Wishy 1968).

The result was the professionalization of motherhood. While it continued to be seen as a crucial endeavor, women were no longer innately fit for motherhood because of their "maternal instincts" or "higher moral principles." Now they were told to study the role, be trained for it. "Doctors and lawyers and clergymen fit themselves to have charge of human lives. Why should not mothers?" queried a writer in *The Cosmopolitan* magazine (Walker 1898:89). Emma Marwedel, a leading proponent of scientific child rearing, urged women to make "science their ally" in preparing for competent mothering (1887:34). And middle-class mothers were urged to "study" their children. "Few mothers . . . have undertaken anything like a systematic study of children," lamented a writer in the *Child Study Monthly*, "though they may have devoted the best years of their lives in training their own" (quoted in Davis 1976:99).

As motherhood was being transformed into a profession for middle-class women, it was soon evident who was going to tell women how to prepare for it—the child study "experts," most of whom were trained in the new discipline of psychology (Ehrenreich and English 1978). But mothers were not equal partners in this endeavor. They were told to take careful notes on their children's development and behavior, to provide the raw data for the "experts" who then devised the rules that mothers were to follow.

Just at the time the maternal role was being "scientized," some saw it as an impediment to women's political participation, using motherhood as an argument against female suffrage. Giving a woman the vote, proclaimed Senator George West in 1887, "would take her down from that pedestal where she is today, influencing as a mother the minds of her offspring." "Woman was created to be a wife and mother," declared another politician of the day, "to manage a family, to take care of children and tend to their early training," not to participate in political life (quoted in Kraditor 1968:194–196). But women's maternal role was cited by others as the reason why they *should* be given the vote. Suffragist Julia Ward Howe claimed that it was entirely appropriate that the "mother of the race, the guardian of its helpless infancy" be allowed to lend her purifying influence to the dissolute world of politics (quoted in O'Neill 1971:96). So while they stood at opposite ends of the suffrage debate, both West and Howe assumed women's political role was unequivocally conditioned by their maternal one.

Contemporary social critics and prescriptive writers disagreed on another issue: whether it was better to have few or many children. Denunciations of small families and of women who limited their fertility became common during the final years of the century. Catherine Beecher (1871:4) deplored the "worldliness which tempts men and women to avoid large families, often by sinful methods, thus making the ignorant masses the chief supply of the future ruling majorities." The stinging class bias here shows up in the concern that "lesser elements" were out(re)producing their "superiors." Another writer of the day, a medical doctor, criticized women who, because of the "trouble and pains of gestation and nursing" and the "temporary privation of social and fashionable enjoyment," come to the conclusion that "children are a nuisance" (quoted in Degler 1980:197). But one physician defended small families: "It is more important what kind of a child we raise than how many. It is better to produce one lion than twelve donkeys" (Trall 1874:5).

Despite this disagreement, the demographic data are clear: the fertility of American women in the late nineteenth century continued to decline. The following figures show the average number of children born to white women during the last decades of the 19th century (Coale and Zelnik 1963:36):

1870	4.55 children
1880	4.24 children
1890	3.76 children
1900	3.56 children

Some 50 to 75 percent of this decline can be attributed to family limitation within marriage—the rest is a result of the relatively larger percentage of women who never married or who married at a later age.

How were late nineteenth-century couples limiting their fertility? Most contemporary observers agreed that between 1880 and 1900 the incidence of abortion declined among middle- and upper-middle-class married women. By that time abortion had been outlawed in every state of the union, and after 1880 American courts began to deal more harshly with indicted abortionists. Scholars now believe that by the last decades of the century married middle-class women were controlling fertility and the spacing of children through contraception rather than abortion, although abstinence and coitus interruptus were probably common as well. What is noteworthy here is that contraceptive devices also had been declared illegal. The federal Comstock Law, passed in 1873, prohibited the sending of "obscene material" through the U.S. mail, and the law specifically defined contraceptive devices as "obscene." Following the federal law, a series of state statutes also sought to limit the availability of contraceptives. Twenty-four states banned the advertising, publication, or distribution of contraceptive information, and another fourteen states made it illegal to inform anyone about birth control devices (Smith 1974; Mohr 1978; Luker 1985).

The legal prohibition of abortion and contraception went hand in hand with fears created by the continued decline in the fertility rate. The cry of "race suicide" was heard in some quarters as the conviction grew that immigrants, nonwhites, and the poor would outproduce the native-born white middle class. The banning of techniques to control fertility can be seen as part of what has been termed the "procreative imperative," the promotion of population growth by influential elites that benefit from the rearing of "quality" children (Harris 1981:81). The still young nation required a large labor force to continue its rapid industrialization and to fulfill the myriad labor demands of its booming white-collar sector. Moreover, a growing population would ensure a larger market for the goods and services being produced in ever greater quantities by American business and industry.

Why, then, despite the obstacles to fertility control and the continued emphasis on the importance of the mother role, did middle-class women have fewer and fewer children? As previously suggested, while children are a decided asset in agrarian societies, large families became less economically advantageous for one segment of the population—the middle class—as industrialization and urbanization progressed. A journalist writing at the turn of the century neatly summarized the social and economic forces making for smaller families among the more affluent: "Children are an expensive luxury. They cost a lot to raise; they are late in getting to work because of the long training they must have; and few parents get anything back from them. What I mean is that nowadays raising children is an outlay, financially speaking" (quoted in Gordon 1977:50).

It is ironic that as middle-class women gained greater control over their fertility and had fewer children, the maternal role as defined by the advice givers of the day demanded an ever greater commitment. Middle-class women who were now having only three or four children were being urged to spend a greater amount of time and energy on each one. The full flowering of "scientific" motherhood in the twentieth century meant that child-care experts provided women with abundant counsel on how to keep busy in the ever narrowing domestic realm.

MOTHER DOESN'T KNOW BEST: 1900–1940

The sentimental view of motherliness as the ever holy, ever infallible power must be abandoned. Motherliness is as yet but a glorious stuff awaiting its shaping artist.
                    Ellen Key, *The Renaissance of Motherhood*, 1914

By the turn of the century the child had become the leading player in the American family, if not in all of society. The ideology that full-time mothering was essential to children's proper development met with little or no dissent in the prescriptive writings between 1900 and 1940. Even during the Great Depression, when economic necessity forced more married women than ever before to take jobs, the experts' relentless insistence on the centrality of the mother role did not abate.

The position of the professional child-care expert, the advisor par excellence on correct child-rearing methods, became more firmly entrenched in the era before World War II. So important was the task of molding the child that it could not be left to mere mothers. To the experts of the day child rearing was no longer a duty or a joy, but a scientific undertaking requiring skill and training.

While motherhood after the turn of the century was still a woman's central occupation, it was no longer her only one. Many middle-class women were joining clubs, including ones that sought social reform. They spearheaded efforts to encourage temperance, reduce infant mortality, educate consumers, protect workers, and promote hygiene. But these activities were not divorced from women's primary role. The movements favoring child labor laws and improved working conditions were clothed, in part, in maternal garb; women were said to care about such matters because of their domestic "instincts." Some historians have labeled this ideological justification for women's social activism "maternalist." Even as women were taking on a more active role in public life, a role that occasionally afforded them limited access to positions of influence in government agencies, their participation in social reform efforts was inevitably justified by their roles as mothers. It was not by chance that the first government office to be headed by a woman was the Children's Bureau, a federal child welfare agency created in 1912 (Ladd-Taylor 1995).

While volunteer work was fine, paid work was unthinkable for "respectable" married women. In 1910 a mere 5 percent of married white women were employed outside the home (Degler 1980). And while it was becoming more acceptable for a "girl" briefly to hold an "appropriate" job before marriage, only "spinsters" could have serious career ambitions. The working mother was particularly anathema, and some of the women active in the social reform movement inveighed against mothers who took jobs. Florence Kelley, an officer in the Consumer's League, an organization that promoted protective legislation, opposed the establishment of day nurseries on the ground that they would make it easier for mothers to take jobs. According to Kelley, working women had fewer children, neglected the ones they did have, and were responsible for high rates of infant mortality, all "intolerable social costs" (quoted in Scharf 1980:17).

As Kelley's vehemence suggests, attacks on the employment of married women were part of a larger concern: the ongoing decline in the fertility rate. In 1900, when child-rearing experts were urging women to have at least four children, the majority of women stopped with four or, more typically, with three. During the first two decades of the century many middle-class couples used birth control, and by 1920 most native-born whites were having only two children (Wilson 1979).

G. Stanley Hall, considered the founder of the child study movement, worried about the impact of lower fertility on women. Their "bodies and souls," he wrote, are "made for maternity," so that they can "never find true repose for either without it." Unless women's education focused on motherhood, female graduates were destined to be "parturition phobics." And small families were not only perilous to women but to children as well. "Being an only child is a disease in itself," Hall wrote, and "to some extent, offspring limited to a pair of children also tend to be feeble" (1904:607, 610, 634). Ellen Key sounded a similar alarm in her best-selling book, *Renaissance of Motherhood.* "Has our race ever been afflicted with a more dangerous disease than the one which at present rages among women: the sick yearning to be freed from the most essential attribute of their sex?" (1914:115).

The best known and most vociferous voice of the day condemning small families was that of President Theodore Roosevelt. In an address before the National Congress of Mothers (1905:4) he proclaimed that the man or woman who "deliberately forgoes" the blessings of children, "whether from viciousness, coldness, or self-indulgence . . . why such a creature merits contempt." Roosevelt was not just referring to childless couples but to those who chose to have only two children. "If the average family in which there are children contained but two children," he fumed, "the Nation as a whole would decrease in population so rapidly that in two or three generations it would very deservedly be on the point of extinction. A race that practiced such a doctrine, that is, a race that practiced race suicide, would thereby conclusively show that it was unfit to exist!" Thus, Roosevelt urged the white middle class to procreate.

At the same time some social critics were decrying higher education for women, correctly noting that women with college degrees were less likely to marry and, if they did marry, have fewer children, on average, than other women. As such, debates about women's education became entwined with the dual concerns of family size and proper mothering. Hall, the child study guru, decried higher education for women because it made them "overdraw" their reserves and lose their "mammary functions," making them unable to nurse; this led to "abnormal or incomplete development" in their offspring. A highly educated woman, Hall wrote, "has taken up and utilized in her own life all that was meant for her descendants." In the worst cases, such women became completely sterile and this "elimination of maternity is one of the greatest calamities . . . of our age." For Hall the solution was to provide women with an education that "fits their natures," to educate women "primarily and chiefly for motherhood" (1911:304–305, 297, 283).

Similar notions about women's education filled the pages of the *Ladies' Home Journal*. In a 1900 issue an article written by an "American mother" criticized higher education for women on the grounds that nine out of ten women became housewives. "I know of no college for women in which nursing, cookery, or any of the practical arts which she will need as a wife and mother can be learned." What sort of education does the "American mother" call for? One that "recognizes the differences between the sexes and trains a girl thoroughly for her womanly work" (1900:15).

Books and popular magazines continued to spew forth recommendations on proper mothering. The advice offered during the first decades of the twentieth century was of two types. Prior to about 1915 women were urged to be moral and loving, perhaps even indulgent toward their children, although the experts insisted that training and study were necessary to do the job really well. But by the early 1920s women were warned against "smother love" and were told to stress discipline and regularity over indulgence; "independence training" became the watchword of the day.

While scientific motherhood was being prescribed by contemporary child-rearing experts, the spiritual glorification of the maternal role—so typical of the previous century—was by no means lost. "As for the mother," intoned President Roosevelt in his address before the National Congress of Mothers, "her very name stands for loving unselfishness and self-abnegation and in any society fit to exist, it is fraught with associations which render it holy" (1905:3–4). The persistent emphasis on motherhood should be seen as part of a continuing effort to answer "the woman question" first raised in the nineteenth century. What was to be the role and position of middle-class women in a rapidly industrializing society now that their traditional productive skills were no longer needed? What were they to do all day to keep them occupied? The answer was still—as it had been at least since the 1830s—the child.

The child, no longer a productive member of society or a "miniature adult," had become "a kind of evolutionary protoplasm, a means of control over society's not so distant future" (Ehrenreich and English 1978:172). And women's job was to shape that future. Why should they not be content? "A woman," editorialized the *Ladies Home Journal*, "will often envy a man his chance to go into the world and make laws. But, in comparison, what is the law-maker to the man-maker?" (Bok 1910:5). Ellen Key (1909:100) also told women to appreciate their noble calling: "Women in parliament and in journalism, their representation in . . . government . . . science and literature, all this will produce small results until women realize that the transformation of society begins with the unborn child, and with the conditions of its coming into existence, its physical and psychical training."

Not only was motherhood a lofty profession, it was also a time-consuming one. Women had plenty of work to fill their days if they followed the directives of the child-rearing experts. A mother, advised Dorothy Fisher Canfield, a popular manual writer of the era, should observe every action of her child at every age, suggesting women reserve a half hour every night before bedtime for "meditation devoted to the cultivation of the scientific spirit as applied to our children" (1914:180). Ellen Key counseled that while it was not necessary to devote every waking hour to child care, "our soul is to be filled by the child." Mothers were to think of their children constantly—while sitting at home, taking a walk, lying down. In order to do this they were told to "limit their social activities" and remain "entirely free from working to earn a living during the most critical years of the child's training" (1909:102).

While mothers were urged to be in constant attendance on their children, what were fathers supposed to be doing? Not much, according to the experts. Most equivocated on the subject of the father's role in child care, and while some paid lip service to the importance of the father in his child's education, none spelled out his duties. A writer in the *Ladies' Home Journal* stressed that "father's failures" are less serious than "mother's mistakes" because fathers are "out of the child's life so much of the time." Nevertheless, she suggested that fathers "forget at times their worldly business" and remember that they are "guiding souls upon their upward and outward way" (Brown 1900:32). An editorial in a 1915 issue of the same magazine suggests the rather narrow duties prescribed for fathers of the era. The writer regrets that many men, when questioned about their children, reply, "That's for my wife." But paternity has limited parameters; a father becomes important only when the child reaches school age. Education takes place "outside the home," so that "it is within the father's scope of interest" (Bok 1911b:5).

Ellen Key, who recommended that all women should be required to take a course on housekeeping and child care "as a condition for the right to marry," worried far less about training men for their parental duties. She called for a greater role for fathers as "educators" of their children, but only when the "care for the maintenance of the family does not press them down to the ground." And she cautioned that while men perform as well or better than women in the world of work, "in the home . . . men cannot supplant the spirit and activities" of mothers (Key 1914:167, 135; Key 1909:86).

SCHEDULING TAKES COMMAND

Won't you remember when you are tempted to pet your child that mother love is a dangerous instrument? An instrument which may inflict a never healing wound.
        John B. Watson, *Psychological Care of Infant and Child*, 1928

Starting around 1920 the child-care literature raised a new and frightening spectre: the dangerous mother. Mothers were potentially dangerous to the health and well-being of their children and ultimately to society at large. In the words of historian Sheila Rothman (1978:212), the prescriptive writings of the period "reduced the competence of the mother to the point where she almost seemed a criminal figure, stunting and warping her child's development."

While it had long been thought that improper mothering could inflict damage on the child, incompetent mothers were seen as the exceptions, not the rule. But under the hegemony of behaviorism, the dominant school of psychology in the United States in the early twentieth century, mothers were assumed guilty of damaging their children unless proven innocent. The cause, said the experts, was women's lack of expertise in "mothercraft." The solution prescribed for this lamentable situation was to rigorously follow the dicta of the experts of the day, a regimen that recommended a highly scheduled, almost military approach to raising children.

The dominant figure in the "mothers are dangerous" school of child care was behavioral psychologist John B. Watson, the author of the best-selling manual, *Psychological Care of Infant and Child* (1928). No advice giver of the day was untouched by his theories. The widely read child-care pamphlets published by the Children's Bureau, an agency of the U.S. government, incorporated his ideas and guaranteed them a large audience. Watson castigated irrational, emotional mother love for its devastating effects. Such love, he argued, led to weak, dependent children, children with "crippled personalities" who would never make it in the tough competitive world of industrial capitalism. Rather than coddling children and overwhelming them with affection, mothers should stress regularity, punctuality, and cleanliness, which would produce the polite, disciplined children, fine-tuned to the needs of business and industry (Hardyment 1983).

Doubting that women could successfully carry out his recommendations, Watson sarcastically dedicated his manual "to the first mother who brings up a happy child." Although children could be reared more "scientifically" away from their parents, the home, he conceded, was here to stay. The task, then, was to work with the raw material at hand, to get the mother "to take a new view . . . of her responsibility for her experiment in child rearing" (1928:7–9). Clearly his dicta were directed at the middle class since he urged potential parents not to have children at all unless they could afford separate bedrooms for each child, a prerequisite for carrying out behaviorist doctrines.

The core of Watson's view of maternity is found in his chapter "The Danger of Too Much Mother Love." "Invalidism," he warns, is on the rise in most American homes because children are being "over-coddled." Mothers should treat their children "as though they were young adults." "Never hug and kiss them," he cautions, "never let them sit on your lap." If a mother simply can not resist showing some sign of affection toward her children, she should "kiss them once on the forehead at bedtime, but shake hands with them in the morning" (1928:80–82).

Watson wrote that he wished "it were possible to rotate mothers occasionally" in order to avoid the development of excessive affection between mother and child. But since this was not a realistic option, children should be left alone for part of the day so that "over-conditioning" would have a chance to die down. Watson realized that his advice would not be easy for some mothers. "If your heart is too tender," he wrote, "and you must watch the child, make yourself a peephole so that you can see it without being seen, or use a periscope" (1928:84–85).

As innovative (not to say bizarre) as Watson's proposals appear, they bore some resemblance to earlier child-rearing prescriptions. The dicta that children should be trained to "stand on their own two feet" and should not be coddled or kept dependent by excessive maternal affection were themes that often appeared in the prescriptive literature of the colonial period. The innovation of the behaviorists was not their advice per se, but the welding of the time-worn dicta of the Protestant ethic to the findings of "science."

Watson's warnings about the dangers of mother love were echoed by nearly every child-rearing expert of the day. The 1925 Children's Bureau pamphlet *Child Management* cautioned its readers that "the very love of the mother prevents her from successfully fulfilling the obligations of her parenthood." The mother who fails to train her child in independence because she gets satisfaction when "he clings to her so tenaciously" will later regret her actions (Thom 1925:3–4). Five years later another Children's Bureau pamphlet delivered the same message in a simple-minded, condescending tone: "Do you want your child's love for yourself? A good mother is happy to see a child happy, no matter where he is. She is a bad mother if she is sorry when he is happy without her" (1930:54).

A major tenet of the Watsonian school of child rearing was scheduling. Children were to be kept on a rigid schedule for feeding, sleeping, toilet training, and nearly all other activities; any deviation from routine was viewed as harmful and was recommended only when a child was sick. The emphasis on regularity is a recurrent feature in all of the prescriptive literature of the period. In child care, wrote Mrs. Max West, author of the first edition of the Children's Bureau pamphlet *Infant Care*, published in 1914, "perhaps the first and most essential habit is that of regularity. This begins at birth and applies to all the physical functions of the baby" (West 1971:37). And the 1929 edition of the pamphlet repeated these instructions: "Through training in regularity of feeding, sleeping, and elimination the tiny baby will receive his first lesson in character building" (Eliot 1929:3).

Infants were to be fed by the clock every four hours. Every edition of *Infant Care* (1914, 1929, 1938) published during the Watsonian era stressed feeding on a rigid schedule. The 1930 Children's Bureau pamphlet *Are You Training Your Child to Be Happy?* gave mothers a "lesson" on how to feed their babies. It was Watson's principles in microcosm written on a second grade level:

> Begin when he is born.
> Feed him at exactly the same hours every day.
> Let him sleep after each feeding.
> Do not feed him just because he cries.
> Let him wait until the right time.
> If you make him wait, his stomach will begin to wait.
> His mind will learn that he will not get things by crying. (1930:1)

Mary McCarthy's novel *The Group*, set in the 1930s, contains a graphic depiction of a young mother trying to follow these dictates:

> The sound of a baby's crying made itself heard in the silence. . . . "That's Stephen again," said Mrs. Hartshorn. "I recognize his voice. He yells louder than any other baby in the nursery. . . ."
> Mrs. Hartshorn looked at her watch. "Can't the nurse bring him in now," she wondered. "It's quarter to six." "The schedule, mother!" cried Priss. "The reason babies in your time had colic wasn't because they were breast-fed, but because they were picked up at all sorts of irregular times and fed whenever they cried. The point is to have a schedule and to stick to it absolutely!" (1963:241–242)

Similarly, toilet training, according to Watson's scenario, was to begin very early and be pursued vigorously. The 1929 edition of *Infant Care* suggested that training could begin when the baby was one month old but must always be started by three months. "Almost any baby can be trained so that there are no soiled diapers to wash after he is six or eight months old," the author of the pamphlet suggested optimistically (Eliot 1929:57). The difficulty of training a baby that young must have dawned on the authors of the revised 1938 edition of the pamphlet. They advised a slightly more realistic schedule: training was to begin at six months and be completed by one year (Children's Bureau 1938).

The behaviorist insistence on regularity and tight scheduling is perplexing unless it is placed within the larger context of "scientific management," an early twentieth-century movement that sought to control labor and increase efficiency in capitalistic production through the methods of science. The goal of scientific management was to dictate to the worker "the precise manner in which work [was] to be performed," a goal that was to be met by management's control over "the decisions that are made in the course of work" (Braverman 1974:107, 118). Thus, just as management was to set the pace, time, and scope of work, the mother was told to schedule and regulate the hours of feeding, sleeping, and elimination. Watson insisted that his methods would train children to be independent, but it is unclear how removal of control over activities—from baby to mother (or worker to manager)—instills autonomy and self-reliance. A more likely goal of the industrial model of child care was the rearing of individuals who fit into a working world that demanded regularity, discipline, and conformity to outside direction.

If Watson's scientific principles were molding children to the requirements of industrial capitalism, they were doing so at the expense of their mothers' time and energy. Watson was unconcerned about the impact his advice had on a mother's workload. After all, maternal convenience was hardly worthy of consideration when so much was at stake. Mother was to spend hours chauffeuring her children to music and dance lessons, sports events, and other activities meant to nurture independence; in her leisure time, she was expected to study the child-care manuals to find out what she was doing wrong. Watson's methods, in fact, increased women's work. "The attempt to develop independence in infants," notes historian Mary Ryan, "was particularly productive of nervous exhaustion entailing as it did the pressure to toilet train an infant by three months; feed the child precisely on schedule; and endure the childish tantrums and long bouts of screeching that were deemed healthy" (1975:347).

A number of Watson's followers tried to explain why "smother love" had suddenly loomed as such a problem. A speaker at the 1930 White House Conference on the Health and Protection of Children offered this explanation: "Freed by labor-saving devices from many of the tasks which formerly kept her occupied, living in a small apartment, she has little to do except exercise close supervision over the children's affairs. As a result, the mother is likely to form such a close attachment to the child that he is robbed of his initiative and spontaneity" (quoted in Rothman 1978:215). The authors of the manual *Parents and Children* agreed with this interpretation. The root of the problem, they claimed, is that the modern mother has more leisure, thus giving her "the opportunity to impress herself too much upon the child . . . her influence is excessive" (Groves and Groves 1928:121).

One might think that with all the danger of overexposure to "Mom" the experts would have called for a greater role for "Dad." In fact, some of them did just that, but within clearly defined limits. "It may be natural and good for young children to be more with their mothers than their fathers, but it is certainly not wholesome for these children to be brought up almost exclusively in the fellowship of their mothers," according to one child-care manual. This is a good example of the way the paternal role was depicted in the child rearing literature of 1920s and 1930s; a dose of father was a healthy antidote to an overdose of mother. Still, to the experts of the day, the paternal role was a decidedly limited one. The authors of *Parents and Children* recommended "a half hour a day of real companionship with the father" and suggested that a father occasionally take his children out to lunch or the theater. "Surely five or six afternoons *a year* spent in this fashion represent no serious drain either upon [his] time or [his] pocketbook" (Groves and Groves 1928:140, 132, 148, emphasis added). The authors of the 1938 edition of *Infant Care* also took a narrow view of a father's duty. "It would be wise," the pamphlet advised, "for the father to help with the care of the baby so that if the mother becomes ill or has to leave home for a period he can meet this emergency until help can he provided" (Children's Bureau 1938:6).

One solution to the problem of excessive mothering was never offered by the experts. None of them suggested women take jobs or have any real interest outside the home. A hobby was all right, but nothing serious or full-time. Watson himself is very clear on this. Writing in a 1927 issue of *The Nation*, he deemed it acceptable for married women to pursue careers so long as they did not have children. "Having children," he wrote, "is almost an insuperable barrier to a career. The rearing of children and the running of a home for them is a profession second to none in its demands" (Watson 1927:10).

The distinction between working women and working mothers was important throughout the 1920s and 1930s. Even those who advocated paid employment for married women drew the line at mothers. "Being there is the greatest contribution we mothers can make in the lives of our children," averred a supporter of vocational training for women (quoted in Scharf 1980:31). The general consensus was that mothers already had a profession. "Baby care," wrote the author of the 1929 edition of *Infant Care*, "is the most important task any woman ever undertakes and she should apply to this work the same diligence and sustained effort that she would give to the most exacting profession" (Eliot 1929:2). In 1924 Vassar College established the School of Euthenics with the avowed aim of raising "motherhood to a profession worthy of [woman's] finest talents and greatest intellectual gifts" (quoted in Filene 1976:32). And the nineteenth-century notion that a woman's career was her children, particularly her sons, was still being touted. As the author of a 1934 magazine article declared: "it is better to be the mother of a Michelangelo than a second rate lady painter; the mother of a Shakespeare, a Dante, or Homer, than a very pleasing lady poet" (quoted in Rupp 1978:63).

The backdrop for Watsonian doctrines included a low rate of employment among married women. In 1920, only 7 percent of married women had jobs, and by 1930 that figure had increased to just under 12 percent. Most married women who worked did so out of economic necessity. They were primarily employed in low-paying, menial positions, and during the Depression many were forced to take whatever work they could find to make up for lost male wages.

During those years the nation's birthrate also reached its then all-time low. Because of Depression-era economic uncertainty, the birthrate plunged, translating into an overall decline of 41 percent between 1900 and 1936. And while popular advice givers and child-rearing experts lambasted mothers who worked outside the home, they did not seem overly concerned that women were having fewer children. Watson, in particular, urged quality rather than quantity in offspring, realizing how difficult it would be for a mother of numerous children to adhere to the strict scheduling and one-child, one-room arrangement demanded by behaviorist doctrine. Then, too, general economic conditions were likely too precarious during the Depression for even the most ardent pronatalist to insist that women's duty lay in giving birth to more mouths to feed.

CHANGING WITH THE TIMES

Depending on the decade, mothers are told to consult the experts or follow their instincts, to show their feelings or disguise themselves in discretion, to allow the twig to bend or train it from the start.
Mother's Day editorial, *New York Times*, May 10, 1981

Three periods emerge in the shifting images of motherhood in the advice literature from colonial times to the years before World War II. In the colonial era the advice of the clergy—the major prescriptive voices of the era—minimized differences in parental roles and duties. Ministers assumed that child rearing was not a discrete task but something that took place amid the daily round of activities that were part of the domestic economy. Parents were told to "raise up" their children together, and aside from the father's role in religious instruction and the mother's duty to nurse her infant, parenting was not a specialized function within the domain of either sex. Nor was there any indication that a special tie existed between mother and child.

This image of generalized parenting began to change during the last years of the eighteenth century. As the country slowly industrialized, women's domestic production began to wane, and the home and the world of work gradually became differentiated. The spheres of the sexes diverged as "work" became associated with men, while women were left in charge of the smaller household domain comprising themselves and their children. The first glimmers of a distinct maternal role began to appear, but the early writings were tentative since the conditions under which motherhood was spotlighted came about gradually. Nevertheless, for the first time we find sermons and pamphlets dealing with child rearing addressed to "mothers" rather than "parents," along with hints of the importance of maternal care for the growing child. The prescriptive writings of these years were transitional. The stern colonial dicta of rearing righteous, God-fearing children directed at both parents were now rarely heard, but the extravagant celebration of motherhood associated with the nineteenth century was yet to come.

By the 1830s as industrialization continued apace, a burgeoning population of homebound middle-class women emerged as the targets of a cascade of maternal advice. These flowery paeans to motherhood contained strong directives. Mothers undertook the herculean job of molding their children into the model middle-class adults of the age. Children required their mothers' full-time care and attention, care that could be provided by no one else. Mothers must perform this task with high purpose and great diligence, for one false move could mark the child for eternity. But if a woman followed the dictates of the advice givers, motherhood would be the most important achievement of her life.

The emphasis on the maternal role and the importance of mother–child ties advocated by the child-rearing experts of the first four decades of the twentieth century was not qualitatively different from that which prevailed during much of the nineteenth century. Styles of child rearing had changed, science had become an instrument for instructing middle-class mothers how to carry out their maternal duties, and the principles of management had been applied to the sphere of child care for the first time. But the focus on the mother as the child rearer par excellence, the insistence that no one else could take her place, and the assumption that women's most important, if not sole, task in life was rearing healthy, well-adjusted offspring had roots deep in the nineteenth century. It was not until profound changes occurred in the roles of middle-class women in the decades following World War II that it behooved the child-care experts and popular advice givers alike to tardily, but momentously, redefine the mother role and the duties it entailed.

MOTHERS DESCEND

The idea of imprisoning each woman alone in a small, separate and self-contained dwelling is a modern invention, dependent upon an advanced technology.

Philip Slater, *Pursuit of Loneliness*, 1976

Something new came over America in the years immediately before and after World War II. The rigid routines of child care recommended by Watson and his followers were displaced by the tenets of the much-lauded and much-damned "permissive school" of child rearing associated with Dr. Benjamin Spock. The goal of child care was no longer to stymie the natural inclinations of infants and small children but to encourage them and give them free rein. Since spontaneity and self-expression were now believed important to the developing child, children would lead and mothers would follow.

Permissiveness did not just apply to child care. It was a harbinger of change sweeping through many arenas of American life. Advice that emphasized laissez-faire methods in child rearing meshed with the postwar economy's reliance on ever rising levels of consumption. Discipline and self-control, qualities that suited a future-oriented work ethic, were replaced by individuality and indulgence, traits in harmony with the consumption orientation of the late 1940s and 1950s. Continued commercial prosperity was partly dependent on the celebration of freedom and excess, and what better way to instill such values than permissive training during the early, impressionable years? It is not mere coincidence that the teachings of Dr. Spock and his disciples appeared at a time of vast consumer output when self-gratification had become the watchword of the day.

How did the middle-class mother fare in this climate of permissive self-expression? Mothers still had primary, if not sole, responsibility for child care and housework, but now there was a novel element in the lives of many moms: a job, typically a part-time job. While it is well known that millions of wives and mothers went to work during World War II, few realize that not all of them rushed back to tend the homefires after the war ended. In fact, the entire setting of this chapter is one in which married middle-class women—including mothers—moved into the job market in greater numbers than ever before.

Rising standards of consumption, inflation, falling male wages, and a boom in that sector of the labor market that had traditionally hired women all played a role in women's ever growing level of employment. The overall trend took different forms during the course of the postwar era. In the 1950s and early 1960s married women took jobs, often part-time ones, to be able to buy the extras—a second car, a major appliance, a college education for their children—that had become synonymous with a middle-class lifestyle. But by the late 1960s, a time of surging inflation, the income of married women had become crucial to the family budget; it helped pay for food, clothing, the house mortgage, and other basic expenses. And by the 1970s and in subsequent decades, the two-income family had become the norm. Owing to the decline of average male wages from the early 1970s on and, with the notable exception of families of highly paid business and professional men, two incomes were and still are the sine qua non for sustaining a middle-class standard of living in this country.

Women not only sought jobs, but the jobs were there for them to take. During the three decades after World War II women were hired for twenty-five million new jobs, and by the late 1970s, two out of three new jobs were filled by women. These figures, in turn, reflect the phenomenal growth of the service and information sectors of the economy in the postwar period (Harris 1981). By the early 1980s service and information jobs outnumbered manufacturing jobs by at least two to one, and the loss of manufacturing jobs has continued ever since.

The types of jobs created over the last forty years were just the ones traditionally held by women—single, childless women for the most part before World War II, but women nonetheless. Secretarial, clerical, and retail jobs, jobs in nursing, elementary school teaching, and social work, all beckoned the middle-class housewife. And she was certainly in demand. Not only could she be paid less than a man—some 25 to 40 cents on the dollar less—but she was literate and often highly educated. She was an employer's dream come true. And because inflation was gnawing away at the family budget, she was available.

Surveying the child-care advice published during the 1940s and 1950s, one would never suspect that growing numbers of children did not have full-time mothers available to cater to their every need. While child-care methods had changed, the ideal mother described by the advice givers had not. They still took for granted an ever-present mother who was to follow the (revised) dictates of the experts. An exclusive mother–child dyad was still thought essential for a child's healthy development. And Mom was still to blame if anything went wrong (Margolis 1995).

The disjunction between the experts' vision of motherhood and the reality of women's lives grew as the 1950s turned into the 1960s. Rising inflation and new white-collar jobs drew large numbers of middle-class married women into the labor market. While in the 1950s a majority of working mothers had no children under age eighteen, by the 1960s increasing numbers of mothers with school-age children held jobs. The turning point came in 1972 when, for the first time, more mothers of school-age children were employed than were not. This trend has continued ever since: the mothers of younger and younger children have taken jobs. And by the close of the millennium over three-quarters of all women with children under age eighteen were employed (U.S. Department of Labor 1980; Gross 1998).

The child-rearing experts' recognition of these trends was slow in coming. Some of the child-care manuals of the 1960s show a dawning awareness that mothers are not home all the time and that fathers have some responsibility for child care. But not until the 1970s did popular manual writers and child-care experts alike awaken to the reality that many mothers had jobs outside the home. For the first time since the early nineteenth century, full-time mothering was no longer viewed as essential to a child's well-being. The hoary dogma that an *exclusive* mother–child relationship was both natural and inevitable came under attack. Mothering was no longer the prerogative of women alone. Fathers, it turned out, had the capacity to mother as well as mothers did if given the opportunity. Indeed, times had changed, but the structural conditions of postwar American society rather than some sudden bolt of understanding on the part of the advice givers were ultimately responsible for this signal redefinition of the mother role.

SPOCK-MARKED MOTHERS AND MOMS: 1940–1960

> Let us, contemporary mothers, together regain that common sense which is yours, which has been yours before you allowed yourselves to be intimidated by the omniscient totalitarians of one denomination or another.
> Leo Kanner, *In Defense of Mothers*, 1941

Tentative signs appeared in the 1930s that child-care experts were starting to question the wisdom of behaviorist dogma. Were early independence training and restricted doses of maternal affection really best for children? "It's perfectly safe to love your children," proclaimed *Parents* magazine. The pendulum had started to swing away from the let-them-cry school of the Watsonian era to the permissive, wean-them-late school of the Spockean age. The detached, mechanical Mother was replaced by the warm and affectionate Mommy. "Self-demand" became the motto of the movement, and by 1940, two-thirds of all the articles in *Ladies' Home Journal*, *Woman's Home Companion*, and *Good Housekeeping* advised mothers to allow their babies to set their own feeding and sleeping schedules. "It is reasonable to feed a baby when he's hungry. It is unreasonable to make him wait," admonished a writer in a 1940 issue of *Good Housekeeping* (Stendler 1950; Kenyon 1940b).

Babies still dominated their mothers' lives; only now it was babies rather than mothers who set the timetable. "Any . . . schedule must . . . take into account the balance of all the infant's natural activities and the life routine must be carefully . . . worked out with this in mind," wrote Dr. Margaret Ribble in her popular pre-Spock manual, *Rights of Infants* (1943:63). We have happier children, concurred a writer in *Good Housekeeping*, "since we have learned to adapt ourselves to the baby's body rhythms and natural inclinations" (Kenyon 1940a:63). The experts' new message was clear: Babies don't need their mothers to schedule them and teach them discipline; rather they need their mothers to trail after them, stimulate them, and meet their emotional needs.

"Mothers," the experts said, "relax and trust yourselves." Women were told to stop beating their breasts in self-reproach and wailing, "I know it's all my fault! What is all *whose* fault?" asked Dr. Leo Kanner in *In Defense of Mothers*. He urged mothers to ignore the so-called experts, whose goal was "to put fear of their particular gods into their audiences." His advice, in contrast, was based on "common sense" (1941:102, 5, 7). So too was that of Dr. Spock, dubbed "the confidence man" (Zuckerman 1975). The first edition of his enormously popular child-care manual was entitled *The Common Sense Book of Baby and Child Care* (orig. 1946). In it, Dr. Spock told mothers to ignore all the conflicting theories and take the anxiety out of child care by following their own instincts.

But maternal instincts could only go so far, and herein lay a mixed message in Spock's advice. He gave mothers quite limited autonomy and, in fact, advised them to consult often with their pediatricians about even the most minor problems of child care. Moreover, his instructions were so specific and simplistic at times as to make a mockery out of his dictum that mothers should follow their own common sense. Here are his instructions on preparing for the baby's bath:

> Before starting the bath, be sure you have everything you need close at hand.
> If you forget the towel, you'll have to go after it holding a dripping baby in your arms.
> Take your wristwatch off.
> An apron keeps your clothes drier.
> Have at hand: soap, washcloth, towel, lotion or powder if you use either, shirt, diaper, pins, nightie. (Orig. 1946:155)

What did the permissive, self-scheduling ethic of the day mean for the caregiver herself? Now that infants were to dictate their demands to mother, her routine was to follow them. As one student of child-care literature noted: "Self-demand, especially when the baby is breast-fed or when it is believed that close contact between the mother and the child at feeding time is important, means that all other activities must be adapted to the child's rhythm and makes it almost impossible to get away from home" (Escalona 1953:212). Dr. Ribble, who recommended that infants be breast-fed every three hours until they were three months old, warned that a mother must "function for her infant for many months because it is not until after the faculties of speech and locomotion have developed that he can cope with any separation from the mother without danger" (1943:21).

Not only good physical care was required. Spock and other advice givers superimposed emotional work on the physical work of caring for a child. Mother must always be mindful of her own behavior so as to ensure a propitious environment for her children's development. She must walk a fine line between too much and too little attention, although during the permissive era too much was better than too little. Sociologist Philip Slater has observed just how all-consuming the maternal role was supposed to be during those years. He paraphrases Dr. Spock's advice to mothers: "You have the capacity to rear a masterpiece. Such an activity is the most important thing you can do and should therefore rightfully absorb all your time and energy" (1976:70–71).

The ideal mother of the postwar era was completely fulfilled by carrying out all the minute and at times tedious tasks of child care, satisfaction that came naturally from her maternal instinct. "Womanly women," wrote Dr. Ribble, "will get unique mental stimulus . . . from contact with the first principles of life" (1943:108). Such a woman was alert to all the nuances of her children's behavior. To stimulate their intellectual growth she spent hours engaging in baby talk and playing games. And she had few or no interests outside her home. In the words of one scholar: "The mother of Dr. Spock's manual is an apolitical person without any social involvements. . . . She exists largely to rear her young and has time off to pursue a few private activities" (Weiss 1977:543).

While Dr. Spock admitted that the demands of motherhood were sometimes trying, he advised mothers who got depressed to "go to a movie or to the beauty parlor, or to get yourself a new hat or dress." Employment was never a solution to maternal malaise:

> Useful, well adjusted citizens are the most valuable possessions a country has, and good mother care during early childhood is the surest way to produce them. . . . If a mother realizes clearly how vital this kind of care is to a small child, it may make it easier for her to decide that the extra money she might earn, or the satisfaction she might receive from an outside job, is not so important after all. (Orig. 1946:63-64.)

The idealized image of the mother–child unit of the Spockean school contended with a strong countercurrent in the popular literature of the period. During the late 1940s and 1950s psychoanalysts and their popularizers discovered that the mother–child relationship was often pathological; its symptoms were problem children and problem adults. To be sure, such ideas were not entirely new. The damned if you do and damned if you don't message is found in the prescriptive writings as far back as the nineteenth century, but it reached new heights of vitriol during the postwar years.

The frightening specters of "Momism," maternal overprotection, and maternal neurosis were first raised in Philip Wylie's best-seller, *Generation of Vipers*. "Megaloid mom worship has got completely out of hand," he proclaimed. "Our land, subjectively mapped, would have more silver cords and apron strings crisscrossing it than railroads and telephone wires" (1942:185). Wylie opened the floodgates to more than a decade of stinging attacks on "Moms." In his book *Maternal Overprotection* (1943), Dr. David Levy concluded—based on a "sample" of twenty women and their children—that overprotective mothers were of two types: 1) submissive or 2) domineering; and they produced children who were 1) selfish and undisciplined or 2) docile, goody-goodies. These "research findings" are a marvel of scientific obfuscation since Levy admitted he found no common behavior patterns in either the mothers or the children he studied, the data on which his "behavioral types" were based!

The mothers-are-dangerous theme was echoed in some of the child-rearing manuals of the day. Dr. Leo Kanner, who defended mothers from the advice of the "experts," still cautioned against the dangers of "smother love." It is, he wrote, "the most egotistically selfish thing on earth. It is a caricature of mother love. . . . Its aim is domination . . . and it forges chains" (1941:40–41). The authors of *It's a Wise Parent* also warned against excessive maternal attention: "We all know women who fancy themselves as sacrificing everything for their children. They are impossible as parents or anything else" (Smart and Smart 1946:8).

A few advice givers suggested that Dad might help solve the problem by undoing some of the damage done by Mom. The father, they noted, was especially important as a masculine role model for his sons, so Dad must always display "appropriate" male behavior. He should not be seen doing the dishes, cooking, or pursuing other "feminine" activities. Fathers were also counseled that their other main job as parent was keeping Mom sexually satisfied so that she would not vent her frustrations on the kids. In the chapter "Live Your Gender!" Dr. David Goodman wrote that "the American mother married to a business-bound husband lives her whole life in her children with the result that she smothers them with excessive care, affection, and protectiveness." And the solution? "If the American mother enjoyed the companionship of a romantic-minded husband, she might be more willing to let her children alone. . . . The truly feminine mother, fulfilled in her marriage to a truly masculine father, does not overprotect, dominate, or over-fondle her children" (1959:54–55).

Family sociologist E. E. LeMasters analyzed these widespread attacks on mothers and claimed they were related to the "emancipation" of women that began during World War I and reached its zenith by World War II, when "the American mother had become the bad guy in our family system." He explained the source of this anger: "When any group of human beings in a society battles its way out of an inferior social position, hostility is always generated." Perhaps, he suggested, "American mothers achieved more equality than they wanted." What they had in mind was a "50-50 partnership" that "turned out to be closer to 70-30 or even 80-20, with the American father having all the fun with the children and the mother all of the headaches" (1970:121–24).

LeMasters implies that the mother's near total responsibility for her children was a recent phenomenon; as we know, this was not the case. I suggest whatever problems may have arisen because of "smother love" were related to the hothouse isolation of American women and children in the home during the first half of the twentieth century. As Barbara Ehrenreich and Deirdre English have pointedly noted in their analysis of experts' advice to women: "It did not enter the experts' minds to question the theory [locking mother and child together exclusively] or to be alarmed at the terrible solitude in which most women were attempting to raise their children; the theory was solid; the home was sacred; it was the women who had failed" (1978:202).

Aside from duties as male role models, the child-care manuals of the 1940s and 1950s disagreed on how much time and energy fathers should devote to their children. But the paternal role was invariably depicted as a mere shadow of the maternal one. Because the father is busy with his job and sees his infant so irregularly—and irregularity is disturbing to a young child—it is often best if the father doesn't come into the child's routine until after the third month, Dr. Ribble recommended. Then he can briefly visit the baby in the morning and evening. After all, Ribble opined, "one mother is really enough—provided she really mothers" (1943:101–102). The author of the *Parents' Manual* disagreed with this restricted notion of fatherhood: "Children need fathers as well as mothers and they need them from the earliest years." Although the mother has "the major responsibility for physical care and routine management," the father and child will get to know each other better if the father "occasionally changes a diaper or supervises a meal." Then the author revealed the bogeyman behind her recommendations: if all control of children falls to the mother, children might "grow up believing that women are born to be the world's real bosses; such a belief tends to breed passive men and aggressive women" (Wolf 1941:46, 222, 218).

And while Dr. Spock addressed *Baby and Child Care* to "loving parents," all of the advice is actually directed at mothers; only a handful of paragraphs in the 600-page volume are addressed to fathers. Moreover, it is clear that not too much help should be expected from men in daily child-care tasks. While it's "fine for fathers" occasionally to give a bottle or change diapers, "there are some fathers who get gooseflesh at the very idea of helping to care for a baby, and there's no good to be gained from trying to force them [since] most of them come around to enjoying their children later when they're more like real people" (orig. 1946:31).

The insignificance of fathers was also reflected in the research done on child care by the scholars of the day. For example, the authors of *Patterns of Child Rearing* sought "to secure reliable information about the varieties of experience that American children have had in their homes with their parents by the time they go to school" (Sears et al. 1957:vi). The authors interviewed 379 mothers for the book, but not a single father. Similarly, only mothers were interviewed for *The Changing American Parent*, this time nearly 600 of them (Miller and Swanson 1958). Perhaps biases like these are what led British anthropologist Geoffrey Gorer to conclude in *The American People* that "in few societies is the role of the father more vestigial than in the United States" (1964:54).

The prescriptive literature on the maternal role during the 1940s and 1950s seems somewhat at odds with its setting. Its discourse on maternal care contradicts the reality that growing numbers of married women—including mothers—were taking jobs. Women's labor force participation zoomed by 32 percent during the war years. Moreover, 75 percent of the new war workers were married, and one-third had children under fourteen years of age (Rupp 1978). During the 1950s—a decade when a woman's desire for a career was seen as a disguised search for masculine identity—more than four million married women entered the labor force, many of them mothers. In fact, between 1940 and 1960 the number of working mothers increased by 400 percent.

The continued emphasis on full-time motherhood coincided with a sharp increase in the fertility rate following World War II. Between 1936 and 1940 the birthrate slowly began to revive from its Depression-era low. The momentum picked up during the war and culminated in the well-known "baby boom" of the 1950s. By 1960 the fertility rate of white women was almost as high as it had been at the end of the nineteenth century, when they were averaging between three and four children each.

Married women must have suffered from cognitive dissonance during the 1950s. While many were taking jobs, child-care experts and the popular media were lambasting working mothers and extolling the "feminine mystique" (Friedan 1974). A married woman has only two jobs, proclaimed Dr. Goodman (1959), one to care for her children, the other to keep her man happy. Agnes Meyer's comment in a *Ladies' Home Journal* article "Children in Trouble" is typical in its condemnation of working mothers. "I find that the upper income bracket child whose mother works because she wants more money, or because she considers it more stimulating, often hates her with a frenzy that he doesn't understand because he feels that his mother prefers this thing called a job to him" (1955:205).

The apparent contradiction between behavior and ideology may be partly resolved by citing the age of women workers. During the 1950s the largest group of women entering the labor force was comprised of women over forty-five years old. Most younger wives were still at home having three or four babies while their older counterparts were taking jobs. The child-care experts were recommending just that. Spock, for example, suggested that after a five- or six-year break when their children were small, mothers could return to work, as long as they were home when the children returned from school. But in an era when a typical woman had three or four children, this meant at least eight to ten years before the youngest child was in school, freeing her to take a part-time job.

The experts' directives were explicit: women were to enter and withdraw from the job market in accordance with the family life cycle. Part-time work was preferable to full-time employment and, under no circumstances, should the demands of a career interfere with a woman's primary responsibility to her children. This advice conformed to the postwar economy's demand for particular types of female labor. As the service sector expanded, large numbers of women were needed to work in offices, retail stores, and banks. These positions were often part-time or temporary, so they did not require the steady work commitment associated with pursuit of a career. Moreover, these "female-typed" jobs usually required little or no on-the-job training; women could take them and leave them at small cost to their employers. At least indirectly, the experts were suggesting that women should be content with the low-paying, part-time, and temporary work available to them because such jobs did not conflict with "good mothering."

The Modern Mother's Dilemma, a popular 25-cent public affairs pamphlet of the mid-1950s, illustrates the neat mesh between the experts' advice and the types of jobs for which middle-class women were in demand. The "mother's dilemma" stems from the early age at which women complete raising a family. As a result, older mothers and young grandmothers find themselves "out of a job." In order to prepare for that day, mothers of small children are advised to keep their hands in any field of interest they had before marriage by reading, going to concerts, subscribing to technical journals, or sewing their children's clothes. The authors cite examples of some of the strategies used by women to keep abreast of their particular field of interest. One woman who wanted to teach when her children were grown went to school one night a week while they were still toddlers to earn credits for a teaching certificate. When her youngsters were in school, she took a full load of courses toward her degree. "Part-time work is the ideal solution for women with school age children," the pamphlet's authors note, and they go on to suggest jobs like file clerk, receptionist, typist, doctor's aide, and lab technician—all low-paying female ghettos—as fields in which part-time employment might be had (Gruenberg and Krech 1957).

These recommendations for dealing with the "mother's dilemma" were reinforced by the authors' depiction of the paternal role. "Fathers get to know children earlier these days since they lend a helping hand." But then a stern caveat was issued: "Let it not be forgotten that Father is still the breadwinner even when the wife works, because his is the chief and continuous responsibility." While father can mind the children while mother cooks dinner, "the thing for Mother to bear in mind is that her husband can't be asked to take over too much. It is more than unfair to expect him to do half the housework as well as carry the load of a full-time job" (Gruenberg and Krech 1957:18–20).

As more and more married women took jobs, the experts approved their actions under certain conditions. Women could work part-time or after their children were grown, but their wage-earning activities should adapt to and never take priority over their primary obligations as mothers. By the 1960s, however, the reality of many women's daily lives had begun to challenge such advice.

TIME FOR A CHANGE: THE 1960S

> Life in America is made up of a tissue of fictions that do not accord with reality, and the omnipresent "Mommie" is one of them that could be very well dispensed with.
>
> Alicia Patterson,
> Address to the Radcliffe College Alumnae Association, 1962

The experts' advice and their vision of the mother role began to change in the 1960s. That decade paralleled the early nineteenth century when, as a result of industrialization, prescriptive writers started revamping the image of motherhood. During the 1960s an increase in maternal employment eventually led to a recasting of middle-class women's roles, including their duties as parents. But those years were also marked by a disjunction between what most of the experts were saying and what growing numbers of middle-class women were doing. This contradiction between ideology and reality—the leitmotif of the era—was not resolved until the 1970s, when feminists and child-care experts alike called for a reappraisal of the old shibboleths about motherhood.

The decade of the 1960s was a period of transition because of the mixed advice that characterized its prescriptive writings. Dr. Spock continued to insist on the need for full-time mother care; that dictum appeared unchanged in the revised 1968 edition of *Baby and Child Care*. Then, too, writers still were voicing concern about the "toxic effect of mother love." Yet, during those years a few experts were discussing the problems created for women by an exclusive mother–child dyad, while others started gathering data that questioned the common wisdom that working mothers invariably harmed their children.

If Dr. Spock clung to his views on the incompatibility of motherhood and work outside the home, others tried to come to terms with maternal employment. "The children of women who are doing interesting work of their own during the day will often find more sensible and sympathetic mothers," psychiatrist Bruno Bettelheim wrote in *Harper's Magazine*. Focusing on the "problems of growing up female," he suggested that "the mother who urges her girl toward intellectual achievement while staying at home herself" poses a contradiction which probably is not lost on the girl (1962:124).

During the 1960s a low-key but steady accumulation of research began challenging the doctrine that working mothers damage their children. In a comprehensive study, *The Working Mother in America* (Nye and Hoffman 1963), the authors concluded that maternal employment per se was neither an index of maternal deprivation nor the profound influence on children's development as once thought. Moreover, the study made the revolutionary suggestion that maternal employment just might have a *positive* effect on children; the children of working mothers were found to be more independent than those of women who stayed home.

Some advice givers of the era were of two minds about working mothers. "Today many women are as deeply and successfully in business and professional duties as are men," Dr. Ribble wrote in the revised 1965 edition of her book. "Yet both can be adequate parents if they put thought, understanding and planning to work" (1965:141). These lines did not appear in the 1943 edition. But the revised edition still distinguishes parental roles: "Perhaps with our new psychological insights into the dynamics of a child's mental growth, the meaning of motherhood and fatherhood may assume its rightful dignity, interest, and joy, and the temporary withdrawal from a career for a woman in order to create and nurture a new life may not be regarded as . . . an unwanted sacrifice."

A telling work of the era is Edith De Rham's *The Love Fraud*. De Rham made the revolutionary suggestion that the solution to the "parasitic relationship" between mothers and children just might be maternal employment:

> If we may assume that the average adult will normally prefer to spend the majority of his or her time in the company of other adults, we may further deduce that the psychological interdependence of mother and child threatens to change the mother's personality in at least two ways: at best she will become childlike herself, at worst she will be transformed into the despised and voracious MOM. (De Rham 1965:132, 158)

While De Rham was suggesting jobs as cures for "Moms," psychoanalyst René Spitz continued the hallowed tradition of blaming mothers for a variety of real and imagined psychosocial disorders. In *The First Year of Life* he identified the "psycho-toxic diseases of infancy." It will come as no surprise to anyone schooled in mother blame that Spitz found all the emotional and physical problems of childhood rooted in a maternal disorder. A common ailment like infant colic, for example, was said to be caused by the mother's "primary anxious over-permissiveness" (1965:206).

Other writers began calling for a greater role for fathers. The 1963 edition of the popular government pamphlet *Infant Care* suggested that "wise mothers let fathers share in the routines of baby care from the beginning." While "some fathers take over certain aspects of care regularly . . . others are more comfortable helping with household chores. . . . But, whichever suits, the father is part of the picture" (Children's Bureau 1963:101, 141, 143). These phrases are absent from the earlier editions of the pamphlet. In a similar spirit, Dr. Ribble's revised 1965 edition of *Rights of Infants* eliminated the passages suggesting that fathers should not have regular contact with their infants until they were three months old. "That her husband is capable and interested in assuming his father role from the start in this joint venture assures a more successful outcome." Also significant is the change in the dictum about baby's needs. The 1943 edition read: "His deepest need by far is the understanding care of one consistent individual—his mother." The 1965 edition was changed to "His deepest need is the understanding and consistent care of his parents" (1965:101, 141).

Still, not all advice givers updated the father role. The pediatrician Haim Ginott, for example, took a traditional approach. In the mid-1960s he was still warning parents that fathers should not become too involved in diapering and feeding their babies because "there is the danger that the baby may end up with two mothers" (1965:169). Ginott aside, a subtle change in the nature and scope of the father role had taken place, a change that foreshadowed the years to come.

The notion that an exclusive mother–child relationship is essential for a child's proper development also was questioned. Anthropologist Margaret Mead (1962:55) wrote that the influential research on the ill effects of maternal deprivation done by John Bowlby (1953), the Dr. Spock of British child care, "was based on a mixed and unexamined set of premises." This was a reference to Bowlby's insistence that there is a "biologically given need for continuity in the mother–child relationship" and that "all interruptions in it are necessarily harmful . . . emotionally damaging, if not completely lethal." Mead pointed out the ethnocentrism of these assumptions: "Actually, such an exclusive and continuous relationship is only possible under highly artificial urban conditions, which combine the production of food outside the home with the practice of contraception" (1962:56). Parenthetically, Bowlby's research on maternal deprivation was done on orphaned and otherwise institutionalized children who were separated from their parents. A member of the British upper class, Bowlby never questioned the child-rearing practices of his own social set, such as hiring governesses and sending boys off to boarding school at a young age.

By the mid-1960s there were tentative suggestions that motherhood was not the only glory in a woman's life and that it was ludicrous, given economic realities, to continue to insist that the maternal role be all-consuming. The best-known and most emphatic declaration on the issue came in 1963, with the publication of Betty Friedan's The Feminine Mystique (1974). Friedan wrote that a woman "must think of herself as a human being first." She must "make a life plan in terms of her own abilities, a commitment of her own to society, with which her commitments as wife and mother can be integrated" (1974:332). Sociologist Alice Rossi also called for a recasting of motherhood as an "important highlight but not as the exclusive basis for a sense of self-fulfillment and purpose in life" (1971:163–164). While women in the nascent feminist movement were the first to propose a revamped mother role, it was not too long before motherhood also was depicted in a new light in the writings of both popular and professional child-care experts.

FATHERS ARE PARENTS TOO:
THE 1970s AND 1980s

I always assumed that the parent taking the greater share of young children ... would be the mother, whether or not she wanted an outside career. ... Now I realize that the father's responsibility is as great as the mother's.

Benjamin Spock, *Baby and Child Care*, 1976 rev. ed.

"Do babies need mothers?" Harvard psychologist Rudolph Schaffer asked in his book *Mothering*. "Yes," he replied, "if it means that they need to be involved in a love relationship and that a limited range of familiar people should provide consistent care throughout the years of childhood. No—if it means that the mother must be the one who gave birth, that no other person can take her place. No again—if we take mothering to involve an exclusive relationship that must encapsulate the child's total social and emotional life" (1977:106).

Dramatic declarations like these first became common in the 1970s, when experts began questioning many of the assumptions that the earlier advice on proper mothering were based. Where were the data that showed mothers were biologically most capable of caring for infants and young children? Where was the evidence that infants bond only with their mothers rather than their fathers or other familiar persons? "Is the capacity to feel maternal emotions and behave in a motherly way restricted to females?" they asked (Wortis 1977:363). Is an exclusive mother–infant arrangement beneficial for either woman or child?

"Mother," declared Schaffer, "*can be any person of either sex*" (1977:103). A child becomes attached to the person who is sensitive, responsive, and emotionally involved. It is these personal qualities, not "blood ties" or sex, that are crucial in developing bonds. Evidence from several studies also suggested that fathers can develop the strong bonds with infants traditionally associated with mothers. Research showed the "mothering instinct is not embedded in the bodies and souls of females alone." Newborns exhibit no consistent preference for one parent or the other, rather it is the person who holds, feeds, and stimulates the baby "to whom initial attachments are made" (Segal and Yahraes 1978:122). Citing this data, Schaffer concluded that there is "no reason why the mothering role should not be filled as competently by males as by females. The father's relative lack of involvement in child care is a cultural rather than a biological phenomenon" (1977:104).

These findings led to criticism of earlier work on mother–child attachment. Some suggested that the studies of René Spitz and John Bowlby were not based on "normal separation" of infants from their parents but on children living in hospitals and orphanages, in other words, children who may have suffered from inadequate stimulation and inconsistent care. One critic accused the two child-care gurus of being "dangerously unscientific" in extrapolating data based on institutionalized infants to "the much more common situation in which infants leave their homes for part of the day, are cared for by other responsible individuals, and are returned again to their homes" (Wortis 1977:365–366).

John Bowlby's assertion that a child is initially unable to form attachments to more than one person—his ever-present mother—also was challenged. "An infant is not confined to just one bond," Schaffer wrote. "Once he [*sic*] has reached the stage of forming specific attachments, he is capable of maintaining a number at the same time" (1977:100). Harvard psychologist Jerome Kagan agreed, arguing that the notion a child can only form a single attachment is "like saying a person can only love one other person. And that's nonsense" (quoted in Glickman and Springer 1978:165–166).

Subsequent studies have shown infants can have multiple attachments that include siblings, grandparents and, most especially, fathers. Nor does attachment to several people imply less depth of feeling: "Love, even in babies, has no limits," Schaffer remarked (1977:100). Most experts now agree that what is important to the development of infants and children is consistent, sensitive care by one or more adults in an environment of love and stimulation, a far cry from the traditional dogma that mother and mother alone could provide such care.

Mother blame also became muted during the 1970s and 1980s. Studies took mothers off the hook on which they had long been impaled: they were not responsible for the variety of children's ills, from schizophrenia to autism and hyperactivity, that had been claimed. "Mothers simply do not deserve all the blame—or all the credit—for what their children become," insisted two child development experts (Segal and Yahraes 1978:74). And where mother blame was still heard, it was usually linked to structural conditions, to the hothouse isolation of the exclusive mother–child relationship rather than to any general failing of women themselves.

The reversal of views on the maternal role was nowhere more dramatic than on the issue of working Moms. Nearly in unison, social scientists and popular advice givers alike began advising women that taking a job did not have the detrimental effect on their children as once thought, so long as high-quality substitute care was available. After an exhaustive review of the literature on the subject, social psychologist Helen Bee concluded that "when the mother is satisfied by her role and adequate alternative care is arranged, the separation of the mother from her child that accompanies maternal employment has no demonstrable negative effect" (1974b:104). The authors of a child development book agreed, noting that "if a mother is happy in what she is doing, then it does not really matter—from the standpoint of how well she brings up her children—whether she chooses to be a homemaker or a worker outside." What about infants and very young children? Does the child's age when mother goes to work make a difference? "Probably not," replied these same authors, "assuming there is adequate and stable substitute care" (Segal and Yahraes 1978:95).

Child care experts now were suggesting that maternal employment just might have some *positive* effects. Studies found that children of working mothers are more self-reliant and less anxious than those whose mothers are home all day. And, the only long-term effect seems to be that by college age, the children of employed women have less stereotyped views of gender roles than those of women who have not held jobs. When the children of working mothers do have development problems, "they seem to be associated more with family instability or inadequate care [when the mother is gone] than with working per se" (Bee 1974b:104).

Nothing is more symbolic of the experts' changed attitude on maternal employment than Dr. Spock's deletion in 1976 of his discussion, "The Working Mother," from the chapter, "Special Problems," where it had appeared in all earlier editions of *Baby and Child Care*. A new chapter, "The Family Is Changing" discussed the "right" of both parents to a career and the qualities to look for in a parent substitute. Moreover, Spock was very forceful in his new-found feminism. "Parents who know they need a career or a certain kind of work for fulfillment," he wrote, "should not simply give it up for their children." He suggested that such parents "work out some kind of compromise between their two jobs and the needs of their children, usually with the help of other caregivers" (1976:37).

Books and magazine columns devoted to working mothers proliferated during the 1970s and 1980s. Most sought to reassure mothers that taking a job was okay. "Good workers are good mothers and vice versa," the author of *The Working Mother* wrote, for "the very qualities which make good workers are those which make good mothers" (Callahan 1972:23). A pamphlet published by the Child Study Association, *The Mother Who Works Outside the Home*, told working mothers that "guilt doesn't have to go with the territory. Working mothers have to remember that they are people themselves, with legitimate needs, and that when these needs are met, they function better as wives and mothers" (Olds 1975:58). Letty Cottin Pogrebin (1974) soothed readers of the *Ladies' Home Journal* when she reported that her interviews with children of working mothers revealed they did not resent their mother's jobs or feel envious of kids whose mothers stayed home.

The climate that molded these revamped attitudes about working Moms also heralded a reevaluation of the effects of alternative child care. Most studies done in the 1970s and 1980s found no differences in mother–child attachment between infants reared at home exclusively by their mothers and infants who spent part of the day in child-care centers. And some former critics of day care withdrew their opposition to it. Jerome Kagan, head of a five-year study of the effects of day care on children, noted that he had once written about its purported evils. "Now I run a day-care center," he said in an interview, "and I changed my mind. All of us have strong prejudices that are religious in intensity but not always based on fact." Pediatrician T. Berry Brazelton no longer saw day care as "taking the child away from the family, but as a way of helping the family through choices, of keeping the family together" (both quoted in

Glickman and Springer 1978:172, 180). Then, too, as psychologist Nancy Choderow (1978) pointed out in her well-regarded study, child care with a few adults caring for a few children—as in good day-care centers—has a longer historical trajectory and is far more common cross-culturally than exclusive mother–child arrangements.

Changing views of the mother role and of the effects of day care on children were accompanied by a surge of research on fathers. The new interest in fatherhood both in scholarly studies and in popular child-rearing literature is evident in my survey of the *Cumulative Book Index* for the years 1950 to 1990. During the 1950s ten books were published on the subject of fathering and fatherhood; during the 1960s eighteen books, during the 1970s, fifty books and between 1980 and 1990, 103 books. Just how few studies had been done on fathers and young children prior to 1970 is clear from the remarks of Milton Kotelchuck, a doctoral candidate at Harvard who did the first laboratory observations of father–child interactions. There was so little research on the topic, he said, that it took him only "a half hour to review all the literature"— and he read "the full articles, not the abstracts!" (quoted in Levine 1976:28).

Prior to the 1970s there was not only a dearth of research on the paternal role, but what little research there was generally focused on father absence and its outcome—the lack of a male role model in the home. "Most of what we know about the impact of fathers," wrote social psychologist Helen Bee, "comes from studies of *absent* fathers." And studies of such fathers certainly "do not tell us much about the positive effects of fathers' presence" (1974a:369, 371). Moreover, "father absence" was defined in a limited way. It meant the lack of a father due to death, divorce, or abandonment; it did not include fathers who were away from home from early morning to late at night or to fathers who worked overtime and on weekends. Even when researchers attempted to measure the impact of fathers on child development, they often assumed that it was "normal for men *not* to interact with their children" (Levine 1976:29).

This truncated view of fatherhood was supplanted by burgeoning interest in father–child interactions and the impact of fathers on their children's development. Kotelchuck's (1972) pioneering research on the nature of a father's ties to his children tried to disprove the theory that "the attachment between mothers and infants was unique or biologically built in." All the earlier research on attachment between mothers and children ranged mothers against strangers, making it appear that the attachment between mother and child was indeed unique. But what about other familiar persons? Kotelchuck wanted to know. What about fathers? His lab experiment found that "infants respond similarly to mothers and fathers," that is, "they will protest the departure of either parent, but not the departure of a stranger." Kotelchuck summarized the significance of his findings: "It becomes clearer and clearer that when another familiar person like the father is introduced into a setting, the presumed uniqueness of the mother–child relationship seems to disappear . . . it becomes obvious that fathers are indeed important to their infants" (quoted in Gornick 1975:10–11).

Not only do babies need and miss their fathers, but fathers need and miss their babies if allowed to have physical contact with them soon after birth. In a study of "engrossment," a sense of "preoccupation . . . and interest in their newborn," fathers permitted early contact did become engrossed in their infants. The authors of the study believe all fathers have the "basic, innate potential" for engrossment and that this "may have important ramifications in the subsequent . . . mental health of the child." Practices that inhibit early contact, however, may lead to "paternal deprivation since potential engrossment may fail to occur" (Greenberg and Morris 1974:526–527, 529, 522–523).

Such findings led experts to begin acknowledging the importance of the paternal role. "The father's involvement—or lack of it—does seem to make a difference," the authors of one child-care manual wrote. "There is convincing evidence," they continued, "that the father's inadequacy or absence can erode the child's emotional well-being and that his wholesome, committed presence can help promote the mental health of his children" (Segal and Yahraes 1978:128,106–107). Paternal influence, the experts concluded, does not seem to be very different from maternal influence in promoting children's well-being. As such, a mother is not always to blame for her children's psychological problems. These "appear to be influenced at least as much by the father's behavior in those studies where investigators have made the effort to study the father's influence" (Hamilton 1977:141).

The dean of American child-care experts, Dr. Benjamin Spock, did an about-face concerning paternal responsibilities in the revised 1976 edition of *Baby and Child Care*. He was "guilty" in the earlier editions of his book, he admitted, of "harboring an underlying sexism" when he assumed that "women will always play the major role in child care." The central tenet of the 1976 edition, which contained a new section, "The Father as Parent," changed dramatically: the mother–child dyad expanded into a triad to include the father. Infants and young children, Spock wrote, require "a sensitive, enthusiastic kind of care if they are to become warm hearted, creative people," but this care can come just as well from "loving fathers" as from "loving mothers" (1972:154–155). He noted with approval that men had begun to participate in "all aspects of home and child care and there is no reason why fathers shouldn't . . . contribute equally to the children's security and development." But, he cautioned, "the benefit is lost if this work is done as a favor to their wives, since that implies that it's really not their work." The father's excuse that he "is not used to the idea of participating in baby care and will wait until the child is more like a human being" will no longer wash. "Valuable time is lost that way," Dr. Spock warned (1976:46–47).

Harvard pediatrician T. Berry Brazelton also lauded the growing involvement of fathers in child care. "No development in our society," he wrote in *Redbook*, "has been better news than the trend toward fathers participating more equally in nurturing the family" (1981:56). Fathers can be as adept as mothers in caring for their children, the experts now claimed. "I see nothing that a mother does (except breast feeding) that a father cannot do," Dr. Burton L. White wrote in *The First Three Years of Life* (1975:256). Parenting is learned, said the experts, and is not the prerogative of either sex.

Many women agreed with this prescription and described their frustration with the "anti-assistance behavior practiced by some fathers when it comes to child care." Such fathers either "spontaneously . . . unconsciously, and unfailingly assign all child care to the woman, or they simply refuse to see what needs doing," wrote the authors of a popular book on motherhood (Barber and Maguire 1975:89). In a *Ladies' Home Journal* article, Letty Cottin Pogrebin told women not to put up with such behavior. "Feeding, cleaning, and dressing a child are not acts of love. They're functions you perform lovingly—and either parent can do them." Women should not feel guilty about "wanting to share the work of child care," she advised, "because that's what it is: WORK—repetitive, tedious, often lonely and exhausting" (1980:152).

While a number of advice givers were expanding the paternal role, others were resoundingly rejecting old definitions of the maternal one. A new genre of popular literature on mothering appeared during the 1970s as women candidly explored the frustration, boredom, and resentment that sometimes went with the job. "We've been taught," wrote the authors of *The Mother Person*, "that mothering is sublime to any complete female, and that's a false lesson to be immediately unlearned" (Barber and Maguire 1975:48). The media depicts motherhood as "easy, fun and vastly fulfilling," thus "creat[ing] a pervasive myth that victimizes every mother," the author of *Mother's Day Is Over* agreed (Radl 1973:3, 6). These women described the mixture of ambivalence and guilt that pervaded their lives because of the "motherhood mystique." "I would die for him," Jane Lazarre wrote of her son in *The Mother Knot*, "but he has destroyed my life and I only live to find a way of getting it back again" (1976:85). While extolling the joys of motherhood, "the community in no way prepared us for a routine which would be thankless, endless, dull, and nerve wracking" (Barber and Maguire 1975:114). Not surprisingly, these authors call for fathers to participate equally in child care, for the establishment of well-run day-care centers, and for an end to society's view of the child as "some greenhouse plant, being pinched and shaped and trimmed by the hands of a single gardener" (Barber and Maguire 1975:217).

It is no mere coincidence that "one child alternative" and anti-natalist tracts began appearing during the 1970s. "Necessity . . . is the mother of the single child," asserted a writer in the *New York Times Magazine* (Moore 1981:26). As more and more married women took jobs, they had their first child at a later age, making it more likely that their first child would be an only child. Moreover, with inflation, the cost of rearing children had risen steadily, putting a premium on smaller families. Not surprisingly, research on only children boomed; between 1978 and 1981 the National Institute of Child Health and Human Development spent two million dollars on eleven studies of only children. Being an only child, it turned out, is neither "a disease in itself," as C. Stanley Hall claimed in 1904, nor are only children mentally or emotionally disadvantaged when compared to their counterparts with siblings. Some research even suggests that only children do better on IQ tests and are more popular with their peers than children in larger families (Hass 1999).

In this climate the "no-child alternative" also had its champions. Two people are an efficient unit that can cope with life better than the usual child-centered family, Alvin Toffler announced in his best-seller *Future Shock* (1970). Betty Rollin agreed in an article, "Motherhood: Who Needs It?" The question, she wrote, is not whether children are sweet and marvelous. The question is, does one want to pay the price for rearing them? Simply put, being a Mom is not for everyone. It is "more dangerous and ridiculous to assume that all women are equipped for motherhood" than to assume that "everyone with vocal chords should seek a career in the opera" (1972:82, 77). This was also the era when the National Organization of Non-Parents was founded, suggesting that, at least in some quarters, the radical de-emphasis on motherhood had come full circle. This option also was reflected in census data; between 1975 and 1995, the percentage of women over forty who never had children rose from 10 to 17.5 percent.

But not all prescriptive writers of the era abandoned traditional thinking on sensitive issues like child rearing and parental roles. Dissent from majority opinion is not surprising given the revolutionary nature of the new research findings and the updated child-care advice that resulted from them. John Bowlby, for one, did not back down from his insistence that an ever-present mother is necessary for a child's proper development. In a 1980 interview in *Ladies' Home Journal* he was still insisting that "looking after a baby or toddler is a 24 hour a day, 7 days a week job," making him "skeptical whether a working mother, unless she is Superwoman, can successfully combine her parenting role with a job outside the home." When asked about women who must work and cannot afford to stay home with their children, Bowlby acknowledged that while inflation is a problem, "it's a question of what you put first—your standard of living or the health and happiness of your children" (quoted in Carro 1980:90).

Similar views were expressed by Erna Wright, author of *Common Sense in Child Rearing*. No child should be "asked to accept long partings from his Mother during his first year," she opined. "If you have to work for pressing economic reasons, and by pressing, I mean you can't meet the food bill by Wednesday—that's different." But a job does not mean a career. "You are not a bad mother just because you want a career," she soothed, "but you are if you allow your ambition to damage your child psychologically." So if your child "resists a babysitter, I'm afraid you'll just have to resign your job" (1973:214–215, 217). The 1980 edition of *Infant Care* sought to instill similar fears in its (female) readers. Although the pamphlet had photographs of both fathers and mothers caring for babies, one of the few specific references to mothers—rather than to parents—was in this passage: "Every mother should carefully consider whether the money and satisfaction she gets from returning to work is worth the cost to her and her family. Good child care is always expensive and poor child care . . . can be dangerous to the baby" (Children's Bureau 1980:54).

The insistence of some advice givers that day-care centers can never meet the nurturing standards of the nuclear family was another element in the dissent from a revamped maternal role. After describing "the disease of nonattachment" in institutionalized children who have been deprived of all mothering, child psychoanalyst Selma Fraiberg concluded this too is the fate of children in day-care centers. "The minimum guarantee for the evolution of the human bond is prolonged intimacy with a nurturing person [and such] . . . insurance must be provided by the mother herself." It is only after age three that "most children can tolerate separation from the mother for a half day." Moreover, it is not until age six that children normally "can manage" a full day's separation with good "mother substitutes" after school hours (1977:56, 84–88). This same line of reasoning was used by Richard Nixon in the early 1970s when he vetoed a federal day-care bill. His veto message explained that such care would "diminish both parental authority and parental involvement with children, particularly in the early decisive years when social attitudes . . . and religious and moral principles are first inculcated" (quoted in Ryan 1975:408).

Some writers refused to abandon traditional thinking about the part fathers play in child rearing. "Your husband's role is just not as important as yours," Wright emphasized in her manual. "No father is ever so emotionally and biologically involved with his children as a mother." While some men "take naturally" to feeding, bathing, and diapering, "a father doesn't love his child any less . . . if he just can't bring himself to help out in this way." Agreeing with prefeminist Dr. Spock, Wright advised there is no use "bullying" a father to participate in child care because he will become "resentful and resistant." All a woman can do is "persuade gently—and appreciate however little or much he does" (1973:69–70).

On occasion women's magazines also rebuffed a redefined role for fathers. Journalist Vivian Gornick proposed an article for *Family Circle* magazine about Kotelchuck's research on father–child ties. But the magazine's editor initially refused her suggestion saying, "You mean you want me to tell our readers that everything we've been telling them all these years isn't true?" (Gornick 1975:11). When the article finally was published, it was heavily edited, so that Kotelchuck's findings were considerably diluted and their significance was unclear. Similarly, James Levine, author of *Who Will Raise the Children?*—a book about "house husbands," single and adoptive fathers, and fathers who share equally in child care—submitted an article based on the book to a women's magazine. The editor promptly rejected it, explaining that "the argument that men make as good mothers as women wouldn't make a big hit with our readers" (Levine 1976:17).

Yet despite such dissent, the 1970s and 1980s saw the most thorough revision of ideas about parental roles since the early nineteenth century. What factors occasioned this momentous shift? Some might argue that the spread of feminism in the late 1960s and 1970s led child-care experts such as Dr. Spock to recant their earlier advice, but this begs the question of why feminism arose when and where it did. A more productive approach is to analyze the women's movement and feminist ideology—including the new thinking on parenthood—as responses to larger social and economic forces in American society that had their roots in the 1950s, the decade when married, middle-class women began entering the job market in large numbers. As more and more women with children worked outside the home, the experts continued to insist that motherhood was a full-time job and the only career a woman should ever want or need. The gap between ideology and reality grew during the 1960s as women's labor force participation rates continued to spiral upward. In 1950 just over 18 percent of women with children under eighteen years old held jobs; by 1960 that figure had climbed to nearly 28 percent and by 1970, it was close to 40 percent (Bureau of Labor Statistics 1980). That Betty Friedan's book *The Feminine Mystique* (1974, orig. 1963) struck a nerve and became a runaway best-seller was not mere chance. "The problem with no name" that Friedan identified in her book was at least partly caused by the growing discordance between the experts' dicta on motherhood and the reality of women's daily lives.

Anthropologists have long known that a time lag can occur between changes in a society's social and economic institutions and shifts in its ideological constructs. The anachronistic child-rearing literature of the 1950s and most of the 1960s—an era when large numbers of mothers could not or would not devote themselves exclusively to their children's care—is an example of such a disjuncture. The overwrought discourse about the need for full-time mothering was sharply contradicted by the reality of women's large-scale entry into the job market. As such, the rise of feminist ideology and the experts' dramatic reversals on child care were tardy responses to basic changes in American society, foremost among them, the employment of married women, particularly those with young children.

The question of why during the last four decades of the twentieth century middle-class wives and mothers took jobs in record numbers is discussed in chapter 6. Here I will only note the results. The year 1972 marked a turning point; for the first time more mothers of school-age children were employed than were not. Another milestone was reached in 1979 when over half—52 percent—of all mothers with children under eighteen were in the labor force; by 1995, that figure approached 75 percent. However, the most salient statistic for our purposes was the astonishing increase in the number of mothers with *children under six* entering the job market. We must look back five decades to put these figures in perspective. In 1950, 12 percent of women with pre-school-age children were employed; by 1960 this figure had risen to 19 percent, by 1970, to 30 percent, by 1980, to 43 percent and by the dawn of the new millennium, nearly 65 percent of all women with children under age six were working outside the home. In short, the number of employed women with young children had increased by almost 450 percent over the last half of the twentieth century (Olds 1975; U.S. Department of Labor 1980, 1998; Gross 1998).

The backdrop for this momentous change in maternal employment was a falling fertility rate. The fertility rate declined rapidly between 1960 and

1980, and during the late 1970s it reached the lowest level ever recorded in the United States. A 1971 Census Bureau survey of young women found that for the first time in American history the ideal family size was fewer than three children (Mandle 1979). A 1978 study of married women aged eighteen to twenty-four noted that they expected to average 2.2 children each, but in that year the average completed family size was actually 1.8; women were having fewer children than planned. Since then the rate has wavered between 1.8 and 2.0, a notable decline from the mid-1950s, when a woman of child-bearing age could expect to have 3.7 children, and the 1960s, when the average was 2.6 children (Yankelovich 1981).

Today one of the fastest growing demographic trends in the United States is the one-child family, which grew in number from 10 million in 1972 to 15 million by 1999. This trend, combined with the rising number of childless couples (almost 18 percent by the dawn of the new millennium), has seen the birthrate decrease to less than two children per family (Hass 1999).

Only children and childless families are due to the higher cost of rearing and educating children, a rising divorce rate, later age at marriage, as well as more women with jobs. A Department of Agriculture study estimated that rearing a child born in 1960 to the age of eighteen cost a family of moderate means $34,300. But the same child born in 1980—with a 10 percent rate of inflation—cost $165,300 from birth to age eighteen. When we add the mother's lost earnings if she stayed home for five years to care for the child and such middle-class amenities as music lessons and summer camp, the cost rises to an astronomical $250,000, a sum that does not include the expenses of a college education (cited in Moore 1981)! A Presidential Commission on Population Growth estimate of per-capita income in the year 2000 provides an up-to-date perspective. The study concluded that if the average American woman had two rather than three children, by the dawn of the new millennium per-capita income would increase by 15 percent. Given these figures, it is little wonder that the one-child and no-child options have become more acceptable.

How do we untangle the relationship between falling fertility and rising maternal employment? Are women having fewer children because they are employed and want to avoid breaks in their earning capacity? Or, with fewer children, are women more likely to take jobs? Economists and demographers do not agree which has causal priority, women's employment or lower fertility rates. But both factors were involved in the middle-class family's attempt to cope with the high cost of living in the 1970s and 1980s. Inflation not only drove up the cost of rearing children, but declining male wages also put a premium on a second family income, an income derived from the labor of wives and mothers.

SOMETHING OLD, SOMETHING NEW: THE DAWN OF THE NEW MILLENNIUM

The expectation of young first-time marrying couples now is that fathers and mothers will co-parent.

Kyle Pruett, Professor of Psychiatry,
Child Study Center, Yale University
(quoted in Lawlor 1998)

By the dawn of the new millennium, most Americans seemed less concerned than they had in the past about the effects of working mothers on children. In 1977, half of all Americans agreed that "a working mother can establish just as . . . secure a relationship with her children as a mother who does not work"; by 1991, two-thirds of Americans agreed with that sentiment. Such shifts reflect ongoing patterns of maternal employment. By the late 1990s, nearly three-quarters of all mothers had jobs, while well over half of women with children age one and under were working or looking for work. And studies find that women today tend to go back to work after only 12 weeks of maternity leave, most because they need the income (Coltrane 1996:203–204; U.S. Department of Labor 1999; Slade 1997).

Then, too, new research suggests that the time loss to children because their mothers work has been greatly exaggerated. Employed women appear to spend as much one-on-one time with their children as at-home Moms, albeit with more of it on weekends and less on weekdays. And working mothers seem to go out of their way to spend more time with their children even at the cost of their own sleep and leisure. Most notably, however, fathers are now making up for part of the lost time. In fact, since the late 1970s the way working men and women spend their time has been converging. In 1977 employed men and women spent 1.8 hours and 3.3 hours a day respectively on child care; two decades later the figures were 2.3 and 3.0 hours a day. As such, children are receiving slightly *more* attention from working parents today than they did twenty years ago, mostly because of changes in fathers' behavior. In the 1970s while working women were frantically coping with double days caring for home and children as well as jobs, their husbands were spending much of their leisure time on themselves. Now fathers are spending more time with their children and less on their own activities (Coontz 1997; Chira 1999; Lewin 1998).

The growing involvement of fathers with their children is also reflected in data on fathers' presence at birth. During the early 1970s, only 25 percent of fathers attended the birth of their children but by the turn of the millennium estimates suggest that 90 percent of fathers were present at their children's birth (Coltrane 1996).

With the mothers of ever younger children taking jobs, interest in the "other" parent continued to flourish. Between 1990 and 1998 alone over 160 books on fathering were published, including titles like *Fatherhood: An*

Owner's Manual (Spangler 1994), *The Expectant Father* (Brott and Ash 1995), *The Daddy Guide* (Nelson 1998), and *A Guy's Guide to Pregnancy* (Mungean and Gray 1994). And, in 1992, a newsletter and Web site, "At-Home Dad," was founded with the aim of "providing connections and resources for the 2 million fathers who stay home with their children," and a few years later the first At-Home Dads Convention was held in a Chicago suburb.

Research on fatherhood also has soared with some surprising results. Contrary to expectations, it is not highly educated professional or business-men breaking new ground in child care but lower-paid, blue-collar men. Most men who are primary caregivers are not single fathers but men in families in which both parents work split shifts. Municipal and service workers—police, firefighters, maintenance workers—are far more likely to care for their children while their wives are at work than men in professional and managerial positions. The care that blue-collar men give their children debunks the stereotype that such men cringe at the very idea of changing diapers. About one-third of two-earner couples with children age five and under have split-shift arrangements; one parent works days and the other evenings so that the primary caregiver is the one not at work. Fathers and mothers not only have more equitable roles in child care with this arrangement, but it saves money by eliminating the cost of day care (Lawlor 1998; F. Deutsch 1999; Collins 1999).

And the number of such fathers is growing. A Bureau of Labor Statistics study revealed that between 1991 and 1996 the number of unemployed men who chose not to look for work because of "home responsibilities" had gone from 4.6 to 8.4 percent, a significant increase since men have traditionally been reluctant to admit that household duties were why they were unemployed. Says James Levine, a researcher on fatherhood, "The number of men at home taking care of their kids is the best-kept secret in American child care (quoted in Marin 2000:18).

Yale psychiatrist Kyle Pruett's 1987 study of families in which fathers were the primary parent found that while most of the men had expected to play traditional paternal roles, but when, for financial or medical reasons, they became the main caregivers, they formed deep, reciprocal nurturing ties to their infants and toddlers. His more recent research, which followed the children of stay-at-home Dads for 10 years, found them slightly above average in social, emotional, and intellectual development (Pruett 2000). Other new research suggests that being there is not enough; fathers have to be active caregivers for children to benefit emotionally from their presence. And active fathering has been found to provide other significant benefits: a sense of competence in girls and reduced drug use and delinquency in boys. Finally, active fathers reduce stress on mothers, particularly if they are employed. Fathers and mothers buffer each other so that both parents are less likely to burn out or feel depressed by the weight of it all (Parke and Brot 1999; Levine and Pittinsky 1998; F. Deutsch 1999).

But more research is needed. James Levine (1999), head of the Fatherhood Project of the Families and Work Institute, points out that most studies of the effects of working parents on children are still being done on employed mothers, *not* employed fathers. This reinforces the mind-set that views child care as primarily a female responsibility. So, too, do "family friendly" policies—flextime and time off to care for a sick child—when they are assumed to benefit mothers, not fathers. Many men, in fact, are loath to take advantage of such policies fearing that to do so would jeopardize their careers. When fathers want to attend a school play or take a child to the doctor, some declare they are "going to a meeting." Despite such worries, under provisions of the 1993 Family and Medical Leave Act, about half a million men annually take some kind of parental leave to care for a child, compared to 1.4 million women (*Gainesville Sun* 1999a).

Interestingly, in the first sex discrimination case filed under that act, a Maryland State Trooper was awarded $375,000 when a personnel manager refused to give him an extended leave to care for his newborn child on the ground that he was a male. Said the manager, "God made women to have babies"; unless the state trooper could have babies, he "could not be the primary caregiver" unless his wife were "in a coma or dead" (Lewin 1999:11).

While fathers may now be more acceptable as caregivers, considerable anxiety is still expressed about the effects of day care on infants and young children. In 1986 when psychologist Jay Belsky reported that children under age one who spent more than twenty hours a week in day care had weaker attachments to their mothers than babies whose mothers stayed home, an alarm sounded. But Belsky himself noted his findings were probably due to the uneven quality of day care in the United States rather than the number of hours spent in it. While poor-quality day care is still of great concern, additional long-term research on 1,300 families found that children's attachment to their mothers was unaffected by whether or not they were in day care, how many hours they spent in it, or the age at which they started. Moreover, at least through age three, no difference was found in language or intellectual ability of children in day care and those who stayed home. The researchers concluded that family life is more important than all other factors affecting the emotional and intellectual lives of children. The influence of familial factors linked to good outcomes in children—mother's education and how well she handles her child's needs, for example—are the same, no matter how much or how little time young children spend in day care. In short, the research suggests that the impact of family is at least twice as great as the influence of day care, whether children spend less than ten or more than thirty hours a week in alternative care (Chira 1996, 1998; *Gainesville Sun* 1999b).

To be sure, not all is sunny and bright in the world of contemporary advisors and opinion makers in regard to updated parental roles and the wisdom of day care. One woman attorney, for example, temporarily lost custody of her two children to her ex-husband when a three-judge panel ruled that her long hours interfered with her maternal role (Petersen 1999). Then there are those who see working mothers as the root of much, if not all, evil. After the random shootings of seven people in a Texas church in 1999, a local resident "explained" the senseless act saying, "We've got too many mothers working, leaving children on their own" (Goodstein 1999:1). And books like *When Work Doesn't Work Anymore* (McKenna 1998), suggesting women must make a stark choice between having a career and "having a life," do nothing to enhance women's sense of well-being. Nor does the TV ad for AT&T cellular phone service that shows a small child saying she wishes she were "an important client" so her mother would spend more time with her.

One new genre of advice that might be termed the "boys will be boys" playbook is something of a throwback to *Ozzie and Harriet* days. Books like *Fatherless America* (Blankenhorn 1995) and *Life Without Father* (Popenoe 1996) call for a return to traditional parental roles. Both decry the cultural message that fathers should abandon their role as manly family "providers" and roll up their sleeves to be diaper changers and bath givers. They denigrate the newfangled notion that to be a good father means to participate fully in child care. Breadwinners are what men were meant to be, these authors aver, and the real problem with contemporary American society is not men who do not "specialize" in nurturing—which, after all, is a woman thing—but absent fathers and fatherless homes, phenomena they blame in part on the positive portrayal of males as child rearers.

Then there are the right-wing ideologues who cannot be classified as part of a backlash since they never approved of a revamped maternal role in the first place. But their censure of working mothers has not been muted. Conservatives James Dobson and Gary L. Bauer write darkly of day care: "Mom, your children's identity will be indelibly stamped with the identity of the significant caregiver. His [sic] security and self-esteem will be permanently affected by his setting" (1990:143). Some conservatives are trying to expand the maternal role even beyond what was called for in the 1950s. In their appeal for "home-schooled" children as an antidote to godless public education, it is clear who is going to devote her days to teaching them: mother herself. But as one commentator points out about this conservative rallying cry, "all the crocodile tears shed over the rights of children to a mother at home are largely saved for the middle class" (Chira 1999:209). The Personal Responsibility and Work Opportunity Act signed by President Bill Clinton in the mid-1990s forced thousands of welfare mothers with young children into the work force.

But these are exceptions, and most child-care experts have indeed changed their tune. In a society where three-quarters of all mothers are employed outside the home—mothers who are having fewer and fewer children and whose income has become essential for maintaining a middle-class standard of living—it would be ludicrous for the advice givers to continue to demand an exclusive mother–child relationship. This is also the setting for the experts' discovery that the average child has two parents. The growing awareness of the importance of fathering and the new research on father–child ties comes at a time when full-time mothering is no longer the norm. Popular advice givers and social scientists alike have abandoned their focus on the isolated mother–child unit and have replaced it with a call for quality and continuity in child care, care that can be provided by a limited number of loving and concerned adults, male and female, in the home or outside of it.

CHILD-CARE ADVICE, SOCIAL SCIENCE, AND THE NATIONAL SETTING

The culture commands that the mother is more important to the child than the father and the social scientists will be damned if they discover otherwise.

Vivian Gornick,
"Here's News: Fathers Mother as Much as Mothers," 1975

Changing ideas about child care are not simple ideological fashions that vary randomly over time, nor are they based on universal truths of a moral or scientific character. Attitudes about parental roles are grounded in and shaped by the conditions under which they arise. While the authors of child-care manuals only appear to be describing the roles that mothers and fathers play in child rearing, they are, in fact, attempting to sustain these roles by providing ideologies or scientific truths that "prove" that the particular child-rearing pattern of the era is part of the natural order.

Early in the twentieth century amateur advice givers were joined by experts from the social sciences in their pronouncements on what was right and appropriate in mothering and child care. But however much we may emphasize the word "science" when referring to social science, we know that social science theory does not arise in a vacuum divorced from external social and economic contingencies. The creation and acceptance of social science theory and research depends on time and place. A relevant example; in 1963 two Scottish psychologists conducted an experiment with sixty infants and, like Milton Kotelchuck, found strong emotional ties between the babies and their fathers. But, according to Kotelchuck (1972), the Scottish study received almost no attention. At best, it was treated as a casual observation. Why? Because research findings made before their time are generally treated as curiosities, not legitimate discoveries worthy of serious discussion. In contrast, Kotelchuck's findings on father–child ties a decade later were not ignored, although, as we know, they were watered down for publication in a mass-circulation magazine. Starting in the 1970s he and others did pioneering research on the importance of the father–child relationship, a time when the recognition of such a relationship synchronized with the deemphasis on the mother–child dyad brought about by widespread maternal employment.

Viewing the mother role through the lens of history and from the perspective of other cultures highlights the degree to which social scientists and advice givers are bound by time and place. There is, for instance, the insistence on the need for an exclusive mother–child unit earlier in this century.

No evidence exists that the lack of such an intense one-on-one relationship leads to maladjustment. If such a singular dyadic relationship were, in fact, essential for healthy development, we would have to assume that prior to the nineteenth century and in many cultures past and present its absence produced damaged children and emotionally stunted adults. We would have to infer that throughout the ages mothers have failed their offspring and that only within the last two hundred years in the United States and other Western industrialized societies have children's psychological needs been met.

The near-exclusive assignment of parenting to women was and, to the extent that it still exists, is a condition of our particular society. It is not found in all human societies, nor did it exist in our own early history. If children only have strong bonds with their mothers, it is because mothers have been the primary or exclusive caregivers in middle-class American homes for the last two centuries, not because of the nature of attachment or because of a child's inherent need. The experts' emphasis on an exclusive mother–child relationship must be seen, then, as an attempt to justify a local and temporary cultural pattern by citing eternal biological verities.

The advice givers' insistence that mothering is a full-time job also is problematic. Child rearing is not a full-time job unless it is made so by the advice of the experts themselves. Throughout most of history and in most societies women have been too busy with other tasks to make child rearing a full-time activity. As sociologist Philip Slater notes, "the idea of devoting the better part of one's day to child care seldom occurred to anyone because few women had the time for it before" (1976:70). But with the gradual demise of domestic production and the contraction and increased isolation of the household, it was not long before advice givers were suggesting just that. If middle-class women were perplexed about how to fill endless hours in the care of children or questioned whether such timeless devotion was necessary, they only had to turn to the pages of the advice books to be assured that no amount of time and effort was too great to invest in their monumental calling.

The authors of advice books and other prescriptive writings are buffeted by the social and economic winds of the day. But the prescriptive dicta put forth in a given era and the material conditions of that era do not always mesh neatly. Because such dicta are gradual responses to shifting social and economic parameters, time may elapse between the prescriptions of the advice givers and the realities of everyday life. When such a disjunction between ideology and behavior occurs, a revision of ideology will not be long in coming. This is precisely what happened in the 1970s. Middle-class wives and mothers went to work in ever greater numbers during the 1950s and 1960s, a fact widely ignored by the child-care experts of the day who continued to insist that anything less than full-time mother care imperiled a child's well-being. At some point the gap between what the advisors were *saying* and what women were *doing* became too great. Enter the experts of the 1970s. We were mistaken, they cried. While some completely reversed their earlier stance on the importance of full-time mothering and the sanctity of the mother–child dyad, others attacked the earlier advice as old-fashioned, misleading, or just plain wrong. During no period in American history was the revision of prescriptive mandates more profound. The times demanded a change and, as in the past, women's advisors responded by updating their views of the maternal role and its duties.

And change has been ongoing. Recent research suggests that the security of infants' attachment to their mothers does not have the lifelong significance once thought. Other events, like divorce and disease, may be more important influences on children's well-being than early bonding with their mothers. And this, in turn, challenges the received wisdom of infant determinism, the notion that the first three years of life determine personality and development and that earlier events in children's lives are always more important than later ones (Blakeslee 1998). One recent controversial book suggests that peers may play a greater role in shaping children than their parents do (Harris 1999). Moreover, noted Harvard psychologist Jerome Kagan now even questions the science on which attachment theory was based, calling it a "morality play" that saw the mother–child bond as an antidote for the ills of the twentieth century (quoted in Chira 1999:70). To be sure, the bond between mother and child does matter, but as journalist Susan Chira put it in her study, "declaring that working destroys or disrupts that bond . . . is not only wrong, but feeds into an ideological crusade with a long and shameful history" (1999:87).

We are now long past the point when full-time motherhood is possible, even if desired, for a majority of women in this country. But what of the future? Will the experts again change their opinions and return to a traditional exaltation of the mother–child unit? Will they again tell women to devote themselves exclusively to child care? If my analysis is correct, the answer must be that it depends. However much we may hope that the thinking and events of recent decades—the changes in women's roles, the realization that fathers are parents too, and the recognition that what children really need is the warm, loving attention of a few consistent caregivers—have permanently revamped parental roles, unless we are soothsayers able to predict the future course of history, we cannot say just how motherhood will be defined in years to come.

GOOD HOUSEKEEPING

Woman should stand behind man as the comrade of his soul, not the servant of his body.
Charlotte Perkins Gilman, *Women and Economics*, 1898

Women's role as guardian of the home has been revolutionized in the United States over the last 250 years. During those years the American family, once a unit that both produced and consumed goods, became a unit of consumption alone. Prior to industrialization, much of what was produced was the responsibility of the housewife whose work was far more varied and crucial to her family's survival than that of her counterpart today. She spun and wove cloth for family clothing and linens; she transformed foodstuffs from their raw state into edible form; she made candles, soap, buttons, and home remedies; and she gardened and tended the family livestock. Laboring under this workload, the pre-industrial housewife spent relatively little time on the tasks we consider central to housework today: cleaning, cooking meals, and doing the family laundry. The lofty standards of cleanliness prevailing in twentieth-century America are of relatively recent origin; colonial housewives spent their time doing far more essential tasks than getting their floors "cleaner than clean" or their husbands' shirts "whiter than white."

Prior to the industrial revolution, men, women, and children worked side by side in and around the household. As such, there was little distinction between "work" and "life," so that women did not have to choose between "work" and "staying home" as alternative careers. Further muddling the distinction between life and work was the fact that most work was task oriented rather than time oriented. Work continued until the task was completed regardless of the time it took. The working day was longer or shorter depending on the chore being performed (Thompson 1967).

THE INVENTION OF HOUSEWIFERY

All of this changed with industrialization. Much of women's traditional work—spinning and weaving cloth, making clothes, manufacturing household items—was removed from the home. But their other tasks remained there: child care, meal preparation, and household maintenance. With the demise of domestic production, women lost some of their economic independence because they no longer produced goods that were occasionally sold or traded. And their work became more elusive. While family members must have readily appreciated the efforts of the wife-mother who made the very clothes they wore, the value of housework in the industrial age is more difficult to measure because it is less visible, less concrete.

How did "work" come to be an activity only done outside the home? And what effect did this have on women's work in the home? How were these changes reflected in the domestic manuals and other sources of advice intended for the homebound woman? These are the questions we will explore in this chapter. The demise of household production, the employment of single working-class women in factories, the resulting servant shortage, and the eventual transformation of the home by public utilities and other modern conveniences were all factors in the transformation of married women into archetypical housewives.

But this sweeping statement should be qualified by social class and geography because as industrialization progressed, the type of domestic work done by middle-class women diverged from that of their poorer rural and working-class sisters. Simply put, the domestic activities of working-class and rural women were affected by the industrializing economy later and to a lesser degree than those of middle-class women. For example, household production continued at least to some extent until the late nineteenth century in working-class and rural homes, while middle-class women, particularly those living in towns and cities, had long abandoned domestic manufacture. Then, too, what came to be termed "the servant problem" in the mid-nineteenth century was eminently a problem of middle-class women; working-class and rural women rarely had the luxury of a paid servant to help them with their domestic chores. Finally, modern amenities like public utilities that had begun to transform middle-class homes by 1900, did not become common in working-class households until about 1930 and in rural areas until after World War II.

The family's primary function also was transformed by the shift from a pre-industrial to an industrial system of production. From a unit that had produced food and other goods necessary to sustain daily life, the family became the principal site for socializing and educating children who would become the workers and managers essential to the industrializing economy. The family's productive activities were now limited to housework and child rearing. Working-class housewives produced and reared future workers—their children—and materially and psychologically maintained current workers—their husbands—while middle-class housewives produced and socialized the children who would become the white collar workers of business and industry.

The domestic labor of women can be analyzed in this way because one of the peculiar features of women's household work is that it does not determine their class affiliation. The social class to which a woman belongs is not a function of her own work; rather it is defined by the class of her husband and the class of the future workers whom she bears and rears. Middle-class women, like working-class women, were each producing and socializing a segment of the next generation. As I suggested in my discussion of motherhood, middle-class women were rearing the long-dependent "quality children" who would eventually take their "rightful" place in the middle and upper echelons of the nation's industrial enterprises. Maintaining a home, planning meals, and seeing to the physical, emotional, and educational needs of their offspring was vital to the grooming process. Middle-class women were also creating sheltered havens to which their husbands could withdraw to rest and restore themselves before returning to the stressful world of early industrial capitalism.

The crucial role of middle-class housewives in the new industrializing economy was not lost on the authors of home and family care manuals. By the mid-nineteenth century prescriptive writers were advising women of the importance of their homebound duties and glorifying the domestic realm, while telling women why they should be content to remain in it. As middle-class women's household production dwindled, a flood of works appeared that proclaimed housewifery a profession second to none. Next to motherhood, housewifery was touted as woman's highest calling, making her dedicated performance of domestic tasks essential not only to the health and well-being of her family but to the nation as well.

COLONIAL HOUSEKEEPING

Cleanly, industrious, perfectly qualified to direct & manage the female concerns of country business as raising small stock, dairying, marketing, combing, carding, spinning, knitting, sewing, pickling, preserving, etc.
Pennsylvania newspaper advertisement for a housekeeper, 1780

Housework was central to the family economy during the colonial period and in frontier regions well into the nineteenth century. It was as necessary for survival and as central to daily existence as any work performed by men. Prior to American independence, some British policies made it difficult for colonists to import all the goods they needed, while other policies inhibited the development of a shop or factory system. Most necessities thus had to be produced at home. The comments of a visitor to North Carolina in 1714 indicate the degree to which such self-sufficiency was dependent on women's work: "The women are the most Industrious Sex in that place, and by their good Housewifery, make a good deal of Cloath of their own cotton, Wool and Flax, some of them keeping their families (though large) very decently apparel'd" (quoted in Earle 1898:252).

Once the British parliament began taxing manufactured goods, colonial legislation was passed encouraging home manufacture of wool, linen, and cotton cloth. The wearing of homespun, in fact, became a badge of distinction and a symbol of defiance of British policies. During the American Revolution home manufacture burgeoned because of the drastic reduction of imports from England, thus forcing colonists from Maine to Georgia to manufacture nearly all of life's necessities. After independence, imports briefly resumed. They then fell again and household production revived, remaining central to the life of the new nation until the 1830s when, with the spread of the factory system, manufactured goods became more widely available (Tryon 1917).

Although there was some variation in the domestic activities of colonial women based on their place of residence and their social class, their work usually consisted of tasks involved in the manufacture of household goods along with those we consider central to housework today: cooking, laundry, and household maintenance. The general rule was the more rural and isolated the household, the heavier a woman's workload. Nonetheless, the basic tasks of town women were similar to those of their rural counterparts, although town dwellers were more likely to buy meat, butter, and cheese and were somewhat less likely to manufacture their own cloth. Even in wealthy households with many servants the "lady of the house" and her daughters assisted with daily chores. The wives of southern planters directed the work of house slaves and helped prepare meals for their families and frequent guests. But unlike women in the northern colonies and on the frontier, wealthy southern women usually did not spin or weave cloth or produce household goods since these items could be purchased with the proceeds from the sale of tobacco. With these exceptions, nearly every article in the house was homemade. The degree of self-sufficiency of many households can be gauged from a farmer who wrote in 1787 that his total annual expenditure was $10, for "salt, nails, and the like. Nothing to eat, drink, or wear was bought as my farm provided all" (Norton 1980; Spruill 1938; cited in Earle 1898:158).

Producing cloth was by far the most important task that fell to colonial women. This was a time-consuming process involving more than a dozen steps before the product was complete. Women did all the spinning, and every household had at least one spinner. Weaving, however, was sometimes done by itinerant artisans who wove cloth for a living (Earle 1898). Once the cloth was finished, it was sewn into household linens and family clothing. All stockings and mittens were knitted at home, and in their spare time women did fancy handiwork; they netted fringes for curtains, embroidered coverlets and petticoats, and engaged in a variety of needlework projects.

Women also were responsible for manufacturing many household goods. They made candles and soap and collected herbs and plants, brewing them into home remedies. They made brooms and buttons and spent hours preserving fruits and vegetables, brewing beer and cider, and smoking, pickling, and salting meat, game, and fish.

Preparing family meals was particularly time-consuming and arduous. Although meals were simple, usually consisting of a single course with little variety, bread had to be baked, cows milked, butter churned, eggs collected, and vegetable gardens tended. Cooking was done on an open hearth, and iron pots—weighing up to 40 pounds—had to be stirred constantly. Perhaps because so much time was spent in food production, little was left over for preparing elaborate dishes or for meal cleanup. The items used at meals were simple and easy to clean. Pewter plates were simply wiped off and wooden tankards rinsed. "There was little to make extra and difficult work—no glass to wash with anxious care, no elaborate silver to clean—only a few pieces of pewter to polish occasionally" (Earle 1898:103).

Given the burdens of home production, women were left with little time for the jobs that are at the core of housework today. Pre-industrial homes were simple, and colonial standards of cleanliness left something to be desired. Travelers in the colonies were often shocked by the filth of rural America. As one historian of the period has written: "It seems clear either that cleanliness was not highly valued or that farm wives, fully occupied with other tasks, simply had no time to worry about sweeping floors, airing bedding, or putting things away" (Norton 1980:11). Clothes were not changed very often, and when they became dirty, they were allowed to accumulate and were washed once a month or, in some households, once every three months. Houses were not cleaned daily or even weekly but *annually*.

Colonial women did not need anyone to tell them how to fill their time or to sing the praises of their work. Since women produced a large proportion of the articles used in the home, their days were filled with activities necessary to the survival of their families. Moreover, housework was done in a social setting. Relatives and friends usually lived within walking distance of one another, and a housewife's older children or perhaps an unmarried sister helped her in the daily round of activities. The colonial housewife performed her work in the midst of life and, in this sense, housework was not a discrete activity. Women were not isolated from the workaday world; they were part of it. Since no segregated domestic realm existed, there could be no specialized directives singling out women's domestic activities for particular mention.

THE ELEVATION OF HOUSEWIFERY: 1830–1870

I am fully confident that if there be a profession or occupation, which is in its nature, truly dignified, & to which philosophy & philosophic instruction are more necessary or more applicable than to almost any other, it is that of housekeeping.

William A. Alcott, *The Young Housekeeper*, 1838

Housekeeping during the early years of the nineteenth century differed little from housework in the colonial period. Between 1790 and 1810 family production enabled the new nation to become independent of foreign imports, particularly the manufacture of textiles for clothing and household use. Embargoes on the importation of foreign goods, along with the westward movement of population, ensured continuing dependence on homemade products. As late as 1820, estimates suggest that some two-thirds of the textiles manufactured in the United States were homespun (Tryon 1917; Clark 1929).

The transfer of production from household to factory occurred in stages. Home manufacture was followed by an "itinerant stage" in which families hired someone to help in the manufacturing process or sent semifinished products to outside establishments for completion. Dyeing mills, for example, would ready wool cloth for sewing. The first tasks to leave the home were usually those requiring the most specialized skills. Spinning was done at home long after weaving had been turned over to the village weaver, and factory-made men's clothes were available long before women's clothes (Reid 1934).

During the final stages of industrialization, production was completely transferred first to small and later to large factories. The timing of these stages followed a general pattern: the longer a community had been settled, the earlier and more complete its transfer to factory production (Tryon 1917). As manufacturing expanded, more and more tasks left the home. Weaving, spinning, tailoring, sewing, butchering, baking, candle and soap making, poultry raising, and gardening were all eventually taken over by commercial establishments. But it was not until the end of the nineteenth or early years of the twentieth century that all these activities moved from home to factory.

In the pre-industrial era the task that most profoundly affected women's domestic work was the manufacture of cloth. Hence, the removal of this time-consuming but essential chore from the home had a major impact on how women spent their day. The first mill that transformed raw cotton into finished cloth was established in New England in 1813, and by 1830 spinning and weaving had been industrialized in most of the older sections of the country. At about this time, itinerant peddlers began selling a variety of goods once made at home—pins, scissors, needles, combs, buttons, and cotton goods. As a result, according to one historian of the period, by 1830 the factory system was sufficiently widespread in New England, the Middle Atlantic, and parts of the West "to relieve the housewives of a great deal of the strenuous labor which their foremothers had been obliged to perform" (Tryon 1917:276).

The decade of the 1830s marked a turning point in housekeeping in the older settled regions of the country, and it was not long before changes in the housewife's tasks were reflected in household manuals aimed at the stay-at-home woman. The differences in tone and direction of the advice givers of the day are highlighted by comparing them to their predecessors.

Household guides of the eighteenth and early nineteenth centuries were simple, straightforward lists of "receipts" (recipes) and directions for making a variety of household products. Most of these manuals were addressed to men and women; the authors took it for granted that both sexes worked together in and around the home. Typical of this genre is H. I. Harwell's *The Domestic Manual.* "The following receipts," he wrote, "are offered to the Public, in the full belief, that among them, every person will find something of advantage to himself" and that even for "the man of wealth and leisure, they will at least afford a series of interesting experiments" (1816:1). The manual appears to be addressed to men since Harwell uses masculine pronouns when he gives advice on such diverse topics as brewing a "fine cordial" of Holland gin, removing stains from cloth, preserving meat and fruit, repairing gun barrels, making furniture wax, wine, and ink, and an ointment for getting rid of freckles!

Another early household guide was John Aikin's *The Arts of Life*, first published in 1803. It consists of a series of letters addressed to "my dear boy" and provides information on food, agriculture, manufacturing, and architecture. Aikin's manual advises his readers on the "arts of life" because he considers it "unworthy of a man . . . to rely upon the exertions of others" (1830:2). What follows is a set of instructions for preparing various foodstuffs, raising crops, and manufacturing flax, hemp, cotton, and wool cloth.

Harwell's and Aikin's matter-of-fact household guides contrast with the prescriptive writings that began appearing around 1830. Lydia Maria Child's *The American Frugal Housewife* is transitional in that it presages things to come. Her manual, despite its title, is addressed to "every member of the family," and while it offers numerous household hints, it is more than a simple list of "receipts." Child's primary aim is to teach frugality, but most noteworthy for our discussion is her call for a specialized "home education for young ladies." Child laments that schools do not teach girls "feminine employments" or "domestic habits" (1831:3–6, 92–96).

A number of themes—many remarkably similar to those of the maternal manuals of the day—began appearing in the household guides of the 1830s and 1840s, all now specifically addressed to women. Like motherhood, housework was elaborated and exalted, and women were advised that their responsibilities were far greater than the mere physical upkeep of their families. Women no longer simply cooked meals and cleaned house, according to Sarah Josepha Hale, author of *The Good Housekeeper* (1839:1); they promoted the "Health, Comfort, and Prosperity" of their husbands and children.

Women were told that they were "naturally domestic" and informed about the duties that had come to be seen as their special sphere. "If a woman does not know how the various work of a house should be done," opined the author of *The Young Lady's Friend* (1836), "she might as well know nothing, for that is her express vocation" (Farrar 1974:33). "For a woman to be domestic is so consonant with every feeling of her heart, & so true to her nature," another manual writer agreed, "that when she is not so it must be the result of a training which has counteracted the designs of Providence" (Graves 1843:24). The home was now woman's province, the world of "work" was man's, a distinction that would have been inconceivable just a few decades earlier.

Despite the supposed "natural" domesticity of women, they required training for their life's work. "Is it not as much a matter of public concern," queried Catherine Beecher in her popular 1841 manual *A Treatise on Domestic Economy*, that a woman be "properly qualified for her duties, as that ministers, lawyers and physicians, should be prepared for theirs?" (1977:31). Just as with motherhood, arguments favoring women's education were couched in terms of improving their stewardship of the home. "Why," asked one advice giver, "should not that science and art, which a woman is to practice her whole life, be studied and recited?" "Domestic education," as Miss Beecher called it, should be taught in female seminaries "on an equal or superior ground to Chemistry, Philosophy, and Mathematics" (1977:44, 46). Arguing along similar lines, the author of an article in *Godey's Lady's Book* (1839:95) suggested that female education should not be limited to the "domestic arts" because the sciences also might be useful in the household. "Take chemistry . . . what an advantage it must be for the lady who superintends the roasting of a leg of mutton to have a thorough knowledge of the nature and action of free caloric!" Study geometry? Of course, since through some acquaintance with it, "a lady may be able to cut out a garment more skillfully than one who is ignorant of that science."

Women were entreated not to underestimate the dignity and importance of their domestic labors. The author of *Letters to Young Ladies* had no doubt it was challenging work: "The science of housekeeping affords exercise for the judgement and energy, ready recollection, and patient self-possession, that are the characteristics of a superior mind" (Sigourney 1841:80). Miss Beecher urged that young girls be taught to respect their future profession. "Every woman should imbibe, from early youth, the impression, that she is training for the discharge of the most important, the most difficult, and the most sacred and interesting duties that can possibly employ the highest intellect" (1977:144). The paramount message here was that a woman does not merely minister to her family's physical needs; the housewife "has more to do than to attend pots and kettles," wrote Reverend William Alcott in *The Young Housekeeper*. "She has the temporal, and, to some extent, the eternal well-being of those around her at her disposal" (1838:52).

Even though a woman's sphere was limited to the home, her influence reached far beyond it. "No statesman, at the lead of a nation's affairs," Miss Beecher wrote in 1841, "had more frequent calls for wisdom, firmness, tact, discrimination, prudence, and versatility of talent" than a woman who systematically performs her household duties (1977:143). For Reverend Alcott, no "mission, foreign or domestic, has higher claims . . . than the mission of the housekeeper" because her duties demand "a degree of self-government and self-sacrifice, which is seldom if ever required of him who goes to India or the Sandwich Islands" (1838:38).

But housekeeping, like mothering, was a double-edged sword. When the work was done well, a felicitous outcome was virtually assured, but woe to the woman who failed to take her domestic chores seriously. All manner of evil could be traced to the "impure atmosphere of filthy apartments" and the eating of "oily, indigestible, or poisonous food." Does not the housekeeper, who is "director and guide of some half dozen children" realize that "her every error—in eating, drinking, conversing—is educating them? Does she not know that she . . . is treading at every moment on the verge of destruction, physical and moral?" demanded the Reverend Alcott. Indeed, many social ills were traced to lax housekeeping. Children "whose appetites have become perverted by exciting food and drink" are the very ones who eventually wind up as "state prisoners." The lack of "domestic virtues" in women led to homes filled with "discontent, irritability of temper, and estrangement of affection" (Alcott 1838:37, 39–40, 43).

And, as with mothering, housekeeping was far too important to entrust to anyone else. Since housework was a "science," it was time "wise and discreet mothers" took it into their own hands, instead of leaving it to "those who have no interest in it" (Alcott:1838:33). This was one reason girls should be taught housekeeping skills from an early age "instead of teaching them the fatal error that it is servants . . . who should do these things" (Graves 1843:47–48).

The "dangers of foreign influence in the home" had become a code phrase for Irish immigrant women who were rapidly replacing native-born women as the primary pool of domestic servants. The declining number of servants—as more single working-class women took better-paying factory jobs—was the backdrop for discussions of the "servant problem," a favorite topic of the manual writers of the day. But there was little agreement on what to do about "the problem." While some domestic advisors took the presence of servants for granted, others felt that a woman who needed them should "not consider it a privilege, but a misfortune" (Alcott 1838:52). Miss Beecher (1977) saw the servant shortage as a blessing in disguise because it forced the daughters of the household to become proficient in all manner of domestic tasks. But at least one manual writer, Eliza Leslie, saw the housewife's role as managerial. She suggested that a well-run household required "the mistress or her representative visit the kitchen at least once a day" to check on the servants' work (1845:227). Here too, as with motherhood, George Washington's female relatives were cited as paragons of domestic virtue. Martha Washington, Mrs. Leslie noted approvingly, accompanied her manservant daily to a Philadelphia market to select food for the family table.

Not only were women to devote their days to the care and sustenance of their families, should they have a moment to spare, some advice givers offered the same sort of time-filling, make-work suggestions that came to characterize the domestic advice of a later era. Reverend Alcott urged housewives to keep a detailed daily journal of all their activities, including their "successes and failures in cooking and other duties" (1838:76). But women were not told to spend every waking minute on the physical care of their families. After all, they needed time for their role as moral stewards of the home. Catherine Beecher, in fact, decried the elaboration of some domestic duties: "The furnishing of a needless variety of food, the conveniences of dwellings, and the adornments of dress, often take a larger portion of time than is given to any other object" (1977:147).

The ideology implicit in this outpouring of advice reflected a dramatic societal shift. Middle-class families went from the relatively fluid sexual division of labor characteristic of pre-industrial America to the sharp dichotomy between men's and women's spheres that arose as the "important" work of society left the home. For this reason, many prescriptive writers of the era treated housework, not as an isolated activity, but as one coupled with the larger issue of middle-class women's role or, what was then termed "the female question." To Catherine Beecher and some of her contemporaries, elevating the status of housework, a quintessential part of women's new domain, was the answer to feminism. Beecher herself opposed female suffrage and saw a scientized and professionalized domestic sphere as the key to raising women's status and power in the home. Feminists who sought to draw women away from "their allotted sphere," who urged them to violate "that Gospel injunction that women should be keepers of the home," would be undercut if only women realized the importance and nobility of their calling (Graves 1843:xiv–xv).

HOUSEWORK AND THE "FEMALE QUESTION": 1870–1900

In the shadows of domesticity . . . women performed myriad social and economic services which neither the husbands' wages nor the employers' capital were able or willing to provide.

Mary P. Ryan,
"Femininity and Capitalism in Antebellum America," 1979

The technological innovations of the last third of the nineteenth century began transforming the domestic tasks of middle-class housewives. A variety of appliances and services first appeared during those years, but as historian Susan Strasser (1982) points out, the invention of these devices should be distinguished from their actual use in the home. While most household labor savers existed by 1900, before that date many were found only in the homes of well-to-do urban families.

Nevertheless, by the end of the century housework had become less arduous for most women as new products and services became more widely available. Clothing a family was far easier as cloth production moved from home to factory. By 1860, almost no housewife spun and wove fabric, and the invention of the sewing machine in 1846—which spread more rapidly than any other laborsaving device—also simplified this once onerous task. Although women's and children's clothes usually were still sewn at home and only the wealthy employed seamstresses and tailors, men's apparel was commonly store-bought after the Civil War.

Food preparation was easier because of the greater availability and variety of foodstuffs. Better transportation and refrigeration meant that fruits and vegetables were less seasonal, and meat prices declined as meat became easier to market. City dwellers could now buy dairy products and, by the 1880s, women living in urban areas could purchase nearly all the items they had "put up" themselves a generation earlier. However, while prepared food was available by the closing decades of the century and stores were stocked with a variety of new products—canned soups, preserves, spices, and condiments—many still considered them luxuries. Only store-bought bread was consumed by all urban classes.

Cooking also was simplified as the open fireplace gave way to the cast-iron stove. While hauling wood or coal and lighting a fire still involved a good deal of labor, stoves were more efficient than fireplaces and shortened meal preparation to some extent. Then, too, many small labor savers—apple corers, eggbeaters, slicers and parers—came on the market during those years.

New sources of water and energy lightened household chores. Probably no task changed more than doing the family laundry. Throughout most of the nineteenth century washing clothes meant chopping wood to heat water drawn by hand. Each article of clothing and household linen was scrubbed, rinsed in clean water, hung to dry, and ironed. Laundry day was so named because doing the family wash did take an entire day. Two innovations helped alleviate this drudgery. Manual washing machines with wringers became more common, and by 1900 commercial laundries were used to some extent by all urban classes.

Running water made life easier for those who had it. By the turn of the century plumbing was fairly common in large cities; it simplified housework by eliminating the need to haul water for doing laundry, washing dishes, and cooking. Moreover, the wider availability of gas and electricity for light and heat cut down on the laborious tasks of carrying wood and cleaning the soot and grime created by coal- and wood-burning stoves.

At first, these innovations were found only in more prosperous urban households, but by the late nineteenth century housework had been simplified for most urban middle-class housewives, who also were likely to have a servant to assist them with their chores. However, the lot of the working-class housewife was quite different. With less money to spend, she substituted her physical labor for middle-class purchasing power. Poorer women, even in cities, sometimes raised their own livestock, kept gardens, and manufactured soap and other items that their more prosperous sisters had long become accustomed to buying.

Still, if the middle-class housewife's burden was dramatically lightened by these innovations, she now confronted a novel and onerous challenge. She had become her family's protector against that recently discovered scourge: the household germ. During the 1880s scientists discovered that material agents, not "bad air," caused disease. This discovery set off a veritable war against the spread of disease through contagion. Never had the dictum "cleanliness is next to godliness" been taken more seriously, and the horrors of poor housekeeping were much discussed by the prescriptive writers of the day. "Moths and dust . . . invade the most *secret* recesses" of the home, warned Helen Campbell (1881:35), author of a housekeeping manual of the era. The housewife was to stand sentinel against this menace. Simple cleaning was not enough; her task was to ferret out germs, to clean all the nooks and crannies where the silent enemy lay in wait. Women who were dilatory house-keepers and did not take these dicta to heart had only themselves to blame if their children or husbands fell ill.

It was not coincidental that as housekeeping tasks were simplified through new technologies, women were urged to strive for ever-higher stan-dards of cleanliness. As the new mechanical devices and the spread of utilities made housework less arduous, the advice givers multiplied the tasks neces-sary to run a proper home. And, if their advice were taken to heart, women's domestic chores would be no less time-consuming. Take indoor plumbing, for example. Before its advent, families conserved water in order to lighten the domestic load. People changed clothes and household linens less often, they bathed less frequently, and dish- and bathwater were reused. But as historian Susan Strasser (1982) notes, "More water meant more washing."

Just as science had discovered germs, so science began transforming the management of the home. Scientific nutrition and hygiene were watchwords of the day, while a scientific approach to homemaking meant the profession-alization of the housewife herself. The new household technology was key; the home was now being described as a "machine" or "laboratory" in which the housewife was the chief technician. An 1881 manual advised a woman "to regard her kitchen as a laboratory in which careful manipulations will pro-duce exact results" (cited in Andrews and Andrews 1974:317). Domestic technology was being touted more as a conveyor of status than as a practical aid in housework.

And status was pivotal. According to the prescriptive writers, the true worth of women's domestic labor would only be recognized when its status was equal to the work done by men. Catherine Beecher and Harriet Beecher Stowe articulated this in their popular household manual which sought to "render each department of women's true profession as much desired and respected as are the most honored professions of men" (1869:15, 13). Just as men are trained for their life's work, women must be trained for *their* life's work. While many businessmen go through some form of apprenticeship, for most women "housekeeping is a combination of accidental forces from whose working it is hoped breakfasts and dinners will be evolved at regular periods" (Campbell 1881:35).

However fanciful and contrived this discourse may seem, it was an ear-nest attempt to deal with the burgeoning "female question." Now that the middle-class housewife had lost nearly all her productive functions, what was she going to do all day? With fewer and fewer things to make, what was to be her purpose in life? In the words of one contemporary commentator: "Once, the household industries gave to the staying-home woman a fair share of the labor, but today there are few and the 'homemaker' suffers under enforced idleness, ungratified longing, and non-productive time killing" (quoted in Gordon, Buhle, and Schrom 1971:32).

The manual writers never considered one potential solution to the female question: paid employment. The idea of married middle-class women taking jobs was out of the question; their domestic advisors deemed such employment incompatible with their principal duties as mothers and homemakers. Nothing must interfere with women's critical role as producers and socializers of a key segment of the next generation. Not only did middle-class women bear and groom the "high-quality" children on which U.S. business and industry ultimately depended, they also provided a variety of free services to their husbands, the present generation of white-collar and professional employees.

After industrialization men of all classes became dependent on wages and salaries that, in many cases, were not sufficient to pay for all the services required to feed, clothe, and house their families. The wage and salary structure of industrial capitalism was—and still is—dependent on the child care, cooking, and cleaning done gratis by women. If their services had to be remunerated, male wages and salaries would have had to be higher or, alternatively, employers would have had to provide free or low-cost restaurants, commercial laundries, and other facilities. Moreover, because many of the commodities bought with male income were not in final, consumable form, women's domestic labor was an essential ingredient in the productive process. The key point here is that women's household labor provided hidden benefits to American business and industry.

While I do not mean to suggest that a conspiracy was afoot among the prescriptive writers of the day, there is no doubt that their pronouncements meshed nicely with the requirements of the new domestic order wrought by industrialization. The advice givers sent a potent message to the now dependent middle-class housewife, a woman no longer engaged in the productive work of life, a woman whose central role was rearing and creating a proper environment for her children. The cult of homemaking was now firmly wedded to the cult of motherhood, forming a powerful ideology meant to ensure that married middle-class women did not question their "proper place."

HOUSEWORK MADE EASY? 1900–1920

To be happy in your work you must idealize it. Cultivate the power of seeing the poetical, the beautiful, and the scientific side of housekeeping.
Ladies' Home Journal, January 1905

The two decades between 1900 and 1920 set the stage for the transformation of the middle-class housewife's role, a transformation that was not complete until the 1920s. During the early years of the century a variety of new household goods came on the market and the housewife's role was managing their consumption. Although perhaps not obvious at first, consumption does involve work. It takes time and the higher the standard of consumption, the more work and time it takes. "Beyond a certain point," writes economist John Kenneth Galbraith, "the possession and consumption of goods becomes burdensome unless the tasks associated therewith can be delegated" (1973:29). Gourmet meals require someone to cook and clean up after them, large houses need someone to maintain and manage them, and large wardrobes need someone to keep them clean and in good repair.

In essence, the core of housework in twentieth century America is buying goods and preparing them for family use. Some have compared the household to a factory; the housewife purchases raw materials on the market and through her labor changes them into a form that her family can use. Or, in the words of an early home economist, "the tasks that remain in the home can less and less be described as making goods, the better descriptive term is making goods available at the time and in the place and combinations desired" (Kyrk 1933:52).

The housewife's role as administrator of consumption should not be underestimated because if her services had to be remunerated, household consumption would necessarily be reduced. Imagine what it would cost to hire someone to choose, carry, clean, service, store, and perform all the other tasks associated with domestic consumption. Without the free services of the housewife, the expansion of household consumption—critical to the growth of the American economy in the twentieth century—would have been sharply curtailed.

Family composition also affects the amount of household consumption. The standard middle-class nuclear family comprised of a married couple and their children is ideal for consumption because it is highly repetitious both in the work required for its maintenance and the goods used to meet daily needs. A housewife typically services only one other adult and a few children. She cooks, cleans, and does laundry for a handful of people—and every other housewife is doing likewise in *her* home. Since each family buys consumer products for its own use, the small nuclear family is tailor-made for consumption. Imagine how much smaller the market would be for refrigerators, stoves, washers, dryers, home furnishings and all manner of other domestic goods if households were larger and there were far fewer of them. In the words of Margaret Mead: "Where one large pot of coffee once served a household of ten or twelve, there are three or four small pots to be made and watched and washed and polished" (1955:248).

By 1900, households numbering ten or twelve people were definitely the exception in most regions of the country. In fact, housewives were performing domestic tasks for fewer and fewer people in ever greater isolation. Families were having fewer children and the practice of taking in boarders declined sharply as the century wore on. In 1900 an average of 4.8 people lived in the typical American home, while by 1930, there were 4.1 people. Parents and children had become the core of family life to the exclusion of all others.

The new domestic technology of the early twentieth century was designed for this small, encapsulated, home-centered culture. The innovations were never meant to remove housework from the home. Improvements in appliances for cooking and refrigeration were for preparing meals at home. Clothes washers were intended for household use and, in the long run, they may have increased housework because, as they became cheaper and more widely available, fewer families sent clothes and linens out to commercial laundries (Cowan 1983).

Economist Heidi Hartmann (1974) has suggested that during the first decades of the twentieth century American business and industry found it more profitable to produce products than to produce services. The returns from manufacturing refrigerators, stoves, and washing machines were greater than from operating restaurants and commercial laundries. As a result, certain services—like doing laundry—returned to the home, while others—preparing meals—were never commercialized because they did not have the profit potential of manufactured goods. And commodity production certainly shifted toward consumer durables during those years; consumer expenditures on them nearly doubled between 1900 and 1930 as production soared. Decreased costs, resulting from mass production, brought a number of consumer products—cars, prepared foods, ready-made clothes, and household appliances—within the range of the average family.

The spread of many household appliances was dependent on the presence of power sources. Few turn-of-the-century homes were wired for electricity, but by 1920, the growth of public utilities led to the electrification of nearly half of all urban and rural nonfarm households. Electric power was important as a source of light and energy. It meant that housewives no longer had to clean and fill oil lamps daily and that they could use the myriad small appliances then coming on the market. Gas for heating and cooking also had become standard in urban households by 1920. Ads for coal- or wood-burning stoves no longer appeared in the *Ladies' Home Journal* and a Bureau of Labor Statistics study of twelve cities found that 86 percent of the households surveyed had gas or electric lighting by that date (Cowan 1983).

Indoor plumbing was invented long before it was widely available in homes since it depended on the construction of public sewer lines and waterworks. Nevertheless, as early as 1900 most people in towns and cities had access to a public water supply and indoor plumbing and hot water spread rapidly in middle-class households during the second decade of the century. By 1920 references to heating water on the stove for laundry or bathing had disappeared from the pages of women's magazines (Strasser 1982; Cowan 1983).

Then, too, a number of household appliances became available for the first time during those years. Washing machines began replacing washboards around 1900, although these early machines were not fully automatic and had to be filled and drained. Iceboxes also appeared in more homes after 1900, as did vacuum cleaners and electric irons. Also by that date, virtually all men's clothing was store-bought, although working-class women still made their own and their children's attire (Wilson 1979; Hartmann 1974).

The expansion of utilities had a far greater impact on housework than the marketing of labor-saving devices. Electricity, gas, indoor plumbing, central heating, and hot water virtually eliminated the most daunting chores of pre-industrial housekeeping. The new methods of cooking and heating were easier and cleaner since they did not involve hauling wood or coal or scouring the heavy grease and grime created by wood- and coal-burning stoves. With running water, particularly hot water, housewives no longer had to fetch and boil water for home use. The convenience of these developments was duly noted by an observer who wrote in 1916 that "any woman—at least any woman who lives within reach of gas and electricity—can banish most of the ordinary cares of housework" (quoted in Wilson 1979:84). But as economist Heidi Hartmann astutely points out, while the spread of utilities changed the way that work was done in the home, "the work itself was not taken out of the house" (1974:154). Housework still required a homemaker.

The transformation of housework through technological innovations varied by place of residence. Modern power sources spread to rural areas more gradually and, even by the late 1920s, cooking with kerosene or wood and kerosene lighting were still the norm in farm households (Hartmann 1974). Such households benefited from the new technology less and later than did urban ones. However, during the first decades of the twentieth century the country was becoming more urbanized; in 1900 nearly 40 percent of the population was urban and, by 1920, over half of all Americans lived in cities. But by the 1930s and 1940s, much of the new domestic technology was widely available even in rural areas. As such, differences in rural and urban methods of good housekeeping, while profound during the first decades of the century, virtually disappeared by mid-century as electric lines crisscrossed the countryside and consumer goods were marketed nationally.

Social class also had an impact on women's domestic labor during the first decades of the century. But, here too, while working-class families could not afford the new household conveniences when they first came on the market, lower prices resulting from mass production soon led to their dispersal across class lines. By the 1920s working-class women were able to buy many of the labor savers that their middle-class sisters already took for granted. Fewer household servants also meant that the day-to-day experiences of middle- and working-class housewives began to converge. In 1909, only one in fifteen families employed domestic servants, and a mere 8 percent had live-in help. The number of servants continued to decline as immigrant women abandoned domestic work for better-paying factory jobs. And despite the overall increase in the U.S. population, between 1870 and 1920 the number of people employed in domestic occupations decreased by 49 percent (Davison 1980; Wilson 1979).

"Do not despair at this turn of events" middle-class women were told; "the servant problem" is actually a blessing in disguise. "The happiest women of my acquaintance," wrote one home economist in 1901, "are the ones independent of servants." Why? Because children learn household tasks and it is from servantless homes that "our best men and women of today have come" (Wade 1901:101). Articles with titles like "How I Plan a Week's Work Without a Servant" began appearing in women's magazines, and readers were reminded that servants were sources of physical and moral contagion (Parloa 1905a). Middle-class housewives were advised how to make do without domestic help and told how lucky they were that technology had finally liberated them from dependence on such "alien" elements in the home.

The claim that household conveniences freed women from their time-worn domestic burdens is an example of the conventional wisdom about the impact of technology on housework. The phrase "labor saving devices" indicates the drift of this orthodoxy. The new appliances were said to have revolutionized the work of the American homemaker because technological know-how practically did away with arduous, time-consuming domestic chores. But is this true? Did the time spent on housework actually decrease with the spread of household conveniences? Or, is it the case that while the nature of women's domestic tasks changed as a consequence of the new technology, the time spent on them did not?

The truth is that despite the availability of "labor saving" devices, fewer servants meant more, rather than less work for the middle-class housewife. Working in an insular sphere, domestic chores were hers and hers alone; now no other adults were present to help out. Where clothes had been sent out to a commercial laundry or done by a hired laundress, a washing machine in the home meant the housewife was responsible for doing all of the family laundry. As historian Ruth Schwartz Cowan points out, the appliances themselves may have changed the very tasks they were invented to facilitate. In her words: "If the washing machine made household laundry simpler, it may also have made it more demanding by raising standards of cleanliness; at the turn of the century very few farmers expected to have a clean suit of underwear every day" (1974:247). But there was nothing inherent in the new household appliances that made the chores associated with them more time-consuming. Rather, greater expenditures of time were encouraged by rising standards of good housekeeping, standards espoused in the popular media and by women's domestic advisors. In the words of one: "Conventional standards as to what is 'nice' have continually demanded cleaner linen, more table service, more carefully ironed garments" (Reid 1934:65).

A never-ending source of work was the ongoing war against germs. An article in a 1905 issue of the *Ladies' Home Journal* cautioned women about germ-carrying dust: "We should be very careful as to how we sweep and dust a room. Once the dust is set in motion there is no knowing where some of the spores contained in it will lodge" (Parloa 1905b:40). Helen Campbell, a home economist, wrote that women's "one great task" was "to keep the world clean" (1907:206), while Ellen Swallow Richards, a founder of the home economics movement, proclaimed: "Cleanness is . . . a sanitary necessity of the Twentieth Century whatever it may cost" (1914:1). The annual spring cleaning of pre-industrial days clearly would no longer do; cleanliness had become a daily pursuit.

Higher standards of cleanliness were only one element of housework that demanded more of women's time and attention. Cooking now involved a thorough knowledge of nutrition, particularly when feeding young children. Bottles had to be sterilized, formulas mixed and heated, and balanced meals planned and prepared. Shopping also took time because of the careful selection of purchases and the time spent traveling to and from stores. "The housewife is the buying agent for the home," proclaimed a *Ladies' Home Journal* article, and she "must take time to spend wisely." She should not distrust the domestic devices coming on the market but should judge each one on its merits "to let the inventions of men save her time and labor" (Heath 1915:2).

While housekeeping tasks changed in nature and relative importance as a result of the revolution in domestic technology, the marketing of labor-saving devices both assumed and assured that much of women's traditional work remained firmly ensconced in the home. Just as lightening the workload was not the aim of the capitalist use of factory machinery, reducing women's domestic responsibilities was not the goal of the manufacturers of household appliances.

A small group of dissenters deplored these developments and tried to thwart the exploitation of women's unpaid domestic labor by proposing that such labor be recognized for what it was (Hayden 1982). The famed late nineteenth-century feminist Charlotte Perkins Gilman challenged the sexual division of labor, arguing that housework was not a fair exchange for women's support from their husbands' earnings; if it were, low-income housewives would get the most support, since they worked the hardest at domestic chores. Gilman insisted that preparing healthy, nutritious meals was a science and should be in the hands of experts. She called for communal kitchens staffed by trained cooks. Housecleaning would be more efficient if it were centralized and done with "scientific skill." Why, Gilman asked, should there be a "tyranny of bric-à-brac" in which women were duty bound "to wait upon these things and keep them clean?" (1898:247, 257).

She and other dissenters found little support, and proponents of the do-it-all-yourself school prevailed. Take housework out of the home, they cried? What would become of children's physical and moral development? What would that do to the home, the one quiet refuge to which the family breadwinner can safely retire after a hard day's work? No, they insisted, no one can replace the solicitous ministrations of the housewife-mother as she selflessly devotes her days to the care and feeding of her family.

The time was ripe for the flowering of the home economics movement. While the new domestic technology was eroding many traditional housekeeping functions, the "science" of home economics provided an ideology that breathed new life into the faltering sphere of domestic labor and bolstered its importance. The canons of the new discipline decreed higher standards of housekeeping that, along with make-work activities, attempted to ensure that whatever time women saved using their new mechanical contrivances would be more than taken up by the elaboration of their domestic responsibilities.

The roots of the home economics (or domestic science) movement go back to nineteenth-century household manuals such as those by Catherine Beecher. But it was not until the Home Economics Association was founded in 1909 and home economics courses proliferated in schools and colleges in the first decades of the twentieth century that the movement really took shape. The new discipline was defined as "the study of the economic, sanitary, and aesthetic aspect of food, clothing and shelter" by the association, which successfully lobbied to have home economics made part of the regular school curriculum (quoted in Jenkins 1979:146–147). Some thirty-five states instituted home economics courses in the public schools, and in 1917 the Smith-Hughes Act provided a federal subsidy for courses to train "girls and women for useful employment . . . in the occupations and management of the home" (quoted in Lopate 1974:56).

Manuals on how to teach the "domestic arts," and home economics textbooks suitable for students at all grade levels flooded the market. Home economists viewed their subject as the essence of a sound female education. The study of home economics for women, wrote the author of a teacher-training manual, "is so vital an expression of her nature that any curriculum that does not include training for the home sphere ignores the very center about which her life revolves" (Cooley 1911:viii). The table of contents of her manual includes such topics as the chemistry of foods and dietetics, cooking and serving meals, bacteriology and biology, laundering, economics, and sociology—a rather odd mix! The author's suggested lesson plans are equally peculiar. One gives instructions for teaching seventh-grade girls the art of sewing aprons. Teachers are told to ask their pupils such challenging questions as "Why are aprons worn? Are all aprons alike? In what condition should cooking aprons always be?" (Cooley 1911:67–69).

The effort to elevate housework into something more than drudge labor is evident in one home economics text written for elementary school children. In a lesson on "dirt and dust" the authors ask their young readers: "Have you ever thought of cleaning as artistic work? Nothing can be beautiful unless it is clean, and you are adding to the beauty in your house as well as its healthfulness in all the sweeping and dusting and washing that are so necessary" (Kinne and Cooley 1919:103).

The study of home economics was used to justify higher education for women, resurrecting the time-worn ideology that homemaking was as much a career as law and medicine. Moreover, professionals were available to teach it. The author of the textbook *Housewifery*, for example, is identified as an "Instructor in Housewifery and Laundering at Teacher's College, Columbia University" (Balderston 1919). Then, too, a good dose of home economics was proposed as an antidote to the problem of "late marriage" among educated women. Quoting a 1911 teacher's guide: "college women would marry earlier in life if their interests were enlisted in the study of problems directly connected with homemaking. . . . Women's study of proper food, proper clothing and shelter . . . benefits humanity more than years of study of Greek and Latin classics." What of the woman who devoted herself to traditional academic subjects? Well, there was the "truly pitiable" case of "a girl of fine mind, a graduate of one of the Eastern colleges for women" who although "perfectly prepared in mathematics" was so totally ignorant of household affairs that she did not know how to sew a shirtwaist, and the only thing she could cook was fudge! (Cooley 1911:247, 251–252).

To the champions of home economics their discipline applied chemistry, physics, and biology to the otherwise mundane world of housekeeping. For Ellen Swallow Richards (1914), the widely acknowledged founder of the movement and the holder of a graduate degree in chemistry from MIT, scientizing housework transformed its importance. The seriousness with which the early home economists crusaded for their cause was evident in the Proceedings of the Second Lake Placid Conference on Home Economics. "Home and social economics have so vital a connection with every branch of education," declared one participant, "that . . . we must carry the whole burden at once, though we feel like Atlas with a world on our backs" (Goodrich 1900:39). Other proponents were more lighthearted about the subject, depicting good housekeeping as an enticing blend of science and art. An editorial in the *Ladies' Home Journal* (January 1905:2) was of this genre: In preparing meals, "if you will use your imagination you can bring up pictures of many lands," its author rhapsodized, while at the same time "you have studies in the chemistry and physics of cookery." And when washing dishes, "the silver, glass, and china should appeal to your aesthetic taste."

Whatever their tone, home economists urged women to question both their domestic standards and their domestic efficiency. Many such experts attacked the housewife's competence and sought to distance themselves from what they considered her amateur way of doing things (Matthews 1987). But their goal was never to give women more leisure time or enable them to work outside the home. Rather, it was to prompt the exchange of some homemaking tasks for others. For example, a participant in the Third Lake Placid Conference criticized women who "wasted time" preparing elaborate dishes that would be consumed in fifteen minutes. "If the time given by many women to fancy cooking were given to studying food values . . . much would be gained" (Wade 1901:97). Efficiency in housework was also intended to "free" women to spend more time helping their husbands with their careers and their children with their homework. It might even allow them to do more charitable work. Critics worried that with all the new domestic conveniences the modern housewife would become "dangerously idle" in the words of an editorial in the *Ladies' Home Journal*. The same editorial criticized women who complained they were "tied down" with housework and child care opining, "what a certain type of woman needs today more than anything else is some task that would 'tie her down.' Our whole social fabric would be better for it" (Bok 1911a:6).

One component of the home economics movement—a scientific management approach to housekeeping—began flourishing after 1910. The home was to be a professionally managed factory, and the housewife was to follow similar principles as those developed by Frederick Taylor for industry. Scientific management was to the realm of housekeeping what John Watson's behaviorist dicta were to the realm of child care. Efficiency and scheduling were key to both. Women were told to analyze how they spent their time, to make lists of all their tasks, and to determine the time required to complete them most efficiently. Women were to stick to a strict schedule and not give more time to a chore than absolutely necessary. This would not only eliminate the need for servants, it would make housework challenging. Where the old housework meant drudgery, "the new housekeeping takes drudgery out of the home," reported the *Ladies' Home Journal*. Moreover, as the housewife follows the dictates of science, her job is "lifted up into a profession" (Heath 1915:2).

"Homemaking" will become an "object of keen mental interest" once the housewife adopts "an efficiency attitude of mind" proclaimed Christine Frederick, whose book *The New Housekeeping* (1913), serialized in the *Ladies' Home Journal*, became the bible of the home efficiency movement. Frederick addressed herself to "refined, educated" middle-class women because housekeeping for the very wealthy and the very poor did not present a problem. After all, Frederick wrote, the wealthy have servants to attend to such matters, and for the poor housekeeping is "less complex" because "society demands no standard from them." She then relates how she became interested in applying scientific methods to household management: "I won't have you men do all the great and noble things!" she told her husband. "I'm going to find out how these [efficiency] experts conduct their investigations . . . and then apply it to my factory, my business, my home." Industrialization, far from taking away women's occupation, Frederick soothed, has put the modern housewife "into even a more responsible position, that of spender and buyer—she has become purchasing agent of the home and of society" (1913:ix, 11–12, 22, 10, 103).

The language of business pervaded the discourse of the scientific management approach to housework. Women were told that because their home appliances were an "investment," they ought to be concerned with their "return on investment" and on their "depreciation" (Frederick 1913:63). The analogy between the home and the business world is also apparent from some of the titles published between 1910 and 1920: *The Home and Its Management, The Efficient Kitchen*, and *The Business of the Household*. In 1913 the National Society for the Promotion of Industrial Education described housekeeping as "a big, vital progressive enterprise, requiring as much skill in the administration of its affairs as a manufacturing plant or a business undertaking" (quoted in Jenkins 1979:145).

One key to making the domestic sphere more businesslike was the efficient use of time. But this first required work: time-motion studies. "Motion study," wrote Frederick, "means close analysis of work, whether it is peeling potatoes . . . or dusting a room." The object was to analyze each task "so that we may learn to do it in a way that is most pleasant and least fatiguing"

(1913:25). Once accomplished, the housewife will be delighted to find that where it took her forty-five minutes to wash eighty dishes, she can, with a more efficient method, wash them in only a half hour. Frederick urged women to analyze the height and arrangement of their domestic equipment and to eliminate needless motions when doing a particular chore. Then, because the housewife's home was her "business," she was urged to keep painstaking records of all domestic affairs. She should not only record household accounts, medical records, and addresses but "toilet and laundry hints, baby hygiene, entertainment suggestions, jokes and quotations" plus make an inventory of all household items. And if this were not enough, she should also keep a pantry record, a preserve record, a linen record, and a library record (Frederick 1913:127).

Just as efficiency and scheduling in child care would give women free time to peruse the manuals containing the latest dicta of the behaviorists, so too, by following scientific methods of housekeeping, women would have more time to study the principles on which their housework was based. It should be obvious that the new, "efficient" methods of housekeeping were not really efficient at all. They actually meant *more* work, rather than less work, because they added a series of new, time-consuming, make-work activities to women's traditional domestic tasks.

The dual efforts to scientize housework and child care during the first decades of the twentieth century were remarkably similar. Like the behaviorists' demand for regularity and discipline in child rearing, the stress on efficiency in housework becomes intelligible within the context of industrial capitalism. The principles of scientific management were not only used to try to mold adult labor to the needs of business and industry, but to shape children into a compliant and self-disciplined future labor force. The work of the home could not be left untouched. If children were to be reared under strict behaviorist guidelines, the home also must be systematized and regulated. What better example for a child than a mother who diligently follows a strict and efficient routine as she prepares dinner, cleans house, and does the laundry?

Given the commitment necessary for a true science of housekeeping, servants were out of the question. "There is a very strong case against the presence of the permanent worker in the home," Frederick wrote (1919:380). Not only were "good tools not always to be trusted in the hands of servants," but it was only in "the servantless household" that the "exact standards" could be followed (Frederick 1913:70). For much the same reason, employment for married women was simply unacceptable. "Our greatest enemy," Frederick proclaimed in 1914, "is the woman with the career" because when she does housework, "she feels she is weighted down" (quoted in Hartmann 1974:195–196). "It is just as stimulating to bake a sponge cake on a six minute schedule as it is to monotonously address envelopes for three hours in a downtown office." Scientific housekeeping was the antidote for professional ambition because "the science of homemaking and of motherhood, if followed out on an efficient plan, can be the most glorious career open to any woman" (Frederick 1913:101, 233).

THE PROBLEMATICS OF
CONTEMPORARY HOUSEWORK

For all their advice about housework, the home economists never discussed certain critical aspects of the domestic domain. The traditional sexual division of labor was never questioned; nor were the personal, social, and economic issues surrounding women's unpaid domestic work ever raised. The contradictions and ambiguities of good housekeeping in the industrial era were simply ignored.

Contemporary homemaking is problematic in several ways. Housewives find themselves in something akin to a pre-industrial setting, one in which the home and the workplace are one. As such, they can never get away from their work; it is always with them because there is always something to be done. Moreover, the housewife, unlike the time-oriented, nine-to-five wage earner of the modern age, is still task oriented. Her workday is organized around the chores she performs. She works longer or shorter hours depending on whether she is doing the laundry that day or preparing a meal for guests. Because her workday is not bound by the eight-hour schedule of the typical paid employee, the plaint is heard that "women's work is never done."

Homemaking may also raise the thorny issue of social status since, the scientific managers notwithstanding, much of the public believes housework is unskilled labor. While it is true that the bare necessities of housework—cleaning and cooking simple meals—involve minimal skill, other tasks, such as gourmet cooking, home decoration, and sewing clothes demand a high level of proficiency. Still, the most basic skills needed for homemaking are nearly uniform across the entire adult female population. As sociologist Theodore Caplow has pointed out, "the same job requirements are imposed on morons and on women of superior intelligence" (1954:260).

The absence of required tasks and the formlessness of the housewife's day can create other difficulties. A woman can decide to vacuum the rugs and wash the kitchen floor and bake a cake—or she can decide not to do any of those things. She does not have to do any of them; she can put them off for tomorrow or next week. Then, too, housework consists of many different tasks requiring different levels of concentration. A woman may switch tasks all day long, going from one to another and then back again. She may be constantly interrupted by a crying child or a ringing telephone or doorbell so that she never finishes the task she had set out to do. And her work may also lack a sense of completion because the same chores are done over and over again, day in and day out. Beds must be made, surfaces dusted, and dishes washed. Yet the products of the housewife's labor soon disappear; beds are slept in, dust resettles, and meals create new sinkfuls of dirty dishes.

Housework is also problematic because it lacks an audience. No one is there to judge or appreciate what the housewife does. She is neither systematically rewarded nor criticized for her performance because there is no public consensus as to what she should do and when and how she should do it. There are no associations that set standards of excellence and sanction those who do not live up to them. The housewife has no means of measuring her performance against those who do the same work, no real way of assuring herself that she is doing a good job. Then, too, her work has no concrete measure of value. Domestic chores, because they are unpaid and done at home, are not recognized by law and custom as real work. A housewife's services are not counted in the Gross National Product, nor does the federal Social Security System recognize them. Since earning money is the primary way the worth of an activity is measured, unpaid labor, no matter how strenuous and time-consuming, is less socially valued than paid labor.

The objection might be raised that domestic chores have always been unpaid, repetitive, and without a sense of closure. But in the pre-industrial era housewives sometimes sold or traded goods they had produced and the seasonal organization of life must have given them some sense of concrete accomplishment. The fall canning and the spring housecleaning were major undertakings that stayed done for a whole year. In the modern period, however, there is no set seasonal routine, no grand enterprise that, when completed, does not have to be taken up again for a considerable length of time.

Also unlike her pre-industrial counterpart, the twentieth-century housewife's work is not noticed because it is intangible. The gourmet meal that she labors over for hours is consumed in twenty minutes, and no one is likely to remark on her newly vacuumed carpet. Almost the only time a woman's domestic activities are noticed is when they are *not* done. A pile of dirty laundry or a muddy kitchen floor or an unmade bed make an impact on the senses that a sparkling clean kitchen or a dust-free living room cannot. What solid accomplishments can the modern housewife point to then? Unlike the pre-industrial housewife who could show off the garments she had sewn or the rows of canned fruits and vegetables she had preserved, the work of the contemporary homemaker is much more difficult to appreciate because it makes no permanent visible change in the home.

Home economists and scientific managers did their utmost to conceal another critical feature of modern housewifery: good housekeeping in contemporary America is simply not a full-time job. Given the ubiquitous domestic conveniences of the average American household, and excluding the time devoted to child care, housework is really part-time work. The real essentials of housework—cooking, cleaning, and doing the laundry—can be done in a few hours a day. Only when women's advisors demand lofty standards of cleanliness, elaborate meal preparation, and various make-work activities is homemaking transformed into a full-time occupation.

The final question is what purpose was served by obscuring the problematic nature of contemporary housework and keeping women contented and fully occupied at home? During the early decades of the century American business and industry became ever more dependent on the production and mass distribution of consumer goods. As such, family life and its consumption patterns became critical to the continued expansion of the economy. But since buying, using, and maintaining consumer items takes time and effort, someone had to take charge of these activities for the family. What better and more appropriate role for the middle-class housewife who had lost many of her traditional domestic functions?

Home economists and scientific managers came up with an ingenious rationale for keeping women ensconced in the home. By elaborating housework, the prescriptive writers provided women with endless but "essential" suggestions of how to fill their time. By equating the home with a business and elevating the housewife to a managerial position within it, they sought to convince well-educated middle-class women of the professionalism of their unpaid labor. And by advising women of the need for high domestic standards, standards that only the full-time housewife could hope to maintain, they sought to disabuse women of any thought of paid employment. Finally, if a woman was bored or discontented with her domestic lot, she was told that she only had herself to blame. A woman's problems, Frederick insisted, stemmed from "her own lack of personal efficiency, not circumstances, fate, or other people" (1913:191). The final irony was that if the modern housewife, surrounded by her labor-saving devices, took the pronouncements of these writers seriously, she probably found herself busier than ever before.

HOUSE BEAUTIFUL

> No laborer in the world is expected to work for room, board and love–except the housewife.
>
> Letty Cottin Pogrebin, "Rethinking Housework," 1978

Common wisdom has it that American women began taking jobs when housework no longer tied them to the home. The ingenuity of U.S. industry is said to have blessed middle-class women with a wider array of timesaving and laborsaving devices than any women in history. Freed from the drudgery of traditional household tasks, they had time and energy to seek paid employment. With her many-cycled clothes washer, multi-gadgeted Cuisinart, and high-suction vacuum cleaner, the modern woman could whirl through her housework in no time at all.

The only problem with this conventional wisdom is that it is not true. More than two decades elapsed between the invention and spread of laborsaving devices in the United States and the massive entry of married middle-class women into the job market. As we will see, shifts in the American economy that led to a marked increase in demand for women's labor, along with women's growing need for jobs to help pay basic household expenses, are far better at explaining women's rising rate of employment than the appearance of so-called "laborsaving" devices.

By the 1920s housewives had become vitally important to American business and industry because increased retail sales partly depended on the middle-class homemaker's supervision of consumption. Economist Staffan Linder has noted the time and energy it takes to consume goods: "As the volume of consumption increases, requirements for the care and maintenance of these goods also tends to increase. We get bigger houses to clean, bigger gardens to look after, a car to wash . . . and a television to repair" (1970:40). But the mass media disregarded the time and work involved in buying, caring for, and using consumer products and, from the 1920s on, the American housewife was widely caricatured as a "lady of leisure" whose many laborsaving devices left her with little to do all day. While a woman's domestic duties had changed, higher standards of cleanliness and an elaboration of housekeeping tasks ensured that the homemaker still spent a great deal of time tending to her family's needs. Despite the availability of modern household conveniences, then, there is scant evidence that housework took less time than it did before American business and industry transformed the home.

The image of "house beautiful" depicted by women's domestic advisors from the 1920s through the 1960s, an archetype that took a full-time home-maker's presence for granted, did not begin to crack until the early 1970s, an era when more than half of all married women were employed. The lofty standards necessary to keep homes beautiful—standards that had been touted for decades—began to succumb to the burden of the double day. Women now held two jobs—one at work and one at home—and no longer needed advice on how to stay busy. As such, for the first time since industrialization, homemaking was no longer a full-time career for a majority of married middle-class women.

SELLING MRS. CONSUMER: THE 1920s–1930s

> The home woman as purchasing agent is essential to present well-being and social progress.
>
> Benjamin Andrews,
> "The Woman as Buyer and Controller of Consumption," 1929

The 1920s were a watershed in homemaking in the United States. The currents present during the first two decades of the twentieth century—the spread of utilities and domestic devices, the growing scarcity of household servants, and women's new role as administrators of consumption—crystallized during the 1920s and set the tone of housework for years to come. And an important new ingredient was added to the domestic pot during the decade: mass advertising. The advertising-laden pages of the women's magazines of the 1920s are testimony to the degree to which buying had superseded producing. "In earlier days," notes historian Ruth Schwartz Cowan, "the young housewife had to be taught to make things well, in the 1920s she had to be taught to buy things well" (1976:152). Business and advertising made a powerful team extolling the joys of the "new freedom" to be found in purchasing the mass-produced goods then coming on the market.

The 1920s housewife had become purchasing agent of the home. By 1929 women bought 80 percent of the products used by their families and business, and advertisers saw women as key to channeling consumer goods into the home. The pages of women's magazines were filled with tips on "wise shopping" and advice on the proper use of the latest household appliances. As Christine Frederick put it, "Mrs. Consumer has billions to spend—the greatest surplus money value ever given to women in all history" and "she is having a gorgeous time spending it" (1929:250). Neither Frederick nor contributors to women's magazines were the least bit reticent about their efforts to persuade women to buy the new domestic products, as witness the effusive praise for woman as consumer in a *Ladies' Home Journal* editorial:

> For the first time in the world's history it is possible for a nation's women . . . to have homes and the means of furnishing them in keeping with their instinctive longings. The women of America are to be congratulated, not only on the opportunity but because of the manner they are responding to it. When the record is written this may stand as their greatest contribution. (Schuler 1928:32)

The new focus on consumption was tied to shifts in the American economy following World War I. Factories devoted to the war industry rapidly converted to the production of consumer goods in peace time. And because of their relatively stable markets and great sales potential, consumer goods industries were the first to become dominated by large-scale enterprises. By the 1920s, two-thirds of national income was being spent on consumer items: staples, canned and prepared food, clothing, furniture, household appliances, and automobiles. Between 1909 and 1927 expenditures for household appliances increased by 500 percent and for ready-made clothing by 250 percent (Ewen 1976).

Buying on credit expanded consumers' horizons and enabled manufacturers to sell far more domestic products than would have been possible were all such items paid for in cash. Installment plans were introduced in the 1920s and brought expensive home appliances within reach of middle-income families. By 1925, 90 percent of all washing machines, sewing machines, and refrigerators were sold on credit, as were 70 percent of all kitchen ranges (Hartmann 1974). As mass production and credit buying became the norm, prices of household appliances declined, and still more families could afford to own them. Electric refrigerators, for example, cost a whopping $900 when they first came on the market in 1916, but by 1929 the price had fallen to $180. As a result, refrigerator sales increased by over 275 percent during the decade, although the icebox was still very common well into the 1930s and in small towns until the early 1950s. Sales of washing machines also boomed as their price fell. Although electric washers made doing laundry easier, the early machines did not go through washing cycles automatically and lacked a spin-dry cycle, so that clothes had to be put through a wringer by hand. Fully automatic washing machines were not available until the 1940s (Cowan 1976; Davison 1980; Giedion 1948).

The prerequisite for such purchases, of course, was the spread of public utilities, but by 1925 about 70 percent of all urban and nonfarm rural households had electricity. After World War I coal- and wood-burning stoves rapidly gave way to gas and oil stoves, and by 1930 cooking with coal and wood had completely died out in urban areas. Indoor plumbing also became common during the 1920s, and just after the war bathroom fixtures were mass-produced for the first time (Cowan 1976; Hartmann 1974).

Kitchen appliances, new food products, and ready-made apparel meant feeding and clothing a family became easier as the decade wore on. By the end of World War I the variety of canned goods was nearly as great as it is today; soup, vegetables, fruit, meat, and beans were available in cans and boxes of crackers, cold cereals, and cake mixes lined grocery shelves. Then, too, by the 1920s housewives were far more likely to buy bread than to bake it themselves (Hartmann 1974). Family clothing also was more often store-bought than homemade. In their study of "Middletown" (Muncie, Indiana), sociologists Robert and Helen Lynd (1929) found that 80 percent of working-class wives and 90 percent of business-class wives did not sew their own or their children's clothes but purchased them in stores.

As new consumer goods entered middle-class homes, domestic servants departed from them. Better job opportunities and higher wages elsewhere meant that only relatively wealthy families could now afford to hire servants. By 1920 a live-in servant was paid an average of $25 per week plus room and board, while her counterpart in 1890 had averaged only $4 a week in wages. The Lynds (1929) reported that business-class wives had half as many servants as their mothers had had three decades earlier and were far more likely to employ a woman who "came in" once or twice a week to clean or do the laundry than to have full-time live-in help.

The dearth of servants was reflected in women's magazines. Ads depicting servants were common in issues of *Ladies' Home Journal* published through 1918, but a decade later they had been replaced by scrupulously groomed housewives who were vacuuming the rug or doing the laundry themselves. In historian Cowan's words: "The ideal housewife of the 1920s and 1930s did not have servants, or to put it another way, the servants she had were electrical, not human" (1976:148–149). The manufacturers of household appliances and their advertising agencies were quick to use the now-servantless home to sell their wares. An editorial in *Ladies' Home Journal* suggested the following trade-off: "The price of a maid for a year, invested in modern household equipment, will run a house so completely and easily that perhaps the maid will never be wanted" (Schuler 1929a). And in her book *Selling Mrs. Consumer*, Christine Frederick noted the connection between consumer sales and lack of servants: "When the wife herself was forced to take up servants' tasks, then she became eager for tools and mechanisms which would save her own hands, her own muscles, her personal time or conserve her appearance" (1929:169).

Economist John Kenneth Galbraith has called the transformation of middle-class American women into "crypto-servants" an economic accomplishment of the first order. The demise of domestic servants, along with higher levels of consumption, "created an urgent need for labor to administer or otherwise manage consumption" (1973:31–32). Hence the "servant-wife," the full-time homemaker who chose products and saw to their upkeep. The housewife's work permitted consumption to expand almost indefinitely, an essential facet in the ongoing growth of the American economy. People were now required to buy not just to satisfy their own needs, but to satisfy the needs of rapidly expanding consumer industries.

But the transformation of women into servant substitutes was not without problems. Domestic servants had low status, did the household's dirty work, and received low wages. Could the middle-class homemaker retain her station in life while cleaning toilets and scouring pots and pans? As Jane Davison noted, "social considerations demanded that a woman's collar seem to be white, though she obviously knew that, out of sight, its lining had a bluish tinge" (1980:93). One way to sever the housewife's identification with the servant class was to dwell on the difference in *emotional* quality between the loving wife-mother and the "ignorant" (read: black or immigrant) maid. According to the women's magazines of the 1920s, housewives did not simply cook for their families; they made them delicious, nutritious meals. Women did not merely scrub floors, they routed out germs, ensuring their family's health. They did not just sew curtains; they created an attractive environment in which their families would thrive. Such loving care and attention to detail could never be provided by hired help; no maid would ever cook and clean with the same degree of emotional commitment as the homemaker herself.

As part of the effort to professionalize the housewife's role and distinguish it from that of hired servant—all the while promoting the sale of consumer goods—women's domestic advisors, manufacturers, and their ad agencies touted the concept of the "industrialized home" in which the work techniques used in industry would be adapted to the household. Frederick told advertisers that "they must educate, train, and transfer a worker from a hand and craft technique over into a tool technique" (1929:180). Just as scientific principles were used to manage labor in capitalist enterprises, so too they would guide the housewife in her daily round of activities. The routines of the factory operative were the new model for the woman at home.

"Household engineering" was the 1920s rubric for scientific management of the domestic sphere (Frederick 1919). "Are you a household engineer?" asked a writer in *Ladies' Home Journal*. "Have you learned that there are ways of taking at least some of the drudgery out of the old, familiar household routine?" she queried her readers (Bently 1925:36). The most widely read manual with advice of this genre was Lillian Gilbreth's *The Homemaker and Her Job* (1928). Gilbreth, an industrial psychologist, and her husband, the subjects of the best-seller *Cheaper by the Dozen* (Carey and Gilbreth 1948), argued that drudgery in housework was due to "wasted energy." Her solution was a detailed study of housework that focused on the time and motion involved in each housekeeping activity. Efficiency was the goal, leading to "the largest number of happiness minutes for the largest number of people" (1928:85).

Gilbreth suggested the "string-and-pin method" to determine "the one best way to do the work" for every homemaking activity. Here an observer follows a worker around with a ball of string and measures the distance the worker travels in completing a task. A plan of the workplace is drawn up, with pins indicating the points where the worker has changed direction. Then the lengths of string are measured to scale and are wound around the pins, showing the path the worker covered. The method can be used, for example, for a time-motion study of after-meal cleanup. A child with a string follows mother while she clears the table, stacks and washes the dishes. The child makes a sketch of the dining room and kitchen and plots mother's path on it. As mother changes her method of doing the dishes, a string of a different color is used to mark her path—a different color string shows her progress. This exercise gauges the most efficient way of doing a chore and may lead to changes in the workplace or equipment to increase efficiency. The "one best way" is written down and posted so that everyone doing the task will perform it in the same way. "No one who has not made such a pin plan," Gilbreth wrote headily, "can know how interesting the process is." If all household tasks were analyzed in this way even "the simplest kinds of work, those classed as 'unskilled labor' may be made skilled" (1928:87, 92–93, 97–98).

Gilbreth never questioned the investment of time necessary to find the "one best way" of doing a task; nor did she raise the possibility that finding the "one best way" might actually take more time than the amount of time saved using the new method. Of course, it was probably the rare housewife who actually followed Gilbreth's suggestions, but the elaboration of homemaking in women's magazines and household manuals of the era seemed meant to ensure that housewives put in a full day's work. In their study of Middletown, Robert and Helen Lynd noted that while the physical labor of housework was less than it had been a generation earlier, "rising standards in other respects use up saved time" (1929:171). This is evident in one woman's response to her husband's claim that contemporary housewives live in a "veritable utopia of leisure" compared to their grandmothers:

> Because we housewives of today have the tools to reach it, we dig every day after dust that grandmother left to a spring cataclysm. If few of us have nine children for a weekly bath, we have two or three for a daily immersion. If our consciences don't prick over vacant pie shelves or empty cookie jars, they do over meals in which a vitamin may be omitted or a calorie lacking. (Hambridge and Hambridge 1930:30)

Other contemporary observers agreed that rising housekeeping standards meant more work for homemakers. This was all to the good, some argued. "Our progressive standards of what is necessary and what is 'nice' are constantly adding work to the housewife's task," wrote one home economist. But this is a mark of "social progress" because it results in better hygiene and diet, more clothing and household equipment, and more "personal oversight of the child by the parents" (Andrews 1923:408, 55).

Even an easy task like making a bed could become labor intensive if the new standard required the mattress be turned twice a week and the bed linen be stripped and aired every day. And new standards of cleanliness meant the housewife did not just do a desultory dusting of the obvious surfaces; she thoroughly dusted everything every day, if she followed the advice of one manual for "new brides" (Wiley 1938). This manual also advised women to move all the furniture once a week in order to sweep under the rugs. Other weekly activities included cleaning and rearranging cupboards; cleaning out the refrigerator; polishing the silver, waxing the floors, dusting doors, window-sills, and dustboards; and cleaning out the closets. The annual spring cleaning was transformed into a monumental undertaking in which the housewife was directed to carry out the bedsprings to be "aired and brushed" along with all the mattresses and rugs in the house. Walls and ceilings, including those in the closet, were to be scrubbed down. Drawers were to be emptied out and washed, as were the inside of chests and cabinets. Faced with these herculean tasks, should a woman doubt the joys of spring cleaning, she had only to remember that it produced a house "with such a hushed and dewy, newborn expression that you want to walk [through it on] tiptoe" (Cannon 1930:101).

Despite these lofty standards, it might be argued that the new laborsaving devices still saved time. But most of the devices were devoted to a single task and simply replaced older equipment; the electric vacuum replaced the broom, and the gas range replaced the fire stove. The core of housekeeping remained firmly entrenched in the home. While a machine might do the work more efficiently, someone still had to be there to operate it. Doing laundry was one task that probably became *more* time-consuming with the advent of new household technology. A 1907–08 survey found that 88 percent of middle-income families hired a laundress or sent at least some of their clothes and linen to commercial establishments for laundering. But by the 1920s, 60 percent of this income group were using washing machines to launder their clothes and linens at home, and by the 1930s, only 15 percent sent any clothes or linens to commercial establishments (Hartmann 1974). The Lynds (1929) pointed out that as washing machines and electric irons became more common in Middletown, commercial laundries had fewer customers. So while the new electric washer made the physical process of washing clothes less arduous, it did not necessarily result in time saved for the housewife who was now doing all the family laundry herself. Not coincidentally, women were told that perfect cleanliness could not be achieved outside the home; commercial laundries could not be trusted to do the job properly (Hoy 1996). Then too, no matter how inexpensive their services, such establishments could not compete with the free labor provided by the lady of the house.

Time-budget studies dating from the 1920s and 1930s also suggest the new domestic devices did not mean homemakers spent fewer hours doing household chores. One study compared two groups of farm wives; one that lacked electricity and indoor plumbing, the other that had both. The women with modern conveniences devoted less time to cooking, washing, and cleaning and more time to sewing, ironing, and child care than the women without them. But the study's most interesting finding was that the women with electricity and indoor plumbing reduced their housework time by only one hour and ten minutes a week—a mere 2 percent of the average time spent on housework (Richardson 1929). No wonder a home economist writing in the 1930s could conclude that "in most families the introduction of better equipment does not at present seem likely to reduce greatly the total working day" (Reid 1934:91–92).

Intent on distinguishing the housewife's job from that of hired hand, women's domestic advisors chose to ignore the long hours and drudge labor that housework entailed, preferring to stress its managerial content. The modern homemaker, insisted an editorial writer in the *Ladies' Home Journal*, "has a many-sided job calling for all the skill and training of a big business executive" (Schuler 1929b:34). Few businessmen, and only those in executive positions, agreed another writer in the same magazine, "have an equal opportunity with the housekeeper for the exercise of dignified executive work" (Bently 1925:12). Despite such discourse, several studies challenged the claim that the housewife was now primarily a manager and consumer rather than a manual laborer. Research showed the bulk of the housewife's day was still spent on routine housework—meal preparation and cleanup, housecleaning, and laundering—with only an average of two and a half hours a week devoted to "purchasing, planning, and supervising" (Richardson 1929:23). The housewife, then, in the words of one contemporary student of the family, was "still predominantly a housekeeper, rather than a household manager" (Lindquist 1931:42).

Nevertheless, women's domestic advisors and their allies in business, industry and advertising were resolute in highlighting what they deemed the housewife's main managerial task: purchasing agent of the home. Training for "successful spending" was a major theme in women's magazines of the day, a time when some two-thirds of all advertising was directed at the "home woman" (Bent 1929). Thrift was out, consumerism was in; buying things meant living "the good life." Editorials, articles, and ads in women's magazines were doing for homemaking in the 1920s what Dr. Spock did for child rearing two decades later: encouraging immediate gratification. Just as discipline and self-control were rejected in child rearing, so too frugality and saving for tomorrow were frowned on in the home. Women were encouraged to go out and spend *now*, to buy the latest model, the newest product. Christine Frederick wrote approvingly of the housewife who "does not hesitate to throw out of her house much that is still useful, even half-new, in order to make room for the newest best." The "old antique worshiping standard," as she called it, became abhorrent as magazine writers emphasized modernity and sneered at traditional methods of housekeeping, especially those that eschewed modern appliances (1929:251, 247). Little wonder that Frederick subsequently became a consultant to the manufacturers of various home appliances whose products she had so enthusiastically endorsed (Horsfield 1998).

The women's magazines of the day also promoted buying through product-testing, mail-order shopping, and promotional schemes, all under the guise of "educating" the consumer. The distinction between advertisements and articles often blurred since both were so fervent in their praise of consumer goods. The author of a *Ladies' Home Journal* piece entitled "Why Housework Is Not Drudgery" boasted that she owned all the latest appliances—a clothes washer, an electric iron, even a dishwasher—a rare item in those days—and explained why she had bought them: "because we like order and cleanliness we have invested in every practical labor saver within our reach in order to get the work out of the way quickly" (Zillessen 1927:127, 133).

Some of the advertising copy in the women's magazines semantically turned consumption into production, attempting to reassure homemakers that they were making a genuine economic contribution to their families. Buying was "a productive act" because it could "multiply many fold the satisfactions from a given income" (Andrews 1929:41). Through wise buying women could save money or make it go farther; in doing so they were creating something of value by providing their families with a higher standard of living. Some ads suggested that "buying" was more creative than "making" because buying involved the freedom to choose from the vast array of products coming on the market (Ewen 1976).

The specters of fear, embarrassment, and guilt were also used to promote the sale of household goods. Historian Ruth Schwartz Cowan described the unfortunate woman who was "embarrassed if her friends arrived to find that her sink was clogged, guilty if her children went to school in soiled clothes, guilty if she didn't eradicate all the germs behind the bathroom sink . . . guilty if her daughter was not popular with the crowd (her mother having failed to keep her dresses properly ironed)" (1976:155). Just as mothers could harm their children by not taking the advice of the child-rearing experts seriously, so too they risked their children's health and well-being if they failed to buy certain products. In a 1925 ad for Grapenuts cereal, an unidentified "famous scientist" told women: "Tell me what your children eat and I will show you what kind of men and women they will be!" And a 1926 ad for Lysol warned women that even "doorknobs threaten children . . . with disease" (cited in Ewen 1976:173–174).

One benefit from using all the new products was widely touted: women would become better mothers because they would have more time to spend with their children. Robert and Helen Lynd (1929:173) cite the following ad for an electric company:

> This is the test of a successful mother—she puts first things first. She does not give to sweeping the time that belongs to her children . . . the wise woman delegates to electricity all that electricity can do. She cannot delegate the one task most important. Human lives are in her keeping; their future is molded by her hands and heart.

The new consumer goods also made for younger, more glamorous wives. To wit, a 1929 ad in the *Saturday Evening Post*:

> I was the woman whose husband gave her each Christmas some pretty
> trinket. The woman whose youth was skipping away from her too fast.
> The woman whose cleaning burdens were too heavy. . . . In one short year
> I have discovered that youth need not go swiftly—that cleaning duties
> need not be burdensome. For last Christmas my husband gave me a
> Hoover. (cited in Ewen 1976:161)

The seduction of this reasoning is obvious: women who bought these products would become better wives and mothers because they would spend less time on housework and more time with their families. Two tacit messages lurked beneath this discourse; women's place was still in the home, and the time saved doing domestic work was definitely not intended for paid work, although volunteer work was okay. In fact, the impossibility of having both a "house beautiful" and a job was a leitmotif running through the prescriptive writings of the era. "The home will suffer a kind of domestic suicide" if the housewife becomes a regular wage earner, warned one home economist (Andrews 1923:409), and Christine Frederick (1913) believed "the new housekeeping" was "a fine antidote against [women's] unnatural cravings for 'careers.'"

Why should women *want* jobs anyway when homemaking was such a creative endeavor? "Offices rarely reflect the personality of those working in them," women were told, "but homes—have you seen one of those new purple and pink bathrooms?" (Cook 1931:12). "Part-time wives are the scourge of present-day domesticity," a critic of "pin money slaves" informed her audience. If fewer women took jobs, there would be "fewer grimy curtains hung askew by careless helpers from Harlem" (Cannon 1930:99).

Even during the Great Depression, when men were thrown out of work, jobs for married women were not considered an option. Why the vehement insistence that, even under dire economic circumstances, women could not be adequate homemakers if they took paid employment? From the mid-nineteenth century on, the influx of immigrants from Europe provided an adequate supply of male labor to fill the jobs available. Prevailing social values expected married men to work to support themselves and their families, while their wives tended the home, producing and rearing their successors. Women's unpaid domestic labor groomed future workers and managers for business and industry at little or less cost than if their services had to be remunerated. Married women were not only unneeded in the labor force; they were already fully employed socializing the next generation. Fearing the consequences for male breadwinners' wages, many working men—some backed by their unions—also strongly opposed the entry of married women into the job market. After all, how would the working man support his family if forced to compete with a vast new supply of cheap labor? It was within this context that women's domestic advisors busied themselves citing all the reasons why marriage and motherhood were incompatible with paid employment.

Housekeeping during the 1920s and 1930s presents a paradox. Despite myriad laborsaving devices, an array of new household products, and the expansion of public utilities, homemaking remained a full-time job. It could have been otherwise. The new technologies could have been rationalized on a large scale. Commercial laundries, widely used during the first two decades of the century, might have increased in number. Commercial cleaning services, employing the latest mechanical equipment, could have been opened. Communal kitchens, with commercial-scale ranges and refrigerators, might have been established (Hayden 1982). None of these things happened. In fact, as we have seen, the new technologies were used in a very different way; they were specifically designed for and sold to the small, individualized nuclear family unit.

Why the preference for the small-scale and private? Was the thought of commercial companies invading the sanctity of the home simply repugnant? Was an incipient version of the feminine mystique responsible for making certain the tasks of feeding and caring for families remained firmly in feminine hands? While a feminine mystique did emerge during those decades, was this ideology responsible for housework remaining in the home? I think not. If we analyze the housewife's role in the larger setting of a burgeoning consumer economy, the new technology's failure to rationalize housework and to liberate women from its demands becomes intelligible. The housewife had a key role to play in these developments. In Stuart Ewen's words, "the agencies of consumption made the wife a part of a corporately defined productive and distributive process" (1976:165). The housewife was in charge of administering consumption, and this was precisely where business and industry wanted her. Without millions of such managers in home after home, buying, using, and maintaining all the new products and appliances, the expanding consumer economy would have expanded a great deal less. Moreover, the small nuclear family was an eminently salable unit because of its redundancy; that is, enormous numbers of domestic appliances could be sold to individual households. These are very likely the real reasons why the very thought of large-scale or commercial housekeeping was so anathema to American values.

All the rhetoric about educating housewives for their new role as "purchasing agents of the home" also should be seen in this light. Did business and industry *really* want women to become careful and informed buyers of their products? This is improbable. Christine Frederick, a primary advocate of advertisers in the 1920s, told manufacturers not to bother explaining to "Mrs. Consumer" how an appliance works because women are not "mechanically minded." In fact, Frederick's depiction of the "general character" of Mrs. Consumer—she is "predominately emotional" and "proceeds more along the lines of instinct than upon theory or reason"—makes one suspect that businessmen and advertisers never really sought an informed female clientele for their products (1929:17, 22, 43). The truth is probably closer to the blunt remarks of one observer of the American scene in 1922: "American business loves the housewife for the same reason it loves China—that is, for her economic backwardness" (quoted in Hartmann 1974:378).

Busy Work and Make-Work:
The 1950s and 1960s

Since World War II, as never before, the business of American housewives has been busyness.

Jane Davison, *The Fall of a Doll's House*, 1980

In the years after World War II public utilities and household appliances
continued their advance across the land. In their wake the ingredients that
went into making a "house beautiful" became more uniform. The electrification of rural areas after the war and the national marketing of household
products made a single standard possible for all American homemakers. Not
only was the new technology available to more families, but there was a lot
more of it. By the 1950s the average home contained seven times as much capital equipment as it had in the 1920s, and older appliances had given way to
newer, purportedly more efficient models. By the 1950s the wringer washing
machine had been replaced by the fully automatic washer, and in the 1960s
the automatic dryer and wash-and-wear fabrics were said to have conquered
the last vestiges of laundry-day woe. Dishwashers also became common as did
small appliances like electric toasters, blenders, and juicers. Convenience
foods crowded supermarket shelves and frozen foods, including that quintessential invention of the 1950s—the TV dinner—jammed store freezers.

Women's domestic advisors persevered in elaborating homemaking, trying to ensure that women devote no less time to housework than they had
thirty years earlier. An endless array of make-work activities were proposed
in an effort to resolve some of the more problematic aspects of housework in
the industrial age. For example, since the fruits of housewives' domestic labor
were not evident, the goal of various suggestions was to make housework
more visible by encouraging women to produce tangible objects for the home.
Women's magazines were filled with directions for crocheting doilies, knitting afghans, and making needlepoint throw pillows.

Advertisers also played to some of the difficulties inherent in modern
housewifery in order to sell products. Manufacturers were told to maintain a
"neat balance" between stressing the laborsaving qualities of their appliances
and claiming that the latest model vacuum cleaner or clothes washer would
save so much time that the housewife would feel "lazy, or uneasy or bored"
and would be reluctant to buy it (Rainwater, Coleman and Handel 1959).
Products like cake mixes were intentionally left incomplete so that by adding
an egg or a cup of milk to the mix the housewife would feel she was part of
the productive process. Convincing the housewife she needed a variety of
specialized products for similar chores would not only increase sales; it would
upgrade and professionalize her status. A mid-1940s report on the preferences of homemakers had this to say: "When [the housewife] uses one product for washing clothes, a second for washing dishes, a third for walls, a fourth
for floors, a fifth for venetian blinds, etc., rather than an all-purpose cleaner,

she feels less like an unskilled laborer, more like an engineer, an expert." The report also pointed out another irksome feature of contemporary housework: the sense that it is never finished. Deep cleaning was the solution since advertising that stressed deep cleaning "holds out the sense of completion" (quoted in Friedan 1974:206, 208).

Many such directives actually increased work and time-budget studies conducted in the 1950s and 1960s finally laid to rest the old saw that modern technology reduced the demands of housework. Despite the vast improvement in household equipment over the four previous decades, not one study found the time spent on housework had declined. Housewives reported spending almost the same amount of time doing housework as their mothers and grandmothers had twenty, thirty, even forty years earlier. In fact, the total number of hours devoted to housework *increased* somewhat over the forty-year period. By the mid-1960s full-time homemakers were doing housework an average of fifty-six hours a week compared to the average fifty-two-hour workweek of their counterparts in the 1920s (Robinson 1980; Vanek 1974).

Some housekeeping tasks took less time, while others took more time. Between the 1920s and the 1960s food preparation and meal cleanup decreased by thirty minutes a day, but this was offset by a half-hour increase in the time spent shopping and record keeping. Housewives in the 1960s, in fact, spent an inordinate amount of time—one full day a week—shopping and traveling to and from stores. They also devoted more time to general home care—an average of twelve hours a week—than housewives in the 1920s, who spent about 9.5 hours a week at these tasks. But the most striking statistic emerging from these studies is the time women spent on laundry; it increased from 5.5 hours to 6.5 hours a week over the period, a remarkable figure given the ubiquity of washers and dryers in homes by the 1960s (Vanek 1978; Walker and Woods 1976).

How does this compare with the time spent on domestic tasks by employed women? In 1966 women with full-time jobs spent an average of twenty-six hours a week on housework, slightly less than half the time spent by housewives. In fact, if we add the time spent on the job to that doing housework, the total workweek of employed women was only 1.5 hours longer than that of full-time homemakers. Why were employed women doing housework in so much less time? They were no more likely to have servants or to receive help from family members than their jobless sisters, nor did they own more domestic appliances (Vanek 1974, 1978). Moreover, there is no evidence that employed women had abandoned American standards of order and cleanliness and lived in homes that were more slovenly than those of full-time homemakers.

A domestic variant of Parkinson's Law helps explain why housewives spent so much more time on these chores than did women with jobs. Sociologist C. Northcote Parkinson suggests "work expands so as to fill the time available for completion" (1957:2). The full-time housewife of the 1950s and 1960s found herself in a quandary: her role demanded that she devote her days to domestic activities that were simply not sufficient to fill her time. But the lack of real work did not necessarily result in leisure because whatever work there was to be done—following Parkinson's law—increased in complexity and importance in proportion to the time available for doing it. The job of homemaking was enlarged, housework tasks were elaborated, and the full-time housewife found herself without a moment to spare. Betty Friedan commented on the busyness of the suburban housewives she interviewed in the late 1950s for *The Feminine Mystique*: "They were so busy—busy shopping, chauffeuring, using their dishwashers and dryers and electric mixers, busy gardening, waxing, polishing" (1974:227). Friedan also reports these women were amazed that once they took a job or found a serious interest outside the home, they could do in one hour what had taken six hours when they were home all day. In other words, without other work requiring their attention, they had transformed housework into a full-time activity.

Doing the laundry is an example of the way in which a domestic task can grow and assume monumental proportions. Clothes and linens can be sorted by color and material and washed separately using different washing cycles and different laundry products. In this way, many small loads of wash are done rather than one large load. Then there are the items that are too delicate for the machine and must be washed by hand. Sheets and towels can be hung on the line to dry so that they smell fresher and get whiter than if dried by machine. The more things that need washing, the more time it takes to load, unload, fold, iron, and put them away. Washing clothes after a single wearing and laundering sheets twice a week are effective ways of increasing the workload. Then, if there is any time left over, the housewife can always iron the family bed linen, towels, and underwear.

There are innumerable ways of increasing the hours devoted to housework. The number of dirty dishes to be washed can expand to the capacity of the dishwasher (human or mechanical) to clean them. Cooking can become a major chore, despite convenience foods, if different dishes are prepared for different family members and homemade baby food or dog food is substituted for the commercial variety. A homemaker can spend a full day making spaghetti and meat sauce using a pasta maker, a meat grinder, and a Cuisinart. "Eat-off-the-floor" standards of cleanliness can take hours to maintain, particularly when there are children and pets in the home.

Women's advisors facilitated a domestic Parkinson's Law by proposing a wide array of superfluous make-work activities to fill the housewife's time. A good example is the column "Hints from Heloise" by Heloise Cruse syndicated in 512 newspapers around the country. Heloise was ostensibly offering hints to save "you, the housewife and homemaker" time and money, but not more than a handful of her suggestions can be justified in these terms. The following examples of hints from Heloise are taken from her newspaper columns and from her book (Heloise 1967). Her method of making mailing labels—by buying gummed wrapping tape and writing one's name and address over and over again the length of the tape—overlooks the fact that such labels can be printed commercially at very low cost. Her suggestion for making Christmas wrapping by sewing pieces of fabric together and decorating them with sequins, beads, and rickrack eliminates the need for the store-bought variety. One hint gives an elaborate method for preparing homemade dog food. At Heloise's suggestion, all sorts of things can be transformed into other things with a little time and effort. Plastic bleach bottles can be made into birdhouses, "cleaning blouses" can be sewn from old towels, bathroom curtains can be created from plastic tablecloths, and a mop can be made from dishrags. Plastic flowers will "bloom again" with a touch of nail polish. Old throw pillows can be made like new by stuffing them with lint from the clothes dryer and covering them with a shower cap or hairdo protector. Heloise even offers an ingenious suggestion for making a planter out of a dish drainer by hanging it on the wall and entwining it with artificial flowers. These hints are difficult to justify on the basis of the money they save unless the time spent by the person doing them has no value (Margolis 1976).

The unimportance of the housewife's time is also evident in Heloise's make-work cleaning tips. Silver polish does wonders for shining curtain rods, she informed her readers. Kitchen cabinets can be emptied, scoured, and lined with layers of waxed paper and silver foil. When one reader wrote to Heloise telling her of her "disgust, shame, and embarrassment" when guests saw the discolored grouting in her bathroom, Heloise provided a time-consuming solution for bleaching it. But she admitted to some limits in the amount of cleaning that was absolutely essential. Heloise advised, for example, it was not necessary to clean under the bed every day. "Girls," she told her readers, "remember that never yet has my husband or a guest lifted up the bedspread to see if I had dusted under the bed."

Many of these hints not only create work; they also get highly visible results and provide an aura of creativity to otherwise humdrum domestic tasks. One of the problems of housework in the modern era is its lack of "conspicuous contribution," that is, housework is difficult to appreciate because it leaves no permanent, noticeable change in the home (Davison 1980:196). But Heloise's "creative" hints have an important advantage over most household chores: they are eminently visible. A dish drainer entwined with artificial flowers hanging on the wall would be difficult to miss!

The comments of one of the British housewives interviewed by sociologist Ann Oakley (1974) indicates the importance of making one's work noticed. "You dust the same thing every day and it's never appreciated," she told Oakley, "whereas if you're decorating something . . . there's something always gained out of it." Oakley suggests many of her informants liked seeing clothes drying on the line for the same reason: "Perfect cleanliness is the commercial ideal, but the clothes must be *seen* to be clean. Public visibility is achieved when the clothes hang out in the garden" (1974:51, 53).

The do-it-yourself movement that boomed in the 1950s was partly rooted in this same desire for visibility. A 1955 *McCall's* article, "Do It Yourself Takes Over," reported that 75 percent of the readers surveyed did their own house painting and 60 percent did their own wallpapering. Advertisers also played to the housewife's need for recognition of her work. One TV commercial showed a woman's husband and children commenting for the first time on the softness of her laundry after she had switched to Downy Fabric Softener. "They notice the difference," she sighs contentedly. In an ad for Folger's coffee an obviously delighted woman is surprised when her husband remarks on the deliciousness of her brew. Still another ad makes this need for recognition explicit; a woman explains that she has switched to a particular brand of cleanser only because its effectiveness has been noticed by her husband, who never commented on her housework before.

Heloise's hints and similar advice are also attempts to surmount another problematic aspect of contemporary homemaking: housewives' resentment of the charge that they do nothing all day. The housewives Oakley (1974) interviewed often expressed annoyance at this allegation. Heloise's suggestions, then, not only lead to conspicuous changes in the home's decor; they also demonstrate the housewife really *is* working. The common wisdom that housework is not real work might be laid to rest if the housewife could point to the bathroom she had wallpapered or the new curtains she had sewn. As Margaret Mead once wrote, the modern housewife is plagued with "the fear that even though she never has any time, she is not perhaps doing a full-time job" (1955:247). Given this anxiety, the time it takes to do a task may become more important than actually accomplishing the task one set out to do.

Marketing reports advised manufacturers of household products and their advertising agencies about the homemaker's worry that her job was not really full-time. A study of working-class housewives concluded that they "need to be busy keeping house—both because they need to feel they are doing something worthwhile and because they have few psychic resources for occupying themselves." The laborsaving aspects of household products should not be overemphasized, the authors cautioned, because "advertising which places too great emphasis on easing the housewife's burden runs the risk of being reacted to negatively because it seems to detract from her personal importance" (Rainwater, Coleman and Handel 1959:214). Manufacturers were warned that appliances that did everything for the housewife would not sell. One study claimed that an appliance that only required pushing a button would stymie the housewife's desire for participation. When asked what she thought about a particular cleaning apparatus, one housewife was reported to have said: "As for some magical push-button cleaning system, well, what would happen to my exercise, my feeling of accomplishment, and what would I do with my mornings?" (quoted in Friedan 1974:207).

Setting high standards and sticking to a routine were other tactics that could make domestic chores seem more like real work. Following a set of rules allowed the housewife to structure her work in a way that is taken for granted by salaried employees. Oakley noted that the housewives she studied were able to specify their standards and daily routines. "The spelling out of rules to be followed," she wrote, "places housework in the same category as other work— there are things that simply *have* to be done" (1976:93). But high standards and following a routine can also mean more work. Oakley (1974) found that while there was no correlation between the number of hours housewives worked and the number of children or appliances they had, there was a correlation between their standards and the number of hours they spent on household tasks.

Caring for the array of modern appliances owned by the typical American middle-class family of the 1950s and 1960s also accounted for some of the time given to household chores. The nature of appliances manufactured for the home contributed to the work required for their care. With more crevices and movable parts than their commercial counterparts, domestic appliances were more difficult to clean and more likely to break down. Appliances used in commercial establishments, in contrast, were designed to minimize care and repair (Glazer-Malbin 1976). And repair, of course, means waiting for the repairman. Anyone who has spent hours waiting to have a phone installed or a dishwasher fixed will appreciate the time required for the upkeep of such "laborsaving" devices. While the promise to show up "sometime between 9 and 5" is convenient for AT&T and Sears, it is a striking declaration that the housewife's time has no real value. In the words of sociologist Philip Slater:

> Housewives are expected to operate without schedules. Repairmen [and] deliverymen . . . have been successful in refusing to constrict their own convenience by making scheduled appointments with housewives, who are expected to wait at home until the workman arrives. Nothing could convey more powerfully the low esteem in which the housewife is held than this disregard of daily scheduling needs. The lowest flunky in the masculine occupational hierarchy is given temporal superiority over every non-working woman. (1974:180)

Although it may seem unfair to blame housewives of the era for the amount of time they devoted to housework or for the dissatisfaction many felt doing it, that is exactly what happened. It was the housewife's fault if she spent all day doing housework and did not have any leisure. She was inefficient and disorganized. Was she unhappy being only a housewife? That too was her fault. There is nothing "inherently disagreeable" about housework, opined contemporary critics, and the "disproportionate odium" that has been heaped on it is a result of "the repeated verbal fouling of their own nests by disordered female theorists and the disorganization of the feelings of women in general" (Lundberg and Farnham 1947:369). "Feminine neurosis" was the diagnosis used to dismiss women dissatisfied with their domestic lot. Sociologist Mirra Komarovsky wrote in the 1950s that "the tendency to attribute the housewife's discontent to personal deficiency is widespread" (1953:116). But with little else to occupy her time, paired with a social ethic requiring that she remain at home and use the small-scale, individualized domestic appliances designed to keep her there, it is little wonder that housewives tried to keep busy doing work that was devalued, work that was frustrating and repetitive, work that, by its very nature, was unfulfilling.

HOUSEWORK VERSUS PAID WORK; OR
WHAT HAPPENED IN THE FEMINIST ERA

To bake one's own bread in this day and age makes about as much sense
as taking a covered wagon to California.
Edith De Rham, *The Love Fraud*, 1965

Good housekeeping in the feminist era has been a mixed blessing for
women. Married women have taken jobs in record numbers and, for the first
time in fifty years, time-budget studies conducted in the 1970s indicated the
average number of hours women spent doing housework had declined.
Make-work domestic tips meant to enlarge the job of the homemaker were
less frequent in women's magazines and domestic manuals; most household
hints actually seemed meant to save time. But in one crucial way good housekeeping had not changed a great deal from decades past. Women, whether
they had jobs or not, were still the primary caretakers of the home. Study after
study documented the phenomenon of the "double day." Despite full-time
jobs and salaries that made substantial contributions to family income, the
sexual division of labor in the home did not change dramatically. Most working women had two jobs: a paid one at work and an unpaid one at home.

One of the most intriguing findings of the 1970s time-budget studies is the
reduction in hours women spent on housework, not just employed women but
full-time housewives as well. In 1965 employed women said they spent an average of twenty-six hours weekly on home care, but by 1975 they were averaging
twenty-one hours a week. Similarly, the 1965 survey questioned full-time homemakers who reported doing household tasks an average of fifty hours a week,
but by 1975 the figure was down to forty-four hours a week (Robinson 1980).
Were women spending less time on housework than they had ten years earlier
because they were getting help from other family members? The answer is yes,
but to a very limited extent. The same survey reported that men increased the
time they gave to home care from nine hours a week in 1965 to ten hours a week
in 1975, a difference of less than eight minutes a day! Whereas women had
done 80 percent of the housework in 1965, ten years later, they were *still* doing
75 percent of it. The time-budget studies conducted during those years all
agreed that women—employed or not—still contributed 70 to 75 percent of the
total hours spent on these tasks; their husbands and children divided the
remaining time about evenly among themselves. The most time men spent on
household chores was 20 percent of that spent by their wives, regardless of
whether their wives were employed or the age and number of children at home.
Men only took over domestic tasks when their wives were unavailable, that is,
when they were away at work (Van Gelder 1979; Hartmann 1981).

Evidence also suggested the husbands of employed women provided little
extra "help" around the house. One study found that on weekends employed
women spent more time than their husbands on housework and a man's leisure time was not diminished by having a working wife (Meissner et al. 1975).

And the findings of a marketing report seeking men's attitudes toward house-work were not encouraging. "The major disadvantage that the typical hus-band perceives in having a working wife," the report noted, "is the effect not upon the children but upon himself: a husband has to spend more time on household chores that he does not like" (Brozan 1980:52). One researcher made the intriguing suggestion that the little housework men performed probably did not compensate for the extra amount of housework their mere presence created. Lending support to this theory is the finding that single women with children spend much less time on housework than their married counterparts, probably because part of married women's time is devoted to "husband care" (Hartmann 1981:383).

In sum, studies done through the 1970s concluded that while the number of hours women spent on housework declined, this was usually not due to a more equitable division of labor in the home. Marketing research that sought men's views of housework confirmed this for advertisers who had considered airing laundry detergent commercials along with beer commercials during televised football games. According to one report, "today's man wants his woman to work at two jobs—one outside the home and one inside the home." Most men "are not willing to lift the traditional household responsibilities from their wives." They would rather buy laborsaving devices than help with the housework themselves. This study reported more than 75 percent of the men interviewed said their wives had primary responsibility for cooking, and 78 percent agreed cleaning the bathroom was "woman's work." But another marketing study found men to be slightly more "fair minded," 88 percent of the men agreeing husbands should at least "help out" with housework if their wives were employed (quoted in Brozan 1980:52).

If not getting help from family members, what accounts for the decline in hours women devoted to housework? Was it the ongoing advance of home appliances? After all, by 1975, 70 percent of American homes had washing machines, 58 percent had clothes dryers, 38 percent had dishwashers, and 5 percent had microwave ovens. But no correlation was found between the number of appliances in the home and the time women spent on housework. The microwave, in fact, was the only appliance that made a difference in terms of time, saving an average of ten minutes a day on meal preparation.

Perhaps the decline in hours given to housework meant less immaculate homes and less spotless clothing. One study found the greatest decrease in hours was, in fact, in general home care: cleaning, doing laundry, and washing dishes. Slight declines were also reported for shopping, record keeping, and doing home repairs. Cooking was the only domestic activity showing any increase in time devoted to it, albeit a very modest increase of four minutes a day (Robinson 1980). Since evidence suggests cooking is the homemaking activity that women enjoy most and cleaning the one they like least, the time-budget data may reflect these preferences.

But spending less time on housework does not necessarily mean lower standards. If we agree that housekeeping under industrial conditions is really part-time work—unless made otherwise—it may well be that since the 1970s women have been maintaining roughly the same standards as full-time home-makers did in earlier decades, but maintaining them by working more efficiently. In other words, the time-budget data may be reflecting the demise of a domestic Parkinson's Law, at least for women with jobs. Women employed outside the home may have become more efficient at housework. Because their jobs occupied so much time, there was no reason to elaborate domestic tasks to stay busy all day. Quite the contrary; given most working women's double day, their dilemma now was finding enough time to do what was essential.

Then, too, since housekeeping standards are elusive and difficult to measure, we cannot determine if simplifying housework is synonymous with lowering standards. Does the woman who prepares a simple but nutritious meal of baked chicken and vegetables, for example, have lower standards than the one who spends hours in the kitchen whipping up a beef Wellington and a strawberry soufflé for dessert? Is the woman who sews all her own curtains a superior homemaker to one who buys them in a department store? Is the woman who changes the sheets once every two weeks rather than twice a week shirking her domestic responsibilities?

A combination of factors accounts for the decreased hours devoted to housework since the 1970s. Housekeeping standards probably have been simplified, and women also may be making more efficient use of their domestic time. It could even be argued the basic ingredients of good housekeeping in years past—"eat-off-the-floor" norms of cleanliness and an elaboration of domestic tasks—were in themselves inefficient. They were inefficient because they were unnecessary; such standards surely far exceed what is required for good hygiene and family well-being.

How did women's traditional domestic advisors, the authors of articles in women's magazines and household manuals, deal with these changes once full-time homemakers were no longer the norm and a majority of married women held jobs? Probably the most typical response was the one found in Alice Skelsey's *The Working Mother's Guide to Her Home, Her Family, and Herself* (1970). "Whether you have been a compulsive housekeeper or the casual sort," Skelsey told her readers, "once you add a job to your life you have to be an *efficient* housekeeper." The chapters on housework emphasized cutting down on domestic chores because "the only necessities are food, clothing and shelter." Beyond these basics and doing laundry "once in a while," cleaning should be based on personal standards because "there isn't any law that says you have to change your sheets once a week." She advised women to give up activities that take more time than is available, like baking bread and sewing their children's clothes.

Another manual of the day advised women to pare down the "list of everything that has to be done in the house. . . . The house will not collapse if the wastebaskets are not emptied every day and the health department won't come after you if your breakfast dishes don't get washed until dinnertime" (Olds 1975:72). Suggestions for saving time and simplifying housework included marketing once a week, using convenience foods, cooking one-dish meals, eating out, and buying wash-and-wear clothes. Other manuals of the 1970s consist of straightforward hints, a type of prescriptive writing reminiscent of the "lists of receipts" popular in the eighteenth and early-nineteenth centuries. The best-seller *Mary Ellen's Best of Helpful Hints* (Pinkham and Higginbotham 1979) is of this genre. It offers a series of tips for cleaning, doing laundry, sewing, gardening, and home repairs—hints that actually seem meant to save time or simplify domestic chores. This and other manuals of the day lack the overwrought paeans to homemaking that characterized much of the advice of earlier decades.

Some prescriptive writers took the traditional domestic division of labor for granted. Skelsey estimated that if her suggestions were followed, women would spend fifteen to twenty hours a week keeping house. But since her book was written for married women who already were employed, one might ask what she thought their husbands' contribution to the work of the home ought to be. Not much. At best, men "help out" on occasion, and Skelsey advised women to consider their husbands' preferences when asking for "help." "Does he like to cook? Does he detest kitchen work? Sleep late on Saturday? Enjoy a big breakfast on Sunday?" A woman should ask her husband to do only the things he enjoys, and then only when it is convenient for him. "If you use your head in asking your husband for help," she told her readers, "it is highly unlikely that you will strip him of his manhood" (1970:18, 44, 49).

But not all manuals of the 1970s assumed a double day for employed women. The author of one insisted that "housework is not 'women's work.'" It is the responsibility of all who live in the home" (Olds 1975:71). Nor is it enough for men occasionally to help out. "Whatever the man of the house does should be seen as his contribution toward the living arrangements of the entire family—and not as help that he gives to you with your job of running the home." Similarly, most domestic manuals were no longer dedicated to "you the wife and mother" as they were in decades past. A 1981 volume of household hints written by Heloise II, the daughter of the late Heloise Cruse, is addressed to "homemakers" rather than "housewives" because, "lots of us are men," bachelors, as well as "house husbands who've changed things around. While their wives work, a lot of them are discovering what us gals instinctively knew—there's something very satisfying about raising kids, keeping a home, cooking, cleaning, and nipping about in search of a bargain" (Heloise 1981:xi–xii). The cartoon illustrations in *Mary Ellen's Best of Helpful Hints* (Pinkham and Higginbotham 1979) also suggested housekeeping was no longer an exclusively female domain. Men were shown chopping onions, flipping eggs in a skillet, peeling potatoes, and looking ruefully at a shrunken sweater just retrieved from the clothes washer.

Even manuals intended for full-time housewives changed their tune. The author of *Women at Home* told her readers that "every woman at home needs to realize that she is not a wife to the house. Rather she is a person with individual interests. . . . A woman faced with guiding a new generation—with her heart and mind, not with her broom." Hire a servant? Fine, "if a woman doesn't care for housework and if housework can be planned for in the family budget, why shouldn't she hire someone to help her with it? No one does everything well" (Cardozo 1976:38, 32). Quite a change from more than a century of advice about the ill wisdom of employing domestic servants!

But not everything changed in the world of prescriptive writing. There was, for example, the anachronistic "total woman" phenomenon of the 1970s. Marabel Morgan's best-seller *The Total Woman* did not say much about housework; most of her advice told women how to please, accommodate, and obey their husbands. But the traditional division of labor in the home was still sacrosanct. For Morgan, housework was exclusively women's work, and her few housekeeping hints were meant to keep hubby happy. She suggested, for example, housewives cook dinner and set the table for the evening meal right after breakfast in order to avoid the "4:30 syndrome," giving them time to take a bubble bath before the man of the house arrived home. Morgan also told women to attend to their husbands' requests at once: "When your husband asks you to do something, he expects it to be done without reminding you. The next time he delegates a job to you, write it down. Give it top priority on your list" (1975:31, 28).

Anachronistic or not, the runaway success of Morgan's book requires explanation. Full-time homemakers were its target audience—women who came of age in the 1950s and 1960s when the role of housewife was largely unquestioned. But by the 1970s, feminist discourse had struck at the core of their deep indoctrination into women's "proper place." Many such women were caught in a bind because, in the words of psychologist Rae André, "their transition to the new way of thinking [was] difficult, or . . . impossible if they were already caught up in the cycle of economic and psychological dependency encouraged—even demanded—by the woman-as-housewife dogma" (1981:44). Morgan's appeal becomes intelligible within this milieu. Her readers wanted to believe her when she told them their role as helpmates to their husbands was an eminently fulfilling one. Yet despite the sales of her book, Morgan probably transformed few adult females into "total women." After all, by the 1970s, the 60 percent of married women who were in the labor force could not lounge in a bubble bath at 4:30 in the afternoon or greet their husbands at the door at 5:00 dressed only in a pink baby-doll nightie and white boots, as Morgan recommended. It is also well to remember that *Mary Ellen's Best of Helpful Hints*, with its straightforward, no-nonsense approach to housekeeping, also was a best-seller of the day.

"HOMEKEEPING," MARTHA STEWART, AND THE 1990S

Housework can't kill you, but why take the risk?

Phyllis Diller

Overshadowing all domestic advisors at the close of the twentieth century is Martha Stewart who has been dubbed "a cross between an arts-and-crafts counselor and Marie Antoinette in shepherdess mode" (Politt 2000). Stewart's empire, a multipronged conglomerate, includes a monthly magazine with a circulation of 2.3 million, a column syndicated in 233 newspapers, a five-day-a-week television show, "Ask Martha" radio spots, a Martha by Mail catalogue, a Web site, and twenty-seven books, with an estimated total worth of $250 million (O'Neill 1999). Her company, with $180 million in revenue in 1998 and a profit of nearly $24 million, went public in 1999 and is now listed on the New York Stock Exchange (Fabrikant 1999).

At a time when the vast majority of married women in this country are employed outside the home, Stewart's popularity is perplexing. After all, in her dreamlike world chickens hatch pastel-colored eggs, gift wrap won't do unless it is homemade, and families make their own soap for Mother's Day. While some see elements of the 1950s feminine mystique in her proposals, journalist Margaret Talbot (1996) suggests Stewart is as much a throwback to the 1850s, an era when the doctrine of separate spheres gave wealthy married women iron-fisted control over their large households and many servants. Stewart likewise is "the undisputed chatelaine micromanaging her estate in splendid isolation."

Elements of the domestic science movement of the late nineteenth century also are evident in her take on domesticity. Like the champions of domestic science before her, Stewart's goal is not to liberate well-educated, middle-class women from housework, but to upgrade and professionalize it. To Stewart, housekeeping poses aesthetic and administrative challenges that demand respect.

Stewart's "homekeeping" projects, as she calls them, caricature timesaving and convenience. Utility is unimportant; elegance is the only measure of worth. And her notions of elegance—what is necessary and aesthetically pleasing—are decidedly elite. Talbot (1996) calls them "a dreamy advertisement for independent wealth." This is evident in her directives. They focus on the mechanics of the project but do not provide information about the time, labor, or costs involved. And cost they do. For example, in *Martha Stewart's Gardening* she lists forty-nine "essential" gardening tools. A staff of fifty who assist her in her projects also goes unmentioned.

Stewart's world lacks the limitations and distractions of everyday life. Leisure time and financial resources are unlimited, and family members are nowhere to be seen. Her world lacks husbands, and children appear only as immaculately dressed and posed props in photo layouts of elaborate Easter brunches or Christmas dinners. Ironically, the intended audience for Stewart's multiple projects are professional and managerial women, one of the most time-pressed groups in America today. Nearly three-quarters of subscribers to *Martha Stewart Living* work outside the home, and many of them hold professional and managerial positions. Although Stewart never suggests women abandon their jobs or careers, the way of life exalted in her directives clearly requires *someone's* full-time attention.

Martha Stewart books and magazines are rife with nostalgia for lost traditions. She pines for the good old days of home production and provides esoteric knowledge to women who have been socialized to buy, not to make. In vaunting a pre-technological house, Stewart is selling "a kind of mass manufactured neo-Luddism" (Sharlet 1999). But most of her audience has neither the time nor the resources to do the "good things" she suggests. One viewer said she watches her TV show for an "atavistic thrill," while another, the wife in a dual career family, explained the attraction: "I love seeing the domestic life that we don't have time to live." Some people need domestic fantasy and Martha Stewart allows them to dream. Still, to others, Martha is anything but relaxing. In one survey, 51 percent of the respondents said they get stressed watching Martha Stewart on television; only 27 percent found watching disasters on the nightly news similarly stressful (O'Neill 1999).

Stewart's nostalgia for the past also underlies her espousal of family values that are more in line with the 1950s than with the contemporary scene. She sees a backlash against working mothers of the 1970s and 1980s who took jobs in large numbers and "forgot about their kids." Now, she opines, people are again interested in setting standards "more conducive to raising good children and maintaining a nice house" (quoted in Holcomb 1998:41). Yet, ironically, Martha herself comes across as a frosty perfectionist, not a warm motherly type who keeps the home fires burning.

Just as this book was going to press, a new household manual appeared, *Home Comforts* (1999) by Cheryl Mendelson, who is described as "a philosopher, lawyer, sometime professor, a homemaker, wife, and mother." While the book—widely reviewed for a household manual—bears some resemblance to the lists of receipts of an earlier era, it also contains the sort of overwrought tributes to good housekeeping reminiscent of nineteenth century tomes. Keeping house well can be very rewarding, readers are told, since it allows them to provide for the physical and emotional comfort of loved ones. The manual, says the blurb, is meant to "induce a greater appreciation for the effort and specialized knowledge that go into keeping house."

The author goes on to give incredibly detailed, make-work directives on everything from sanitizing drains and sponges, to disinfecting dish towels, vacuuming upholstered furniture every week and hauling mattresses out of the house twice a year to air. As an Amazon.com reviewer put it, the manual is "a relentless paean to obsessive practice," noting pointedly that if she followed even a minority of the author's suggestions, "I'd be dead by now." And as social critic Katha Politt (2000) observed in *The Nation*, "anti-feminists have been chatting it up as proof that working women are wasting their lives."

Despite the overblown efforts of the Martha Stewarts and Cheryl Mendelsons of the world, by the end of the millennium most housework advice actually tried to ease its burdens and save time. This is evident from some of the recent titles offering housekeeping tips: *How to Avoid Housework* (Jhung 1995), *Don't Be a Slave to Housework* (McClellan 1995), *Is There Life After Housework?* (Aslett 1992), *Too Busy to Clean?* (Barrett 1998) and *Clean It*

Fast, Clean It Right (Bredenberg 1998). The overriding goal of these manuals is to save time keeping the house in order, a saving of up to 75 percent according to one author (Aslett 1992). The new books all adopt a light-hearted, humorous approach to the tasks at hand, one warning against the "perils of perfection," including "mopping migraine," "dustpan depression," and "sweeper's shoulder" (Jhung 1995:8). The common message: housework, while perhaps necessary, should definitely not be taken too seriously.

There is also the question of who does it. With so many women employed outside the home, some manuals recognize that times indeed have changed. In a chapter titled "The Fine Art of Delegation," one manual writer approvingly quotes a psychologist who believes that if the whole family shares the home, the whole family should care for it. She tells readers to "reject ownership" of household appliances, suggesting appliances and cleaning equipment should always be referred to as "ours," *not* "mine" (Jhung 1995:28). But not all such tomes depict a revolution in gender roles; some are clearly intended for women only. One manual devotes a section to "getting help" from your spouse. Despite the sex neutral title, the advice is actually how to get husbands to "help out," the author advising women not to "nag" and to be "certain that what you ask is fair" (McClellan 1995:40).

Perhaps some readers are taking the time-saving hints to heart because there are strong signs the long hours of working women's double day are now a bit shorter. By 1995, employed women were averaging 15.6 hours a week on housework, down from the twenty-one hours a week recorded twenty years earlier (Bader 1999). By 1997, women reported doing 2.8 hours of housework on workdays, down a half hour over the course of two decades. And men appeared to have taken up some of the slack; they increased their workday contribution by one hour to 2.1 hours over the same period of time (Lewin 1998). Such figures reflect the fact that the gap is closing in the way employed men and women spend their time at home. In 1977, men spent only 30 percent as much time as women on workday chores, but by the mid-1990s they were spending 75 percent as much time (Lewin 1998). Research indicates husbands do a greater share of housework—and child care—the longer the hours their wives work and the greater their wives' contribution to total household income. As couples get accustomed to both spouses working, men appear more willing to take on a greater share of household tasks (Pittman and Blanchard 1996).

What has been called the "privatization of housework" also helps explain why working women are spending fewer hours on chores associated with the home. Privatization is not limited to hiring someone to clean the bathroom and do the laundry, but to services that actually substitute for the act of being home. For those who can afford it, companies like Les Concierges will send someone to wait for the repairman or the cable installer or take the cat to the vet. For about $15 an hour and up a whole raft of companies provide services that "subcontract the personal" (Bader 1999).

Despite the increasing use of such services, especially among middle-class families, who does what around the house remains a source of contention. Forty-three percent of the women in one study wanted men to do more household chores, and a survey by the Soap and Detergent Association found half of those questioned had argued about housework and 10 percent had separated over issues like whose turn it was to clean the bathroom (Lewin 1998; *New York Times*, January 28, 1999). Yet research also suggests about 20 percent of working women are "gatekeepers" who limit their husband's participation in housework and child care, possibly in an attempt to reinforce their own identity as mothers. Some are unwilling to abandon traditional gender roles, while others are perfectionists who feel no one can do the job as well as they can (Kelly 1999).

WHEN IS WORK NOT WORK?

Since the onset of industrialization in the United States, the most salient feature of housework has remained unchanged: housework is not considered work. Even today, with the spread of feminism and the massive entry of women into the job market, when women do chores at home they are not considered to be "working." Indeed most economists label as "work" only those activities that contribute to the Gross National Product. Yet it is estimated the unpaid domestic services of women equal about 25 percent of the GNP (André 1981). But, it is argued, housework does not produce anything of *monetary value*. Housewives may bake bread or sew clothes, but these products are for family use, not for sale on the market. This attitude is also reflected in the way housework is treated by some federal policies and government agencies. A housewife's services are covered by neither Social Security nor unemployment insurance. In computing Social Security benefits, for example, the years spent at unpaid household labor are not counted. Housework, unlike other types of work, is quite simply nonwork.

This trivialization of domestic labor is an ideology that flies in the face of reality. Housework can be a full-time job. Its hours are often no shorter than those of paid work, and housework involves not only time but physical labor. Cooking family meals, cleaning house, and washing clothes are all indisputably work. When these services are paid for, no one denies they are work. And without the free labor of housewives and the double day of employed women, families could not live as well or as cheaply as they do. One study estimated that about half of the American family's disposable income comes from the unpaid work of family members, mostly wives and mothers (Sirageldin 1969). But housework continues to be trivialized because to do otherwise would be very costly. If women did not provide free domestic services, employers either would have to pay higher wages to enable employees to buy these services or business, and industry would have to invest large sums to underwrite inexpensive cafeterias, day-care centers, and laundries. If men, women, and children had to provide these services for themselves as individuals, many hours now devoted to jobs, schooling, and leisure would have to be redirected to domestic labor. The care and feeding of the present and future labor force and the maintenance of its living standard is the real function of housework, one that, given its importance to the economy, comes very cheaply indeed.

Housework also involves the administration of consumption. Without the time and effort that millions of American women devote to selecting, using, and caring for the plethora of domestic conveniences and devices on the market today, consumption would be greatly reduced. This is the real reason why no major reorganization of housework has occurred over the last century. Each individualized nuclear family continues to be responsible for satisfying its daily needs for food, shelter, and child care, and women continue to bear the primary burden of meeting these needs. Still, with the increasing necessity of two-family incomes, a necessity that has propelled millions of married women into the job market, the time may soon be upon us when millions of American husbands will wonder, as they make their way down the aisles of the nations' supermarkets, "What shall I make for dinner tonight?"

WHEN IS WOMEN'S PLACE
IN THE HOME?

The doctrine that women belong in the home never carries more conviction than when it is allied with "proof" that women's activities outside the
home are detrimental to the health and welfare of their families, and to
the country as a whole.

Ann Oakley, *Woman's Work*, 1976

Working women have received much attention over the last three
decades. As the number of women with jobs climbed past the 50 percent mark
for the first time in American history, prescriptive writers, pundits, and poli-
ticians pondered why married, middle-class women went to work and what
impact their jobs had on home and family life. While women have entered
and left the labor market before, their current high rate of employment
requires explanation. What are the reasons for the varying job rates of American women and the shifts in attitude toward working women that accompany
them? Under what conditions is the time-worn adage, "woman's place is in
the home," vehemently asserted or fervently denied?

There are multiple causes for changing attitudes toward women and
work. Among the most important is the demand for female labor. A strong
link exists, for example, between women's work during wartime and an ideology that regards such work as acceptable, even patriotic, and not in conflict
with women's domestic role. This ideology reflects sharp increases in the
need for a female labor force resulting from the scarcity of male labor during

periods of national and international conflict. Apart from wartime, women's expanding job rates also correlate with a more general demand for female labor. Economist Valerie Oppenheimer (1970) has shown that separate job markets exist for male and female labor and that the rise in demand for women workers grows out of an increased need for workers in typically female occupations—clerical work, for example. In fact, a huge increase in jobs in the "female" sector of the labor market is one reason why women's employment rate has grown so dramatically over the last thirty years.

Women also take jobs when standards of consumption are rising. At such times additional family income is needed to buy the consumer goods that have come to be associated with middle-class lifestyles. Women's employment is met with grudging approval because their work is seen as an extension, not a contradiction, of their domestic role. Women are working to buy "extras" for their families, thus contributing to their well-being.

High inflation similarly motivates middle-class women to take jobs as their earnings become indispensable for maintaining the family's standard of living. Under inflationary pressures women work not merely to buy extras but to help pay for such basics as food, home mortgages, and health care. For the same reason, a decline in male wages beckons women into the job market. Women's income fills the gap created by lower male wages, ensuring that their families' quality of life is not compromised. Under such conditions ideologies that see unbridgeable conflicts between a woman's job and her family's welfare begin to fade and demands for equal pay for equal work take on new vigor.

What about the other side of the equation? What conditions make for low job rates among married women and attendant attitudes decrying women's work outside the home? Contrary to popular wisdom, widespread unemployment does not necessarily mean low work rates for women. Economic conditions that prevailed in the United States in the early 1980s, for example, belie any direct link between the two; at that time the highest level of unemployment in three decades coincided with a record number of women holding jobs. But it is true that during certain periods of economic crisis, like the 1930s, women workers were condemned for taking jobs away from male breadwinners. Ironically, despite the virulent attacks on working women during the Great Depression, the female labor force actually grew during those years as women, out of sheer economic necessity, sought to replace lost male wages.

Women's job rates seem to be lowest during what might be termed "neutral" periods—times when unemployment and inflation are not high, male wages are not falling, nor is there a substantial demand for female labor. The 1920s was such a period; despite that era's much heralded political and sexual emancipation of women, their employment rate remained low; the proportion of women working increased by only 1 percent over the preceding decade.

While I do not mean to depict women as puppets buffeted about by irresistible economic forces, evidence suggests that the size of the female labor force is, in fact, influenced by the factors mentioned above: the scarcity of male labor during wartime, rising patterns of consumption, high inflation, lower male wages, and labor demand in "female" occupations. The data also suggest that attitudes about the propriety of employing certain classes of women—wives and mothers, the middle-class and middle-aged—adjust to rather than cause changing work rates for these groups. Although attitudes sometimes lag behind the reality of rising female employment, as in the persistence of the feminine mystique in the 1950s and much of the 1960s, attitudes themselves have never initiated changes in the rate at which women take jobs. Viewing shifting ideologies about women and work as the prime movers in women's job rates obscures the causal processes that enhance or inhibit women's employment. It fails to ask the vital question: "Under what conditions do these changes occur?" But if we agree that positive or negative attitudes about working women are the result rather than the cause of women's varying rates of employment, then the reasons for these changes must be sought elsewhere.

The wider lenses of anthropology and history provide useful insights for our more focused inquiry into women's employment in the United States and the diverse attitudes that accompany it. They tell us, for example, that the belief that women have been "liberated" to work outside the home only within the last three or four decades is untrue. It is based on the premise that a sharp dichotomy between home and workplace has existed since time immemorial. But, in fact, such a distinction is relatively recent; it does not predate the industrial era. In economies based on horticulture and domestic production the problem of reconciling "home" and "work" did not exist because men, women, and children all lived and worked in the same place. As such, the pronouncement that "women's place is in the home" could only develop after the home and place of work had become separate. Similarly, the concept that child rearing and housework are full-time activities, is also quite recent. During a significant portion of human history the labor of able-bodied women was too valuable to devote to full-time child care. Child rearing was not considered a distinct activity, but something that took place amidst the myriad tasks needed to sustain life.

A cross-cultural and historical perspective also reveals the relative infrequency and recency of women's exclusion from productive activities. In the majority of hunter-gatherer and horticultural societies—which, after all, were the primary modes of production for most of human existence—women are very much involved in productive activities. Some anthropologists argue that the provider-male/domestic-female division of labor first appeared in agricultural societies (Martin and Voorhies 1975). But even in agrarian societies, such as colonial North America, women were engaged in production and the later preoccupation with the "appropriateness" of women working did not arise.

Finally, with few exceptions, only comparatively affluent sectors of society can afford the luxury of full-time housewife-mothers. As such, the ideology of women's economic dependence is both class linked and geographically limited, one that first arose among the middle and upper classes living in the eastern and southern regions of the United States. As sociologist Robert

Smuts cogently notes, "a family had to have the means to support its women in sheltered idleness before it could come to believe that this was their natural state" (1971:137). Such an ideology was incompatible with the harsh demands made on pioneer women who helped settle the Great Plains and far western frontiers. And, given the economic realities of their lives, relatively few African-American women were able to be full-time homemakers. Black women have always worked in far higher proportions than their white counterparts. Ultimately, then, during much of American history the doctrine that women's place is in the home could be translated into practice only by a limited portion of the population.

HOME INDUSTRY AND MILL INDUSTRY: THE COLONIAL PERIOD AND THE EARLY NINETEENTH CENTURY

Prior to the nineteenth century most men and women worked together on the land and in the home with much overlap in the type of work performed by each sex. Labor power was particularly precious during the early years of settlement, and a rigid segregation of gender roles would have been impractical. As one historian of the period put it: "Where a new world was being made women could not stick to the kitchen, let alone the boudoir" (Thompson 1974:103). This does not mean that male and female tasks were interchangeable. Men typically did most of the agricultural work, while women were in charge of home industry.

Home manufacture was key to women's income. Many of the items they produced at home were sold or traded, especially textile goods. Women made lace, sewed, spun, and wove articles for sale. By the second half of the eighteenth century yarn and cloth were in great demand and, working under a commission system, women produced these items at home. Although it is not known how many women were involved in these activities or what they earned, spinning and weaving provided women's most important source of income prior to the establishment of the factory system (Abbott 1910).

Besides home production, women were also engaged in shopkeeping, running taverns and "ordinaries" (inns), midwifery, nursing, teaching, domestic service, trading, and printing. While precise figures for the colonial era are scarce, we know that many women active in these occupations were widows. Moreover, since tradesmen, shopkeepers, and artisans typically worked out of their homes, married women presumably assisted their husbands with these enterprises. In the South women sometimes ran plantations in their husbands' absence, and a study of tort cases during the colonial period has shown that women had intimate knowledge of their husbands' businesses (Spruill 1938; Morris 1930).

The number of women employed in these activities in the eighteenth century was greater, relative to the size of the labor force, than in the nineteenth century. There were more female shopkeepers and businesswomen during the colonial period, for example, than there were by the 1830s (Lerner 1979). Why was this so? Explanations vary. One suggests that in the late eighteenth century when skilled labor was in short supply a large increase in the demand for goods made positions available to women. Another cites the lack of consistent cultural restrictions that might have barred women from certain nondomestic activities (Brownlee and Brownlee 1976). But the question arises: Why were such cultural restrictions ill defined in the late eighteenth century and strengthened some decades later?

Still, in the colonial era it was women's central role in the domestic economy that was acknowledged by commentators. The Boston pastor Benjamin Wadsworth wrote in 1712 of the division of labor: "The husband should endeavor that his wife should have food and raiment suitable to her. . . . The wife also in her place should do what she can that the man has a comfortable support" 1972:29). To Cotton Mather (1741), a virtuous woman was one who "seeks Wooll and Flax, and Works willingly with her hands" (1978:7). In short, industry was praised in both sexes. While by tradition men were seen as the principal providers, discourse about women's "secondary" role was little heard given the reality of a household economy based on the interdependence of the sexes. It was not until the advent of commercial farming, wage-earning, and extra-domestic manufacture that women's economic role, in the words of historian Nancy Cott, "appeared singular, their dependency prominent" (1977:22).

When textile mills were first established in New England in the early nineteenth century, many of the jobs in them, especially spinning and weaving, were deemed particularly well suited to women. These tasks had been done by women at home and were traditionally regarded as "women's work." The early factories, then, did not open up new occupations for women; they transferred their work site. Girls and unmarried women made up a large percentage of the operatives of the new textile mills. As early as 1827, 90 percent of the employees in the famed cotton mills of Lowell, Massachusetts, were females and, by 1832, women outnumbered men by 110 percent in the cotton industry as a whole (Baker 1964).

Nevertheless, women's prominence in the early mills mostly stemmed from a shortage of male labor rather than convictions about women's suitability for work in the mills. Men could easily become freeholders, and opportunities for financial success were far greater in agriculture than in factory work. Until the 1840s the relatively low wages and low status of factory employment offered few incentives to men, while cheap land farther west and skilled jobs at higher pay in New England beckoned. Thus, the exodus of men from New England to farms in New York State and the Great Lake territory spurred the employment of women and children in the New England mills.

The establishment of manufacturing is problematic in agrarian societies with low worker productivity—such as then existed in this country—because most available labor is devoted to producing food and other primary agricultural products. In fact, contemporary critics expressed concern that if men were employed in factories, agriculture would suffer. Years earlier, George Washington wrote to General Lafayette that he would not allow the introduction of manufactured goods to prejudice agriculture and, he added, prophetically: "I conceive much might be done in the way of women, children and others without taking one really necessary hand from tilling the earth" (quoted in Kessler-Harris 1981:8). Thus, as long as land was inexpensive and agriculture profitable, problems caused by the scarcity and higher cost of male labor were resolved by employing women. While work in the mills was indeed attractive to women because the pay was higher than in domestic service, mill owners could still hold down costs by paying women lower wages than they would have had to pay men. The reduced cost of labor, in fact, allowed American mills to compete successfully with the British textile industry.

Given these conditions, the stamp of approval for women's factory work came from many quarters. Since the new mill work involved traditional "female" skills, some supported hiring women by arguing it was merely an extension of work that women had always done. Contemporary moralists advocated mill jobs for women warning that those who did not take them "were doomed to idleness and its inseparable attendants, vice and guilt" (Baker 1964:5–6). Some mill owners even made the outlandish claim that one reason for establishing the textile industry was to save "respectable" women from poverty and idleness. And statesmen endorsed women's factory work, Alexander Hamilton hailing it on the grounds that it permitted the development of manufacturing without taking men away from the fields. Communities were said to gain by women's mill employment because it would reduce the burden of poor women and children on society and the nation as a whole would benefit by making "women a source of wealth rather than an encumbrance" (Abbott 1910:56).

FROM FACTORY TO HOME: THE NINETEENTH CENTURY

Industrial employment for women, at least for unmarried women, was acceptable as long as male labor was scarce, as it continued to be during much of the first half of the nineteenth century. Women who took factory employment were generally young, working class, and overwhelmingly single. As such, they were peripheral to the slowly evolving prescriptive discourse extolling a distinct female domestic sphere, a discourse explicitly directed at married, middle-class housewives.

While the total number of women employed and the number in each industry is unknown—industrial jobs were not delineated in any U.S. census prior to 1850—in the early decades of the century women were concentrated in the hand trades. These were small-scale enterprises with much of the work done at home, in shops or small factories that had little or no machinery. Technological advances had relatively little impact on productivity in the hand trades, but they did require many workers, making labor costs a high proportion of total costs. The low wages paid by employers in their effort to keep costs down were too meager to attract male operatives who could find more remunerative positions elsewhere. But women, with far fewer alternatives for paid employment, were willing to accept the low wages offered.

By the 1840s women and children no longer provided a supply of unskilled labor sufficient to meet the growing demands of industry. The need for such labor led to the first great wave of immigration from Europe, and many employers sought out Irish, German, and French Canadian immigrants who were willing to work for even lower wages than native-born American women. In the textile mills in Lowell, Massachusetts, for example, in 1845 only 7 percent of the labor force was foreign born, but by 1852 more than half of the workers were immigrants. Female immigrants partially replaced American-born women in factories, but since immigration from Europe and Canada was predominantly male, the percentage of men in factories increased sharply in the 1850s. And this trend continued, contributing to the gradual decline in women's factory employment throughout the remainder of the century (Kessler-Harris 1975; Brownlee and Brownlee 1976).

The cotton industry, with its concentration of female employees, illustrates these changes. Between 1810 and 1820 when the industry was in its infancy, women and children accounted for 87 percent of cotton mill operatives. But as the century progressed, the proportion of men working in cotton mills steadily increased. In 1850 women made up 64 percent of the industry's labor force and in 1900, 49 percent. By that year a majority of the cotton industry's labor force were males of foreign parentage, a group that scarcely existed to compete with female labor during the first quarter of the nineteenth century when the mills were being established (Abbott 1910).

Why were women replaced in an industry they had dominated from its very inception? Elizabeth Abbott (1910) analyzed the factors leading to the decline of women in the cotton mills. As the mills became more mechanized, heavier machinery requiring work at increased speed and strength favored the employment of male operatives. Then, too, the supply of male labor increased as immigration from Europe continued, and more men were willing to work at low wages in the mills. Finally, the number of educated women seeking such employment declined as higher-status, white-collar jobs in teaching, offices, and shops opened up. Abbott rightly argued that change in the male labor supply was the most decisive factor, contending that if male labor had remained scarce, mill machinery would have been modified for use by female operatives.

The Civil War marked a turning point for women in the textile industry. The shutdown of mills during the war led women to seek work elsewhere, and when the mills reopened after the war, female workers were largely displaced by male immigrants. Then, too, at about this time barriers to hiring women for skilled factory positions solidified. From the late 1850s on, most craft unions sharply restricted women's membership; union leaders argued that women lowered wages and took jobs away from "male breadwinners." Since craft unions accounted for a majority of union membership during the last half of the nineteenth century, such barriers effectively shut women out of union participation (Brownlee and Brownlee 1976).

Once again, opinion makers came to the fore on the issue of women and work and, from the mid-nineteenth century on, loud and often well-known voices decried women's factory employment. Theodore Roosevelt claimed women's physical delicacy made them ill suited for such work and feared its effects on the "race and the nation": "If the women do not recognize that the greatest thing for any woman is to be a good wife and mother, why, that nation has cause to be alarmed about its future." Others expressed similar views. In 1875 the chief of the Massachusetts Bureau of Labor Statistics declared: "Married women ought not to be tolerated in the mills at all . . . for it is an evil that is sapping the life of our operative population, and must sooner or later be regulated, or, more properly, stopped." Two years later the head of the Boston Central Labor Union opposed women's factory employment as "an insidious assault upon the home; it is the knife of the assassin aimed at the family circle" (quoted in Baker 1964:84). These sentiments seem odd at first because in the nineteenth century very few married women were employed in mills or anywhere else outside the home; throughout the century the female labor force was overwhelmingly young and single.

Such fulminations against women's employment were a pivotal facet of the doctrine of separate spheres that relegated women to the home and men to the world of work. This arrangement and its supporting ideology well served the interests of nineteenth-century business and industry. The middle-class ideal of full-time homemaking was one to which thousands of poor, immigrant, and nonwhite working women could aspire. The discourse on feminine domesticity encouraged such women to view their jobs as temporary, as brief interludes before they attained their true calling as wives and mothers. Workers without strong commitments to long-term employment were less likely to protest exploitation and low wages. And a docile, transient labor force is difficult to unionize. Believing their life's work to be elsewhere, women had fewer incentives than men to fight for better working conditions. The doctrine of separate spheres also allowed women's income to be treated as supplemental, a useful assumption that justified the nineteenth-century practice of paying women one-third to one-half the prevailing wage paid to men. Finally, the cult of domesticity stigmatized men with working wives, a powerful incentive for men who were the sole support of their families. Long hours, perhaps under difficult conditions were the price many men had to pay if they were to keep the respect conferred on those with dependent wives (Kessler-Harris 1975).

The barriers to hiring women for skilled factory jobs created a pool of educated women who sought work elsewhere. As the nineteenth century progressed, more professional and white-collar positions in teaching, nursing, libraries, and offices became available, and native-born, middle-class women flocked to them as alternatives to factory employment. One consequence was the feminization of these fields. When male labor was scarce during the Civil War, for example, the demand for women teachers increased, and school boards with meager funds enthusiastically hired women who could be paid less than men. Campaigns were waged to recruit women whose dispositions, it was said, were uniquely suited to teaching the young and, by the end of the war, more women than men were public school teachers. As public education continued to expand and men were hired for more lucrative positions in business and skilled trades, primary and secondary school teaching became predominately female. By 1870, two-thirds of all teachers were women, and by 1890, women held more than three-quarters of all teaching jobs (Baker 1964).

Nursing, too, once a largely male preserve, saw an influx of women during the Civil War. And, here again, low wages and relatively low status—nurses were classified as "domestic workers" until the late 1800s—made nursing unattractive to men who had other job options. Librarianship was also becoming a female job ghetto. Since public libraries were supported by tax dollars and private donations, they were expected to keep labor costs down and spend most of their income on books and periodicals. Given the limited opportunities available to them elsewhere, educated women willing to work for low pay quickly staffed these burgeoning institutions. In 1878, two-thirds of all library workers were women, and by 1910 women held nearly 80 percent of all library jobs (Garrison 1974).

Why were teaching, nursing, and librarianship among the few professions that came to be identified as particularly suited to women? Local governments and private charities—the primary employers of teachers, nurses, and librarians—lacked the financial wherewithal to compete with farms, factories, and other businesses for male labor. But educated women, barred from other professions, were available in large numbers.

For similar reasons office work and retail sales also absorbed substantial numbers of middle-class women. Willing to take skilled secretarial and clerical jobs for lower wages than men, women first entered offices during the Civil War, when male labor was in short supply. The invention of the typewriter in 1873 increased the demand for women in business and commercial offices, and they soon dominated clerical and secretarial positions. Women were also being hired for retail sales. Here, too, an educated work force was essential; literacy in English and knowledge of arithmetic were prerequisites for such positions. Middle-class women again provided employers with a relatively cheap pool of skilled labor. The Victorian image of women as consumer specialists meshed well with the belief that women were adept at sales, an idea not unrelated to the low cost of hiring them.

Late nineteenth-century attitudes toward women and work varied according to women's status. Unmarried women could be employed in certain "suitable" occupations, but married women were not to work outside the home except in the most dire economic circumstances. The cult of domesticity gave married women primary responsibility for care of home and family, duties that could not possibly be fulfilled if they held jobs. A study of employed married women living in one county in Massachusetts in 1880 bore this out; it found the *only* condition making a woman's work both necessary and socially acceptable was her husband's inability to earn a living (Mason, Vinovskis, and Hareven 1978).

Moralists and opinion makers of the era used several arguments to make their case against women's employment. Perhaps most powerful was the conviction that the female body was delicate and easily impaired by unfeminine activities. Azel Ames, a physician, claimed in *Sex in Industry* (1875) women's jobs not only disrupted their menstrual cycle and, hence, their fertility, but were dangerous to their general health and sanity as well. In 1900 Edward Bok, editor of *Ladies' Home Journal*, cited similar objections: "It . . . is a plain, simple fact that women have shown themselves naturally incompetent to fill a great many of the business positions which they have sought to occupy. . . . The fact is that not one woman in a hundred can stand the physical strain of the keen pace which competition has forced upon every line of business today" (quoted in Davies 1975:285).

Others opposed jobs for women on the grounds that they were intellectually and temperamentally unsuited for paid work. Women were said to have certain mental and emotional proclivities essential to their roles as wives and mothers; industrial and professional employment could impair these qualities and cause mental breakdown. Then there were the moral arguments against women in the labor force. Women were naturally pure, modest, and lacking in passion, according to this reasoning, but these traits, like so many feminine qualities, were easily corrupted. To preserve them, women should not be exposed to tempting and compromising situations such as unsupervised association with men at work.

Equally potent was the suggestion that women's employment would upend the "natural" order of society, giving them undue power. This was an expression of the now familiar anxiety about who "wears the pants" in the family. The timeworn dictum that working women take jobs away from men and deprive male breadwinners of their livelihood was a leitmotif of this discourse. Not coincidentally, such claims were most loudly asserted during times of economic uncertainty. As sociologist Robert Smuts notes, "every depression brought a resurgence of the complaint that working women were stealing jobs that belonged to men" (1971:19).

A final line of argument was directed at the male relatives of employed women. Simply put, female employment reflected badly on them. Men who "permitted" their wives, daughters, or sisters to work were either unable to support them, powerless to control them, or unconcerned with protecting them from the dangers of the world outside the home. Having a working wife or daughter, especially in middle-class families, was a sign of a man's failure; he was expected to demonstrate his success by keeping his female relatives idle.

To some extent these attitudes reflected the actual rate of women's employment in the late nineteenth century. While women did work in facto-ries, offices, schools, and shops, they were exceptions to the rule. The major-ity of women, particularly married women, made home and family full-time careers. Between 1870 and 1900, only 15 to 20 percent of American women worked outside the home and the figures for married women were much lower; by 1900, less than 4 percent of married white women held jobs. Even in factories—the largest employers of women not in domestic service—an 1887 Bureau of Labor study found only 4 percent of female operatives were married. Similarly, only one in twenty-five female schoolteachers was mar-ried, in part, because many school districts had policies against hiring married women (Brownlee and Brownlee 1976; Degler 1980).

In the late nineteenth century African-American and immigrant women were the only married women who worked outside the home in significant numbers. The 1890 census reported that 25 percent of black married women had jobs and in Lowell and Fall River, Massachusetts, about 20 percent of for-eign-born and first-generation married women were employed in the textile mills. That economic necessity was the primary reason married women took jobs is supported by the fact that in 1890 more widows than wives were employed outside the home (Smuts 1971).

The great majority of employed women in the final decades of the nine-teenth century were either nonwhite, foreign born, or young and single. More-over, for young, unmarried women work was temporary; almost all white women who had jobs gave them up when they married. Even among married women without young children to rear or much else to do, very few were employed. Once a girl became a woman and married, she automatically stayed home.

THE FACTORY AND THE OFFICE: THE EARLY TWENTIETH CENTURY

Victorian condemnation of working women was somewhat muted during the first two decades of the twentieth century as more women took jobs. Their increased numbers were due to both greater demand for unskilled and semi-skilled labor and, in many cases, from the inability of male wages alone to meet family needs. As a result, between 1900 and 1919, the female labor force grew by 50 percent. Many of the new workers were immigrants who were more likely to be employed than their native-born counterparts. The typical female worker had changed somewhat since the turn of the century, but in 1910, 60 percent of women workers were still young and single. A U.S. Bureau of Labor study in that year also demolished the myth of women as "pin money" workers; it found many families heavily dependent on the wages of their female members (Breckinridge 1933).

The 1905 census indicated that women in industry were still heavily con-centrated in a few fields—textiles, clothing trades, cigar making, printing, boot and shoemaking, all labor intensive operations. Employers hired female operatives, particularly those of foreign birth, because budding industries needed a supply of inexpensive labor to turn a profit. Poor, unskilled immigrants, in turn, willingly took such jobs since their survival often depended on all family members earning a paycheck. A 1915 report on women and children in industrial jobs in the U.S. cited the connection between the employment of women and low wages: "Almost everywhere women predominate in unskilled work, probably because they could be secured for this at wages which would not attract men" (quoted in Baker 1964:81).

While employers welcomed cheap immigrant labor—male and female—many contemporary social reformers and labor leaders viewed it with alarm. Immigrants, they said, lowered wages and living standards, made it difficult to improve working conditions, and hindered the unionization of factory operatives. Working women also were targets of those who feared the social consequences of a cheap labor supply. Public moralists—worried that there were not enough jobs for men—renewed their plaint that women's proper place was in the home. Nor had the moral argument against employing women been laid to rest. The Chicago Vice Commission claimed in a 1911 report that women's employment, their entry into politics, the decay of the family, and rising rates of prostitution were all related (cited in Smuts 1971).

Aside from factory jobs, in the early years of the twentieth century most employed women worked as domestic servants, on farms, and in a handful of professions. Teaching and nursing still accounted for most women professionals; 76 percent were in one of those two fields. The number of women in sales and office positions doubled in the first decade of the century, and by 1910 office work had become a female ghetto; women held 83 percent of all typing and stenographic positions in that year (Davies 1975). The expansion of business offices meant the rapid growth of low-level, dead-end jobs that, nevertheless, required an educated work force.

This employment picture changed dramatically with the outbreak of World War I. The demand for labor during the war opened new jobs to women, and the customary and legal restrictions against hiring them quickly fell. Large numbers of women worked in munitions plants, as streetcar conductors, elevator operators, theater ushers, furnace stokers, and in some sales and clerical positions once held exclusively by men. The number of women employed in steel and iron foundries increased threefold during the war and, for the first time, the U.S. Public Health Service employed women as medical doctors. Still, as historian William Chafe (1972) points out, the war did not result in a large net increase in the number of employed women. Only about 5 percent of those who took jobs during wartime were new to the labor market. The rest were working before the war and simply moved from lower-paying jobs to higher-paying ones vacated by men after the outbreak of war.

While the sight of women welding and laying railroad tracks probably disturbed some people, by the second year of the war women working in once all-male occupations were generally accepted. Even that bastion of domesticity, the *Ladies' Home Journal*, published laudatory articles on women factory workers. Yet such stamps of approval were decidedly temporary; the unstated assumption was women would abandon their "masculine" jobs as soon as hostilities ceased. And so they did. With the return of the troops, many women were let go from jobs they held during the wartime emergency. In Detroit women streetcar conductors were fired en masse, in New York twenty women judges lost their positions, and by 1919, a Women's Bureau study noted women were prohibited from taking examinations for 60 percent of all civil service jobs. In the same year, the head of New York's Central Federated Labor Union loudly proclaimed that "the same patriotism which induced women to enter industry during the war should induce them to vacate their positions after the war" (quoted in Chafe 1972:53).

The relatively brief duration of the war meant the demand for women workers was short-lived. Hence, their jobs during wartime did not produce a large permanent increase in the number of working women. A few new positions—elevator operator and theater usher, to name two—remained open to women after the war. But women's job prospects actually had changed little following the war. They fell far short of any expectation that a break with tradition during wartime and the intervening suffrage movement might permanently improve women's status as workers. It did not.

SEXUAL EMANCIPATION AND THE FEMININE MYSTIQUE: THE 1920S

The widely heralded emancipation of women in the 1920s was an emancipation with well-defined limits, and the freedom to pursue a career was not among them. The feminine mystique—not yet named or discussed—was nevertheless alive and well during the age of the flapper. Employment figures bear this out. Between 1920 and 1930 the number of working women increased by only 1 percent, and most women still gave up their jobs when they married. Nor did women's jobs change very much. Those in industry still did unskilled, low-paid, dead-end work, and few women belonged to labor unions. The white-collar and professional positions held by women in the 1920s were much like those at the turn of the century. Most women in business still had secretarial, clerical, and sales jobs, and the great majority of female professionals were still teachers and nurses. In medicine and dentistry women actually *lost* ground; in 1900, some 11,000 female physicians and dentists were in practice, but by 1920, there were fewer than 10,000 (Filene 1976).

Attitudes toward women and work also were reminiscent of earlier times. The credo of the 1920s that single women might work at suitable jobs for a while and then retire after marriage was a holdover from 1900. A Department of Labor report on a conference on women in industry cited this consensus: "Practically every speaker recognized that women's interest in industry was at best only temporary, a stop-gap between whatever girlhood lay behind her and marriage" (quoted in Rupp 1978:61). A majority of Americans appeared to agree. In a 1924 survey of some three hundred men, 65 percent concurred with the statement, "the married woman should devote her time to the home" (Pruette 1972:100). Even the most open-minded opinion makers of the day approved of careers for married women *only* if they remained childless. And highly successful women were still primarily identified through their domestic role, as witness this 1923 headline: "Woman President of Bank Does Housework in Her Own Home."

These attitudes coincided with bans on hiring married women. The *New York Times* reported in 1928 that when the Long Island Railroad reduced its work force because of economic problems, married women with employed husbands were the first to be let go. Even in "feminine" fields like teaching, most school boards refused to hire wives, and about half of the nation's school districts required teachers to quit when they got married (Oppenheimer 1970). Such policies existed despite studies showing that 90 percent of women with jobs were helping to support their families. In fact, during the 1920s, one in four working women was her family's principal wage earner. Still, the myth that women work only for "pin money" endured as a handy rationale; it relieved employers of guilt when they refused to hire married women, failed to promote them, or paid them less than men.

The women's magazines of the 1920s glorified the domestic realm and published articles by prominent women who urged readers to seek fulfillment in it. In an anonymous article entitled "I Wish I Had Married and Found Life," written, according to the editors of *Good Housekeeping*, by a woman of "great fame," the author mentioned her highly successful career, but added poignantly: "I count my gains small beside my losses. I have no mate, no child, no home—only substitutes for them" (Anonymous, 1923). A 1927 article in the *Ladies' Home Journal* attacked the "career woman," asserting a good marriage was a woman's best career if she wanted to be "deeply, fundamentally, wholly feminine." And the following year an editorial in *McCall's Magazine* proclaimed the American woman could "arrive at her true eminence" only as a wife and mother (quoted in Chafe 1972:105).

The authors of these prescriptive pieces did not initiate antagonism toward employing married women; rather, they mirrored the reality that relatively few married women held jobs. And they reinforced and rationalized women's exclusion from the workplace. Moreover, the depiction of the archetypical American woman as a full-time homemaker rested on the tacit assumption that she had a husband to support her in this role. Poor women, African-American women, immigrant women, divorced women, all women who, of necessity, went to work, were absent from the national dialogue on the satisfactions of domestic life.

The 1920s were a paradox for American women. While it was the first decade of women's suffrage, women did not form the powerful voting block feminists had expected, and disappointingly few women were elected to political office. It was the era of the emancipated flapper with her bobbed hair and short skirts who smoked in public and demanded the same rights to sexual self-expression as men. But the gendered division of labor remained intact. And career women were still scorned as brazen dissenters from the prescriptive dictum that women's lasting fulfillment lay in home and family.

WORKING WIVES AS "THIEVING PARASITES": THE DEPRESSION YEARS

The onset of the Great Depression in the 1930s dashed whatever hopes feminists still had for female equality in the job market. Under conditions of widespread unemployment opinion makers of various stripes took it for granted women would give up any career ambitions they had and stay home. This would ensure the few jobs available went to men, the presumed family breadwinners. Married women workers who did not toe the line "are holding jobs that rightfully belong to the God-intended providers of the household," proclaimed a Chicago civic group. "Women's place is not out in the business world competing with men who have families to support" (quoted in Filene 1976:155). The hostility to working women was so fierce that one reason the Women's Bureau was established in the U.S. Department of Labor was to convince the public that women not only had the right to work but most did it to help support their families (Goldin 1990).

Although the number of women with jobs increased by some 500,000 in the 1930s and more married women than ever before were employed, these were by no means signs of personal liberation. Quite to the contrary; in an era of high male unemployment, the statistics indicate that women sought jobs because their incomes had become essential to family survival. Women took whatever work they could find to replace the wages of unemployed husbands or supplement meager household income. During the Depression years more than half of all American families had incomes of less than $1,200 annually, and it was the poorest sectors of society that supplied the bulk of female labor; in 1930, black and immigrant women accounted for 57 percent of all women workers (Chafe 1972).

Despite the great hue and cry against working women, by 1940 the percentage of women with jobs was 25 percent higher than it had been in 1930; for married women the rate had increased from 12 to 15 percent. Sociologist Ruth Milkman explains this apparent contradiction between advice and behavior as follows: The labor market's segregation by sex meant men and women occupied different job niches, and during the Depression, most female occupations—clerical, trade, and service jobs—declined less and later than predominantly male occupations in manufacturing. Then, too, because so many men were unemployed, women who had been housewives were driven to take whatever work they could get. Thus, Milkman concludes, "it was not possible for ideological forces to successfully push women out of the labor market. Such behavior was in direct opposition to [women's] material interests" (1976:81).

But these statistics do not reflect the profound social disapproval that confronted married women who took jobs or the general restrictions against hiring them. The American Federation of Labor, for example, urged business and industry to adopt hiring policies that discriminated against married women whose husbands were employed, and in many cases they did just that. By 1939, 84 percent of all U.S. insurance companies had bans on hiring married women with similar restrictions in force in 43 percent of public utility companies, 29 percent of manufacturing concerns, 23 percent of small private businesses, and 13 percent of department stores (Oppenheimer 1970).

Not just the private sector embraced such policies. Under the guise of anti-nepotism rules, the federal government legislated that two married people could not both hold government jobs. Although "people" referred equally to men and women, 80 percent of those fired as a result of this legislation were wives. Bills restricting the employment of married women were also introduced in twenty-six state legislatures. One New York assemblyman proposed a law that would heavily tax the personal income of married women, freely admitting his intention to drive them out of the job market. Although such legislation passed only in Louisiana, the reason for its failure was not lack of public support—a 1939 poll found over two-thirds approved of such legislation—but questions about its constitutionality (Cantril 1951). Finally, during the 1930s bans on hiring married women as teachers were even more widespread than a decade earlier. A 1930–1931 National Education Association survey of 1,500 school districts found that 77 percent refused to hire wives and 61 percent required women to resign from their teaching posts when they married (Degler 1980).

The women's magazines of the era did their part in heaping scorn on women who sought jobs, to say nothing of careers. Readers of the *Ladies' Home Journal* were told "your career is to make a good marriage" (Lane 1936:18), and the same magazine applauded the decision of a talented woman writer who had given up her career to devote herself full-time to the care and feeding of her husband (Thompson 1939). The conflict between marriage, motherhood, and career was a popular theme in the fiction of the *Saturday Evening Post*. While single heroines might have careers, they inevitably abandoned them after marriage (Honey 1976).

Given previous hostility toward employed women, women workers became convenient scapegoats for those unwilling or unable to comprehend the complex forces that led to the Great Depression. "Pin-money workers"—working women with employed husbands—were scathingly denounced as "thieving parasites" and "menaces to society." A 1937 public opinion poll found 82 percent of those sampled disapproved of working wives (Cantril 1951). And the provisions of the 1935 Social Security Act were a powerful statement of prevailing attitudes toward working women. The legislation assumed men were the sole support of their families, and women received social security benefits only as wives, not as workers in their own right. In short, although animosity toward working women was hardly an invention of the depression years, it reached new virulence as more and more Americans were thrown out of work and breadlines became a common sight.

FROM ROSIE THE RIVETER TO THE LOST SEX: THE 1940s

The year 1940 was a baseline in the United States, ground zero for women's employment which, after that date, underwent a profound transformation. In 1940, the typical female worker, like her counterpart in 1900, was young and single, and the vast majority of women still left work when they married. Only 15 percent of married women and only 9 percent of those with children held jobs. And the drumbeat extolling domesticity was as loud as ever. In 1940 the *Ladies' Home Journal* carried an article by well-known journalist Dorothy Thompson, who urged women not to follow in her professional footsteps. And, she added, "I have an increasing respect for those women who stick to their knitting" (1940:25).

By 1940, in the words of sociologist Robert Smuts, "the general case against women's employment had become a specific case against the employment of wives and mothers" (1971:145). And the case was not just talk. Policies discriminating against married women peaked in 1940, the last year of the Depression, when only 13 percent of the nation's school districts would hire wives and bills restricting their employment were introduced in twenty-five state legislatures (Oppenheimer 1970). But whether married women went to work or stayed home ultimately hinged on their husbands' income; most wives who worked had to. In 1940, only 5 percent of women with husbands earning more than $3,000 annually were employed, while one-quarter of those with husbands earning less than $400 a year had jobs (Cain 1966).

In 1940 women were employed in the same types of jobs they held earlier in the century, although by that year far more did secretarial and clerical work and far fewer were in agriculture and domestic service. Women were still vastly underrepresented in managerial positions, and most professional women were still teachers and nurses. In industry, too, the picture had changed little for women; the majority still worked at low-paying jobs in plants producing consumer goods.

The attack on Pearl Harbor abruptly transformed the status quo. With broad public approval, World War II ushered an additional 6.5 million women into the job market as the demand for workers in war-related industries rose sharply and the male labor supply contracted. The imbalance between supply and demand pushed wages up at the same time family income was falling, the result of millions of men being drafted. Women, the largest untapped labor reserve in the nation, rushed in to fill the breach, trying to recoup lost family income by taking well-paid industrial jobs never before available to them.

The outbreak of war not only ended serious opposition to working women but marked the onset of a massive campaign by business and government to bring women into the job market. The mass media encouraged public support for women workers by depicting Rosie the Riveter as nothing less than a national heroine. Newspapers, magazines, and radio programs praised women who took jobs and extolled their contributions to the war effort. They questioned the patriotism of women who refused to work and made employment in munitions plants and other war-related industries appear glamorous. And, once again, the *Ladies' Home Journal* demonstrated its adaptability to the shifting needs of the nation by featuring a female combat pilot on its cover!

The Office of War Information's Womanpower Campaign suggested women who did not take jobs be made to feel responsible for prolonging the war. If a woman worried what her friends and neighbors would think if she went to work in industry, she should be told that, "the neighbors are going to think it very strange if you are not working. They'll be working too . . . any strong, able-bodied woman who is not completely occupied with a job and a home—is going to be considered a 'slacker' just as much as the man who avoids the draft." One federal agency even advised employers to recruit women for war work by telling them it is "pleasant and as easy as running a sewing machine or a vacuum cleaner" (quotes from Rupp 1978:97, 96).

This campaign initially was aimed at single women, but as the war went on and more workers were needed, employers in business and industry threw out the old rules against hiring married women and turned to them to fill vacancies. The Office of War Information pointedly queried these women: "Are you being old-fashioned and getting by just being a 'good wife and mother'?" (quoted in Rupp 1978:242). These efforts were an evident success since fully 75 percent of women recruited for war work were married.

An unforeseen consequence of the war, then, was a seismic shift in the profile of women workers. In contrast to her predecessor, the typical working woman during the war was a middle-aged wife who was also likely to be a mother. In fact, one-third of new women war workers had children under fourteen. And by the end of hostilities in 1945, close to half of all working women were married and a majority were over thirty-five (Filene 1976). Moreover, given a critical labor shortage that made war work synonymous with patriotism, public attitudes toward working women—particularly married women—were bound to shift. Whereas working wives met with overwhelming disapproval in opinion polls in 1937, only five years later, some 60 percent of those surveyed agreed married women should take jobs in war industries and another 24 percent approved of wives working under certain conditions (Cantril 1951).

The demand for workers during the war also upended tradition in the jobs women were hired to do. Women worked as stevedores, blacksmiths, lumberjacks, and crane operators. They serviced airplanes, read blueprints, repaired roads, and worked in foundries. Women not employed in war industries drove taxis and buses, became stock analysts, bank officers, and chemists. By far the largest increase of women—460 percent by the end of the war —was in defense plants. Their numbers doubled in manufacturing, and the rolls of female employees in the federal government grew by two million (Degler 1967).

World War II's impact on women's employment can be gauged from a few figures: Between 1940 and 1945, an additional 6.5 million women took jobs so the proportion of employed women went from 25 to 36 percent, a greater increase than during the preceding four decades. The statistics for married women were even more dramatic. During the war the proportion of working wives rose by 50 percent (Cantril 1951). As a result, for the first time in American history married women made up a majority of the female labor force.

The real significance of these employment gains is that—unlike those of World War I—they were not immediately wiped out once the war was over. A 1945 survey found over 60 percent of women war workers planned to keep working and, contrary to expectations, only 600,000 women voluntarily gave up their jobs with the cessation of hostilities. Moreover, as early as 1947 women had begun returning to the job market in sufficient numbers to start making up for their job losses in the immediate postwar period. But it was not until the mid-1950s that women's employment rate again reached peak war levels (Rupp 1978).

Still, because some feared a wave of postwar unemployment and recession—fears that never materialized—opposition to women working revived from its wartime dormancy. Doubting there were enough jobs for both women and returning veterans, some companies resurrected prewar bans on hiring wives. Under the Selective Service Act veterans were given priority over war workers for jobs and, when factories converted to peacetime production, thousands of women, especially those in heavy industry, were fired. As a consequence, in the first months after V-E Day, 60 percent of all wartime employees who lost their jobs were women and, by November 1946, two million women had been dismissed from their wartime positions. Aside from reimposing bans on hiring wives, some employers changed age requirements and fired women over 45; men, however, could remain on the job until 65. These practices resulted in a layoff rate for women that was 75 percent higher than for men (Mazerik 1945).

The media and opinion makers joined in the re-energized campaign to rid the workaday world of women and return them to hearth and home. Critics of women's employment cited an increased incidence of juvenile delinquency during the war, blaming it on maternal neglect. Magazines and newspapers were filled with stories about the sad fate of "latch key" children and other domestic woes caused by working Moms. One Florida senator told wives and mothers to "get back in the kitchen" to make room in the job market for returning war veterans (quoted in Chafe 1972:177). Soon after V-E Day the company newspaper of a Portland, Oregon, shipyard—28 percent of whose employees were women at the height of the war—carried an article entitled "The Kitchen—Women's Big Post-War Goal!" (Skold 1980:67). Even before the war ended, the *Saturday Evening Post* featured an article by a woman printer and labor veteran who advised "the ladies to give up their beachhead in man's industrial world when the war is over." She went on to compare her own career unfavorably to homemaking: "I know plenty of women who have gotten more out of life just by being feminine and taking a short cut to Shangri-la by way of the altar" (Roe 1944:28).

Diatribes against working women culminated in the publication of the noisy misogynist tome *Modern Woman: The Lost Sex* (Lundberg and Farnham 1947). The book blamed virtually every contemporary social ill on women who left home to take jobs. The "independent woman" who wanted a career was a "contradiction in terms," the authors wrote. Women's employment was a disguised search for masculine identity, a highly neurotic condition that divorced women from their true selves. Women are by nature dependent on men, and the formula for their happiness is acceptance of this innate passivity. Only one scenario ensures female contentment: child rearing and domesticity.

Despite public pressure to go back home, many women stayed in the work force, and it is clear why they did so. The postwar period was marked by high inflation and for many families two incomes were now essential to sustain a middle-class standard of living. How else to satisfy rising consumer demand for a new car or home or household appliances? Then, too, women benefited from a labor shortage brought on by the relatively few young people then entering the job market, a result of the low birth rate that prevailed in the 1930s. Women, including wives and mothers, went to work in ever greater numbers as labor demand grew and inflation and consumption desires put a premium on additional family income.

By the late 1940s, a woman's job was reluctantly approved as long as the goal was providing her family a better quality of life. Wives who took jobs to assist their families conformed to traditional views of women as "helpmates." But woe to career women with personal ambitions or to wives who took jobs to "fulfill themselves"; both met with stunning condemnation. Even in the lives of well-known and talented women the domestic role always took precedence. A 1949 *Ladies' Home Journal* article on acclaimed poet Edna St. Vincent Millay was accompanied by a photo of her cooking the family meal. As Betty Friedan (1974) noted in 1963, women's magazines of the day would only accept articles about women who were not *really* housewives if they were made to *sound like* housewives.

MANY JOBS, BUT ONLY ONE VOCATION: THE DOMESTIC FIFTIES AND EARLY SIXTIES

Ideology and practice seemed to be on a collision course in the 1950s. The feminine mystique celebrating the joys of home and family flourished at a time when more women than ever before were taking jobs. While articles in women's magazines affirming the delights of domesticity were aimed at mother-housewives, these were precisely the women going out to work, a trend so marked that by the end of the decade the typical woman worker was a middle-aged wife and mother. But, as we will see, the collision was more apparent than real. Much of the discourse on women and work was attuned to the era's specific labor needs.

A few figures highlight the shifting composition of the female work force during those years. Between 1950 and 1960 over four million married women took jobs, accounting for 60 percent of all new workers. In 1960, 30 percent of married women and 35 percent of women with children were employed. In other words, between 1940 and 1960 the proportion of wives with jobs doubled and the number of working mothers almost quadrupled. Women workers were also older; by the late 1950s, the median age of employed women was 41. And their class affiliation had also changed. In 1940 married women with jobs were mainly working class, but by 1960, the employed wife was just as likely to be well-educated and middle class (Degler 1967; U.S. Department of Labor 1975).

A sketch of that era's views on women and work is contained in a 1957 report by the National Manpower Council: "Americans have not generally disapproved of women participating in paid employment," the report noted, but public opinion polls show "Americans overwhelmingly disapprove of having the mother of young children go to work when her husband can support her." Moreover, "both men and women take it for granted that the male is the family breadwinner and that he has the superior claim to available work, particularly over the woman who does not have to support herself" (quoted in Kessler-Harris 1981:143–44).

In the 1950s and early 1960s most mothers of young children lived these sentiments and did not work outside the home. Middle-class women's typical job history was sequential. After finishing school, a majority of women worked until marriage or the birth of their first child. Then they left the job market only to return when their youngest child had entered school. By 1956, nearly half of all mothers with school-age children were employed at least part of the year. And, so, in the age of the feminine mystique married women were indeed taking jobs, but they were more likely to be older women with school-age or grown children.

These employment patterns and the attitudes that accompanied them harmonized with the need for female labor. Throughout the post–World War II era women workers were in ever greater demand, a result of growth in those sectors of the American economy that primarily employed women. Economist Valerie Oppenheimer (1970) has shown that because the job market is partially segregated by sex, a separate demand exists for *female* labor. "Female-typed" occupations have certain distinct features. They are low paid and require some skill but have little or no on-the-job training. Once a job is labeled "female," it tends to remain that way unless a labor shortage develops or there is a radical change in the nature of the job. Secretarial work, nursing, elementary school teaching, and certain types of retail sales are all female jobs by virtue of the preponderance of women workers in them, more than 70 percent in each of these examples.

During the postwar period demand for workers in these job categories skyrocketed; in the 1950s alone their workforce grew by nearly 50 percent. This expansion was part of a larger shift in the nation's occupational structure from one based primarily on manual and blue-collar labor before World War II to service and white-collar labor in the postwar years. The white-collar-service sector of the American economy, unlike the blue-collar-manufacturing sector, was not unionized, and this helps explain its rapid growth. Because the cost of non-unionized white-collar labor was relatively low, private sector employers found it more profitable to expand the production of services than the production of goods. Well over half of all jobs in the service sector have wages in the low range of the national pay scale and only 17 percent pay wages in the upper range. In contrast, 33 percent of jobs in manufacturing are in the low wage range, while 26 percent are in the upper range (Harris 1981).

Thus, one reason so many women took jobs in the 1950s was that so many new jobs were available to them. Not only were there more jobs, but employers were used to hiring women for these types of jobs and women were accustomed to having them. The figures are unambiguous. Most women entering the job market in the 1950s were employed in sex-segregated service occupations. Half were in fields in which at least 70 percent of the employees were women, and almost 60 percent were in fields in which the majority of employees were women (Kreps 1971).

And, as we know, many of these new employees were older, married women. Oppenheimer explains why this was so: "Employers have often turned to married women and older women not so much because they have independently discovered the worth of such women but because they cannot get enough young single women" (1970:171). From about 1940 on, the proportion of young single women in the U.S. population declined. Several factors accounted for the shifts in age and marital status: a drop in women's age at marriage; fewer women who never married; the general aging of the population; and an increase in the average number of years women spent in school. Thus, just as the demand for women workers was on the rise, the pool of young, unmarried women—the traditional source of female labor—was shrinking. Employers turned to older, married women to fill the breach, and these women, responding, in part, to opportunities never before available, took jobs in record numbers.

It will come as no surprise that employers' chilly stance toward hiring middle-aged wives quickly dissipated once there were too few young unmarried women to meet their labor needs. This was especially evident in primary and secondary education, which experienced severe teacher shortages because of the postwar baby boom. Simply put, school boards did an about-face. Recall that in 1940 only 13 percent of the nation's school districts would hire married women as teachers, but by 1950, 82 percent of them were hiring married women to teach, and by 1956, 97 percent were doing so (Oppenheimer 1970).

But making jobs available to women was not enough. Women also had to want the jobs. As more families needed additional income to afford the array of consumer goods then becoming the sine qua non of a middle-class lifestyle, more wives went to work. But not all wives took jobs to buy "extras." In the

1950s many families were middle income *only* because of the wife's monetary contribution. In 1956, for example, 70 percent of families with annual incomes of $7,000 to $10,000 had a second wage earner, usually the wife. That women's employment neither declined during the relatively severe recession of 1957–58 nor revived, the old saw that married women were "stealing" jobs from male breadwinners indicates how much women's earnings had come to be seen as a normal and necessary part of their families' income (Filene 1976). In short, women's expanded role in the workforce reflected both greater demand for their labor and increased need for their earnings in a consumption-driven economy.

But in the 1950s having a job was entirely different from pursuing a career. While working women received grudging approval as helpmates providing their families with extras like a second car or a college education for their children, career women were absent from this social ethic. In the women's magazines of the day career women were stereotyped as unhappy, frustrated creatures secretly longing for the security of home and family. A content analysis of the fiction in these publications detected a similar theme: "The new feminine morality story is the exorcising of the forbidden career dream" (Friedan 1974:46). And this "exorcism" seems to have worked; a poll of college women in the 1950s found that less than one-quarter of them planned to turn their work experience into a career (Ryan 1975).

Combining home and career were out of the question. A woman might work to supply her family with "things," but lasting fulfillment came from her domestic role. "Whether they work at outside jobs or not, today's young mothers find their greatest satisfaction in home, husband, and family," proclaimed the *Ladies' Home Journal* (Scott-Maxwell 1958b). An article in the *Atlantic Monthly* decreed that while women have "many careers, they have only one vocation: motherhood," lambasting women who work but "do not have to." They were to blame for a range of social ills from teenage crime to sexual immorality (Meyer 1950:28–29). An author in *Life* magazine even questioned the mental stability of such women, noting pointedly, "In New York City the 'career woman' can be seen in fullest bloom, and it is not irrelevant that New York City has the greatest concentration of psychiatrists" (quoted in Hymowitz and Weissman 1978:325).

The theories of Helene Deutsch (1944), a Freudian psychoanalyst, were popular in those years. According to Deutsch, a normal woman represses her masculine instincts for self-realization and identifies with the outside world through her husband and children. Deutsch held polar views of women; they were either healthy homemakers or neurotic, career-driven feminists. A Deutsch-influenced psychologist writing in the *Ladies' Home Journal* was concerned about higher education's ill effects on the female psyche: "When a girl goes to college and cultivates her mind, this may stimulate, even inflate, her masculine side and she can become avidly intellectual with a strong power drive, and then it is easy to become a doctor or lawyer who is hardly feminine at all" (Scott-Maxwell 1958a).

Women's work and the attitudes it invoked in the 1950s are an instructive example of how women's roles and discourse about them can be mutually reinforcing. Partly in response to the demand for their labor, more women than ever had jobs. But approval of their employment was decidedly conditional. It was all right for women to work to pay for extras to sustain their families' lifestyle, but it was not all right to feel the job was important to their own self-fulfillment and well-being.

This posture meshed nicely with the demand for a particular type of labor. Large numbers of women were needed to work as clerks, secretaries, in retail sales, and in other sex-segregated occupations. Many of these jobs were temporary or part-time and most were dead-end. They did not require the steady work commitment usually associated with pursuing a career, nor was such commitment likely to lead to advancement. Moreover, temporary or part-time work fit well with women's entry and withdrawal from the job market, a pattern coinciding with their family's life cycle. They could work intermittently—before marriage or after the children were in school—at small loss to their employers. Recall that one characteristic of "female" jobs is they require little or no on-the-job training. Traditionally women were not hired for work that required such training because employers saw them as "poor investments" who could not be counted on to stay on the job. Many occupations with concentrations of women workers do, in fact, require special skills, but they are acquired by women on their own prior to being hired, not on their employers' time or expense. This is certainly true of secretarial work, teaching, and nursing.

Women's employment in the 1950s and early 1960s did more than meet the labor needs of business and industry; it also made an ever increasing level of consumption possible. A 1956 study found that families with working wives tended to be more in debt than those with full-time homemakers. The debt usually was for a car, refrigerator, or other household appliance suggesting women were working to pay for specific items. This also explains why many worked part-time (Degler 1980). As such, women were not only "administrators of consumption" in their role as housewives; they were producers of the wages that allowed greater consumption as well.

THE OTHER FAMILY BREADWINNER: 1965 TO 2000

Thanks largely to working Moms, the income of married couples with children rose more than 25 percent between 1969 and 1996. If it hadn't been for women's financial contribution, the increase would have been just 1.5 percent. Women had indeed become the other family breadwinner, and dual income families are now the norm in this country. Today so much of the typical middle-class family's consumption is dependent on women's earnings that one must wonder what the consequences would be for the American economy were large numbers of women ever to return to full-time domesticity, a *very* unlikely event in any case.

Working women today have similar profiles to those who began taking jobs in the postwar era; they are mothers and wives, the middle class, and middle-aged. Only now there are many, many more of them. A few figures highlight this. In 1960, 38 percent of all adult women held jobs, a figure that rose to 46 percent in 1975, and 60 percent by the late 1990s. More striking is the increase in employed mothers. In 1960, 39 percent of women with school-age children had jobs, in 1975 the number was 55 percent, and by 1995 it had reached nearly 77 percent. The statistics are even more remarkable for women with children under age six, today one of the fastest-growing segments of the work force. In 1960, only 19 percent of them held jobs, in 1980, 47 percent were employed and by the late 1990s, 65 percent of mothers with children under six worked outside the home, as did 62 percent of those with children under age three, and 58 percent with children under age one (U.S. Department of Labor 1999; Chira 1999).

One aspect of the female employment picture has not changed nearly as much. Women remain heavily concentrated in traditionally female occupations; 80 percent of working women still are employed in only 20 of the 420 occupations listed by the Department of Labor (Coltrane 1996). By 1997, women still held 98 percent of all secretarial jobs, 96 percent of receptionist positions, and 69 percent of those in retail sales. Today, one out of every five working women is a teacher, office worker, or cashier (U.S. Department of Labor 1998, 1999). And it is just these service positions that have burgeoned during the final decades of the twentieth century. In fact, predictions about future job growth also cite female dominated fields: teaching, nursing, office work, and data entry.

The outlook for women in the professions is more mixed. While they still dominate nursing—92 percent of nurses are women—and elementary and secondary school teaching—75 percent of all teachers are women—they have made notable inroads in other, traditionally male, professions. At the dawn of this millennium 28 percent of the nation's lawyers were women, 27 percent of medical doctors, 20 percent of dentists, and almost one-third of veterinarians (ftp.bls.gov/ pub/s...1.requests/lf/AAT).

Percentage of Jobs Held by Women		
	1970	1998
Managers & executives	16.7	44.4
College faculty	28.6	42.3
Economists	11.4	46.3
Psychologists	38.5	62.1
Pharmacists	12.0	44.0
Veterinarians	5.2	32.5
Architects	3.6	17.5

Source: Hacker 1999.

And these figures are expected to increase since women account for even higher percentages of those currently enrolled in professional schools.

These professions aside, most middle-class women workers are still found in jobs needing what Oppenheimer (1970) terms "middle quality labor," labor that requires a fairly high educational level and considerable skills, such as secretarial work, nursing, and teaching. But women tend to predominate only in those middle-quality occupations that are at a competitive disadvantage in terms of salary scales. Women are employed at bargain rates because more educated workers in several female-dominated occupations are not paid proportionately higher salaries. Indeed, by 1998 the median earnings for full-time women workers was still only 76 percent of what men earned (U.S. Department of Labor 1999). Thus, the ongoing segregation of the labor force by gender allows employers to determine wage scales according to the sex of their employees and to disregard education and training in female-dominated fields.

The presence of relatively low-paid but skilled female workers in white-collar positions contributes to the sex segregation of the job market. As one economist put it, "employers are not simply looking for cheap labor, but for cheap *female* labor" (Kreps 1971:38). Others have suggested that women's inferior wages are directly linked to the highly sex-segregated structure of the labor market in this country (Stevenson 1975). As such, "equal pay for equal work" will not result in the elimination of sex differentials in pay scales if the majority of men and women continue to do different kinds of work. Further, the concept of equal pay for work of "comparable value" is still considered revolutionary. In the mid-1970s a U.S. district court judge dismissed a case that raised the issue, commenting, "I am not going to restructure the entire economy of the United States!"

As the demand for workers in several traditionally female fields continued to escalate, the supply of potential women employees also rose as declining male wages put a premium on a second family income. Median family income has not gone up since the early 1970s, largely because the real wages of 80 percent of working men have lost ground and, by the turn of the millennium, four out of five American households were taking home a thinner slice of the economic pie than two decades earlier (Thurow 1999; Johnston 1999). The only reason most households have not suffered financially is because of the greater work effort of family members, most particularly wives. During the 1980s wives increased their working hours an average of 28 percent and since 1994 almost one million women a year have upgraded their job status from part-time to full-time. By 1998, three-quarters of women workers were employed full-time. In sum, women's increased work effort has occurred simultaneously with a decline in men's real hourly wages. Hence, increases in annual income stem mainly from more work rather than higher wages. Families may, in fact, be worse off than in the past. Instead of receiving regular pay increases to sustain their standard of living, they have to put in more hours to maintain it (Mishel, Bernstein, and Schmitt 1999; Uchitelle 1999b).

Because of these conditions, the two-income family is now the norm. By the late 1990s, only 28 percent of American families had one wage earner, and many of these were single-parent households. Working wives' average contribution to household income grew from 26 percent in 1979 to 40 percent by 1998, underlining the importance of their earnings. Another telling statistic: In 1997 the median income of married couples with employed wives was

$60,670, significantly higher than the $36,960 for those with full-time home-makers (Uchitelle 1999a; U.S. Department of Labor 1999).

By the late 1970s and early 1980s such economic realities were molding public opinion into accepting women's place, albeit a low-paying one, in the work force. But the fact of women's employment preceded its broad approval by several years. In a 1960 public opinion poll only 34 percent of those queried approved of married women working, but by 1978, 70 percent approved, with over 80 percent of those under thirty-five supporting the idea. Similarly, when asked "Is it more important for a wife to help her husband's career than to have one herself?" more than half of those queried in 1977 agreed with the statement, but approval fell to 36 percent in 1985 and only 29 percent by 1991 (Coltrane 1996).

The women's magazines of the 1960s and early 1970s also were slow to reflect the record numbers of wives and mothers taking jobs. The first recognition that many married women either had jobs or sought them appeared in a 1963 *Ladies' Home Journal* article entitled "I'm Going to Get a Job." While the article was meant for "mature women" with older children, it was a fledgling sign of shifting discourse. Children gain in "self-reliance what they miss in maternal attention," the author suggested, and the children and husbands of employed women are "proud and excited by their new careers" (Hoffman 1963:107). Later in the decade articles like "One Day Beauty Make-over for Women That Work" and "Twenty Part-time Jobs for Women" became more common. But the issue of jobs for wives and mothers still met with some strong dissent in the pages of the *Ladies' Home Journal*. In an article called "Jesus and the Liberated Woman," Billy Graham opined that sex roles are divinely ordained, men's natural role is breadwinner, while "the appointed destiny of real womanhood . . . [is] wife, mother and homemaker (1970:42). Parenthetically, the article received a huge response from the magazine's readers, most of it very critical of Graham's views.

But by the mid-1970s, even that bastion of domesticity had finally succumbed to reality and recognized the major role jobs were playing in the lives of readers. Columns by Sylvia Porter ("Spending Your Money") and by Letty Cottin Pogrebin ("The Working Woman") became regular features of the magazine and articles with titles like "Going Back to Work? Helpful Tips from Women Who Have," "Tips on Easing the Morning Crunch for Working Mothers," and "When She Earns More Than He Does" appeared with increasing frequency. The magazine also introduced a "Women of the Month" feature that reported on successful career women, only incidentally mentioning their domestic lives. And by 1977, the *Ladies' Home Journal* was billing itself as a magazine for "the woman who never stands still . . . she's growing a family, an exciting career, and a creative way of life that's hers and hers alone."

In the final years of the twentieth century most of women's domestic advisors not only gave their stamp of approval to working mothers and wives, but much of their advice suggested ways women could cope with their multiple and sometimes, conflicting roles. During the 1990s, for example, the *Ladies Home Journal* was filled with articles like "Working Mothers Aren't Alone in Their Struggle to Balance Career and Children—Here's Help for Working Fathers Too," "The Balancing Act of Home and Office," and "When Your Child Doesn't Want You to Go to Work." And so while the past three decades have witnessed the entry of women, particularly wives and mothers, into the labor force in unprecedented numbers, popular opinion only belatedly noticed this turn of events. While the media initially devoted much space to "bra burning" and other supposed atrocities of the women's movement, little attention was paid to the reality of women's work, which had set the stage for the revival of feminism.

During the post–World War II era traditional ideologies about women and work were gradually transformed. Consumerism, inflation, falling male wages, and an increase in demand for labor in female occupations all created a virtual revolution in women's employment activities. As more and more wives and mothers went to work and as the two-income family became standard, a great awakening occurred, and the fact of women's financial contribution to their families was finally given some of the recognition it deserved. What historian Carl Degler (1967) called "a revolution without ideology" now had one. Spurred on by feminism, a movement that was itself partly a response to the reality of work in women's lives, women's domestic advisors, public opinion, and the popular media belatedly acknowledged that perhaps women's place was not really in the home.

WHERE DO WE GO FROM HERE?

[T]he anti-feminist backlash has been set off not by women's achievement of full equality, but by the increased possibility that they might win it.
Susan Faludi, *Backlash*, 1991

Has a basic revolution taken place in the roles of American women? Have the material underpinnings of American society changed to the extent I have suggested, and can this account for shifts in the work women do and the way it is perceived? There is little agreement on these matters. Some insist that in most ways social life still follows traditional patterns. This view can be summarized as follows: The family is here to stay, and women's position in it as primary nurturers and domestic workers continues essentially unaltered. Women are having fewer children but, in time, the birthrate likely will rise again. Women with jobs are secondary and impermanent breadwinners; primary family income always has been and remains dependent on male wages. This mystification of what has been happening in the United States over the last three decades appears to me to be an empty variant of the philosophy *la plus ça change, la plus c'est la même chose*.

Such claims ignore the vast numbers of married women, including the mothers of young children, who now work outside the home. They also overlook the relatively low birthrate and the incidence of single-parent house-holds. Have these trends really had so little influence on women's traditional roles? While this nostalgic philosophy may be comforting, given the massive changes in the foundations of American society, it is naive to suppose that women's roles and the discourse surrounding them are frozen in an inviolate time warp.

There is no doubt that the domestic and public lives of American women have been transformed in important ways. But what of the future? Will there be a backlash? Have things "gone too far" in the restructuring of gender roles in this country? Does the anti-feminism of the Pat Robertsons, Dr. Lauras, and other pundits who receive so much time on the nation's airwaves portend a wave of reaction against women and some of their newfound gains? Once again, from the perspective of cultural materialism, the answer must be that it depends on a variety of infrastructural conditions. If this is to be a consis-tent analysis based on a particular set of theoretical principles rather than on reassurance or wishful thinking, then this is the only possible answer.

Despite this somber statement, I do not see a return to the traditional family of earlier decades. It is very unlikely that we will go back to the scenario of some bygone era when Mom was a full-time housewife and Dad brought home the bacon. By the late 1990s only 7 percent of American families con-formed to that convention: breadwinner father, homemaker mother with two or more children (Card and Kelly 1998). In most households the wages of married women are simply too important to family income, too crucial to maintaining any semblance of a middle-class standard of living, to be readily or willingly forgone. This is why men's and women's career patterns are con-verging. Today an increasing percentage of women—like men—work full-time, year-round even after having children. Moreover, by the late 1990s more women said they would prefer to work outside the home than in it, and over half asserted they had "careers," not "jobs" (Holcomb 1998; Boxer 1997).

And current employment trends are expected to continue. Estimates sug-gest that by the mid-twenty-first century women will constitute just under half—47 percent—of the U.S. labor force. This is likely because women are a majority of workers in the three occupations forecast to have the greatest future job growth—service, administrative support (including clerical), and professional specialty. The highest growth rates are anticipated in health and personal service occupations, also composed primarily of women (Kutscher 1991). These trends, combined with expected declines in higher-paying man-ufacturing jobs—most of which are held by men—will further narrow the gender wage gap. In short, average male wages will continue to fall, making a second family income even more indispensable. As a result, the one-wage-earner family model will be increasingly difficult to achieve, and projections indicate that in the years to come dual-earner couples will outnumber single wage-earner families by two to one (Coltrane 1996). For all these reasons, I do not believe the inroads women have made into the labor market will be reversed. Any major shift in women's employment presupposes a broad range of prior economic and social changes that cannot be brought about by even the most vociferous anti-feminist rhetoric.

But why the conservative assault on working women? Political scientist Zillah Eisenstein (1982) suggests the ultimate goal of the anti-feminist ideologues of the secular and religious right is to drive married women out of the work force because women with jobs and their own monetary resources threaten the status quo. Eisenstein argues that whether women demand equality at home or not, they certainly demand it in the marketplace—*no* working woman opposes the demand of equal pay for equal work. Women's call for equality not only has the potential to disrupt the inegalitarian structure of the labor market with its female job ghettos and 76 cents to the dollar wages; it also makes women more likely to question the sexual division of labor at home. Still, I seriously doubt social conservatives will have much success imposing their dependent female/working male vision of the family on the population at large. The economic conditions for it are simply not present.

What about the attempt to limit women's reproductive rights? The women's movement and, most especially, its call for reproductive choice gnaw at the foundations of traditional patriarchal structures. The pronouncements of conservative commentator William Kristol make this point loud and clear. Abortion, he says, is the "bloody cross-roads of American politics. Abortion is where . . . sexual liberation (from traditional mores) and women's liberation (from natural distinctions) come together. It is the focal point for liberalism's simultaneous assault on self-government, morals and nature" (quoted in Sullivan 1998:50). Of particular note is that Kristol does *not* cite the saving of "innocent human life" as a pretext for his fierce opposition to abortion.

A recent study lends credence to Kristol's stance by demonstrating a link between the severity of a state's abortion laws and the status of women in the state (Schroedel 2000). The lower women's status, as measured by education levels, ratio of female to male earnings, percentage of women in poverty, percentage of female legislators, and state mandates that insurers cover minimum hospital stays after childbirth, the more stringent the state's abortion laws.

The same study also suggests that the charge that anti-choicers' concern for children begins with conception and ends at birth is not far off the mark. Despite anti-choice rhetoric about the need to protect the weakest and most vulnerable, the study found that anti-choice states are "far less likely than pro-choice states to provide support for the poorest and most needy children." They spend less money per child on a range of services, from the adoption of special needs children to foster care to welfare to education. As such, there is "virtually no support" for the anti-abortion claim that opposition to abortion is all about caring for kids (Schroedel 2000).

But whatever the actual agenda of those who oppose reproductive rights, their ultimate success is highly unlikely. While they have managed to get federal legislation passed—the ban on Medicaid payments for abortion—that curtails the reproductive freedom of poor women, there is virtually no chance that Congress will adopt a general prohibition on abortion through a vehicle like the Human Life Amendment. In fact, by the close of the millennium many Republicans were retreating from their hard-edged stance against abortion, believing that to retain control of Congress and regain the White House, they would have to temper their pro-life zeal (Berke 1999). And the entire issue is likely to be settled, perhaps once and for all, when "the little white bombshell"—RU 486, the French abortion pill—becomes widely available in the United States. The pill makes abortions possible in the earliest weeks of pregnancy so that they are cheaper and easier to get, and perhaps more socially and politically acceptable as well (Talbot 1999).

Abortion will remain legal for the same reasons we will not return to the day when the three- or four-child family was the norm. Given the current cost of living, children are expensive to raise, particularly if a woman gives up her job to care for them. The much heralded baby boomlet of the late 1980s and early 1990s should not be misconstrued as the resurrection of the era of the 3.2-child family. The slight increase in the birthrate is the result of that cohort of women who delayed having children until their thirties or early forties and are now having one or two. The average number of children per woman is *not* increasing. The "procreative imperative" has been broken, and the protestations of the right wing alone are not about to revive it.

Today the completed fertility rate of American women is as low as it has ever been, and more married women than ever before are employed. What does this mean for the maternal role? As we have seen, most child-rearing experts have backed away from their call for an omnipresent Mom to ensure children's proper development. One recent advice manual even argued mothers should hold jobs outside the home to preserve their own identity and enhance their offspring's independence (Peters 1998). No, an exclusive mother–child dyad is no longer seen as necessary for healthy offspring, and Dad has returned to the child-rearing stage as a central player. Moreover, the myth that children are inevitably damaged by alternative forms of child care, including day-care centers, has been laid to rest.

Could the current dicta of the child-rearing experts only be a fad that in time will be supplanted by a revival of the call for full-time maternal care and renewed invectives against "working" mothers? Once again, I doubt it, given women's present commitment to the job market and the high cost of rearing children—phenomena that give no indication of being reversed. Since my entire analysis suggests the ideological underpinnings of women's roles reflect the productive and reproductive conditions that prevail when they are propounded, the maternal ideal of an earlier era cannot be resurrected without major changes in the foundations of American society.

What about housework? Perhaps one hopeful sign is that the Future Homemakers of America, founded in 1945 with the goal of teaching adolescent girls how to keep house for their future husbands, recently changed its name. The national organization—which began admitting boys in 1973—decided its new name, Family, Career and Community Leaders of America, was more appropriate to the times. Nevertheless, it is still true that the sexual division of labor in the home does not yet reflect the reality of women's widespread employment. In what sociologist Arlie Hochschild (1997) calls "the stalled revolution," women's roles in the family have changed more than men's roles. While women are working as many hours as their husbands, many still come home to the double day of household chores and child care. Reflecting this disparity, over half of working mothers in one survey said they wished their husbands would spend more time with their children, and 43 percent felt similarly about household chores (Lewin 1998). It is also true that as long as a majority of Americans live in small encapsulated nuclear families—and there is no indication this is changing—housekeeping tasks will continue to be the responsibility of individual households.

But there has been a major shift in both the definition of good housekeeping and the time devoted to it. With the notable exception of Martha Stewart, the day is long past when the pages of women's magazines are routinely filled with a mind-boggling array of make-work activities. The emphasis is now on *time-saving*, not *time-spending* hints. Women's domestic advisors no longer insist on "eat-off-the-floor" standards of cleanliness and seem to feel a little dust never hurt anyone. Moreover, because the double day has become routine for many employed women, they are indeed spending less time on housekeeping tasks. Nowhere is this more evident than in meal preparation. Not only are there more convenience foods on the market than ever before and more fast food alternatives, but the suggestion "let's go out to eat" is no longer reserved for special occasions. Estimates suggest one out of every two meals are now being eaten away from home.

The reasons that women are spending fewer hours on housework are not entirely clear. Are they using more outside services? Are they receiving more help from their husbands and children? Are they working more efficiently? Are their housekeeping standards less lofty? Or are their laborsaving devices really saving labor for the first time? Whatever the cause, it is reasonable to suppose that if present employment trends continue, the time spent on housework will decline still further.

Some may be disturbed that I have not highlighted the role of the women's movement in the transformation of gender roles in this country. Common wisdom has it that a feminist ideology influenced women to take jobs and led to the demand for a more equitable division of labor at home. I do not mean to diminish the importance of the women's movement in these protests against the status quo, nor do I doubt the power and influence of feminist discourse. Feminism has indeed made women question the low pay and segregation of female labor and the unfairness of the double day. Nevertheless, I argue women's consciousness was raised on these and other issues by the material conditions of their lives, by the disjunctions between ideology and reality, the very disjunctions that also led to the feminist revival. Viewed from this perspective, the women's movement is ultimately a result rather than a cause of women's discontent.

As a cultural materialist I believe neither feminist ideology led to changes in women's roles in this country, nor will conservative ideology see a return to what some see as "the good old days." The folly of an idealist interpretation of women's roles will be apparent if we imagine the following scenario. Let us suppose there is a large and influential group of American men conspiring for a return to nineteenth-century gender roles. They vehemently assert that women's place is in the home, that the loss of full-time mother care lies at the root of the nation's problems, and that the women's movement is a dire threat to "traditional family values" and must be thwarted at all costs. Can any informed person seriously believe such a group of individuals could succeed in imposing their program on large numbers of women? The strength of their convictions will do nothing to change the complex series of material factors that are the basis for the revolution in women's roles and the renewal of feminism.

Where then do we go from here? Despite an occasional note of pessimism about the future roles of American women, I am not arguing "the more things change, the more they remain the same." I find that philosophy to be deeply conservative, for it seeks reassurance, not illumination about the ongoing transformation of American society. The soothing claims that the family will always be with us, that it has not really changed, and that women will always take primary responsibility for child care and housework because it is in the "nature of things" are ideological stances based more on wishful thinking and uneasiness with the current order than on close analysis. These reassurances neither analyze nor explain the major shifts that have occurred in women's roles in this country. They are conservative obfuscations of what is taking place in American society today. All such efforts should remind feminists of the truism that, in order to change the world, we must first understand it.

REFERENCES

Abbott, Edith. 1910. *Women in Industry*. New York: D. Appleton.

Abbott, John S. C. 1833. *The Mother at Home*. New York: American Tract Society.

———. 1842. Paternal Neglect. *Parent's Magazine* 2 (March).

Aikin, John J. 1830. (Orig. 1803.) *The Arts of Life*. First American ed. Boston: Carter & Hendee and Waitt & Dow.

Alcott, William A. 1838. *The Young Housekeeper*. Boston: George W. Light.

Ames, Azel. 1875. *Sex in Industry*. Boston: J. R. Osgood.

An American Matron. 1972. (Orig. 1811.) *The Maternal Physician*. New York: Arno.

An American Mother. 1900. Is a College Education Best for Our Girls? *Ladies' Home Journal* 17 (July): 15.

André, Rae. 1981. *Homemakers: The Forgotten Workers*. Chicago: University of Chicago Press.

Andrews, Benjamin R. 1923. *Economics of the Household*. New York: Macmillan.

———. 1929. The Home Woman as Buyer and Controller of Consumption. *Annals of the American Academy of Political and Social Sciences* 143 (May): 41–48.

Andrews, William D., and Deborah C. Andrews. 1974. Technology and the Housewife in Nineteenth-Century America. *Women's Studies* 2(3): 309–328.

Anonymous. 1923. I Wish I Had Married and Found Life. *Good Housekeeping* 77 (November): 141.

Aries, Philippe. 1965. *Centuries of Childhood*. New York: Vintage.

Asahina, Robert. 1981. Social Science Fiction. *New York Times Book Review*, August 16, p. 15.

Aslett, Don. 1992. *Is There* Life *After Housework?* Cincinnati, OH: Writer's Digest Books.

Bader, Jenny Lyn. 1999. Relying on the Competence of Strangers. *New York Times*, April 1, pp. B1, 11.

Baker, Elizabeth Faulkner. 1964. *Technology and Women's Work*. New York: Columbia University Press.

Balderston, Lydia May. 1919. *Housewifery*. Philadelphia: J. B. Lippincott.

Barber, Virginia, and Merrill Skaggs Maguire. 1975. *The Mother Person*. New York: Bobbs Merrill.

Barrett, Patti. 1998. *Too Busy to Clean?* Pownal, VT: Storey Books.

Beauvoir, Simone de. 1952. *The Second Sex*. New York: Alfred A. Knopf.

Beckwith, George C. 1850. The Fate of Nations Dependent on Mothers. *The Mother's Assistant* 15 (January): 45.

Bee, Helen L. 1974a. On the Importance of Fathers. In *Social Issues in Developmental Psychology*, ed. Helen L. Bee, pp. 367–377. New York: Harper and Row.

———. 1974b. The Effect of Maternal Employment on the Development of the Child. In *Social Issues in Developmental Psychology*, ed. Helen L. Bee, pp. 97–106. New York: Harper and Row.

Beecher, Catherine E. 1829. *Suggestions Respecting Improvements in Education*. New York: Hartford, Packard, and Butler.

———. 1977. (Orig. 1841.) *A Treatise on Domestic Economy*. New York: Schocken.

———. 1871. *Woman Suffrage and Woman's Profession*. Boston: Hartford, Brown and Gross.

Beecher, Catherine E., and Harriet Beecher Stowe. 1869. *The American Woman's Home*. New York: J. B. Ford.

Belsky, Jay. 1986. Infant Day Care: A Cause for Concern? *Zero to Three: Bulletin of the National Center for Clinical Infant Programs*. Washington, DC.

Bent, Silas. 1929. Woman's Place is in the Home. *Century* 116: (June): 204–213.

Bently, Mildred Maddocks. 1925. Household Engineering Applied. *Ladies' Home Journal* 42 (April): 36, 145–147.

Berke, Richard. 1999. G.O.P. Retreating From Hard Stand Against Abortion. *New York Times*, June 21, pp. 1, 13.

Bernard, Jessie. 1974. *The Future of Motherhood*. New York: Penguin.

Bettelheim, Bruno. 1962. Growing Up Female. *Harper's* 225 (October): 120–128.

Blakeslee, Sandra. 1998. Re-evaluating Significance of Baby's Bond with Mother. *New York Times*, August 4, pp. C1–2.

Blankenhorn, David. 1995. *Fatherless America*. New York: Basic Books.

Bloch, Ruth H. 1978a. American Feminine Ideals in Transition: The Rise of the Moral Mother, 1785-1815. *Feminist Studies* 4(2): 101–126.

———. 1978b. Untangling the Roots of Modern Sex Roles: A Survey of Four Centuries of Change. *Signs* 4(2): 237–252.

Bok, Edward. 1910. Editorial. *Ladies' Home Journal* 27 (June): 5.

———. 1911a. Editorial. *Ladies' Home Journal* 28 (October): 6.

———. 1911b. Why the Wife Alone? *Ladies' Home Journal* 32 (September): 5.

Bowlby, John. 1953. *Child Care and the Growth of Love*. Baltimore, MD: Penguin.

Boxer, Sarah. 1997. One Casualty of the Women's Movement: Feminism. *New York Times*, December 14, sec. 4, p. 3.

Braverman, Harry. 1974. *Labor and Monopoly Capitalism*. New York: Monthly Review Press.

Brazelton, T. Berry. 1981. On Becoming a Family. *Redbook* 156 (February): 53–60.

Breckinridge, Sophonisba. 1933. *Women in the Twentieth Century*. New York: McGraw-Hill.

Bredenberg, Jeff. 1998. *Clean It Fast, Clean It Right*. Emmaus, PA: Rodale Press.

Brott, Armin A., and Jennifer Ash. 1995. *The Expectant Father*. New York: Abbeville Press.

Brown, Barnetta. 1900. Mothers' Mistakes and Fathers' Failures. *Ladies' Home Journal* 17 (February): 32.

Brown, Judith K. 1970. A Note on the Division of Labor by Sex. *American Anthropologist* 72(5): 1073–1078.

Brownlee, Elliot W. 1974. *Dynamics of Ascent*. New York: Alfred A. Knopf.

Brownlee, Elliot W., and Mary M. Brownlee. 1976. *Women in the American Economy*. New Haven, CT: Yale University Press.

Brozan, Nadine. 1980. Men and Housework: Do They or Don't They? *New York Times*, November 1, p. 52.

Buchan, William. 1972. (Orig. 1809.) *Advice to Mothers*. Reprinted in *The Physician and Child-rearing: Two Guides, 1809–1894*. New York: Arno Press.

Burns, Jabez. 1851. *Mothers of the Wise and Good*. Boston: Gould and Lincoln.

Cain, Glen C. 1966. *Married Women in the Labor Force*. Chicago: University of Chicago Press.

Calhoun, Arthur W. 1960. (Orig. 1918.) *A Social History of the American Family*, vol. 2. New York: Barnes and Noble.

Callahan, Sidney Cornelia. 1972. *The Working Mother*. New York: Warner.

Campbell, Helen. 1881. *The Easiest Way in Housekeeping and Cooking*. New York: Fords, Howard, and Hubert.

———. 1907. *Household Economics*. New York: G. P. Putnam.

Canfield, Dorothy Fisher. 1914. *Mothers and Children*. New York: Henry Holt.

Cannon, Poppy. 1930. Pin Money Slaves. *Forum* 84 (August): 98–103.

Cantril, Hadley. 1951. *Public Opinion, 1935–1946*. Princeton, NJ: Princeton University Press.

Caplow, Theodore. 1954. *The Sociology of Work*. Minneapolis: University of Minnesota Press.

Card, Emily, and Christie Watts Kelly. 1998. *New Families, New Finances*. New York: Wiley.

Cardozo, Arlene Rossen. 1976. *Women at Home*. New York: Doubleday.

Carro, Geraldine. 1980. How to Raise Happy, Healthy Children. *Ladies' Home Journal* 97 (October): 90–92.

Chafe, William H. 1972. *The American Woman*. New York: Oxford University Press.

Child, Lydia Maria. 1831. *The American Frugal Housewife*. 6th ed. Boston: Carter, Hendee, and Babcock.

———. 1972. (Orig. 1831.) *The Mother's Book*. New York: Arno Press.

Children's Bureau. 1930. *Are You Training Your Child to Be Happy?* Children's Bureau Publication 202. Washington, DC: Government Printing Office.

———. 1938. *Infant Care*. 5th rev. ed. Children's Bureau Publication 8. Washington, DC: Government Printing Office.

———. 1963. *Infant Care*. 11th rev. ed. Children's Bureau Publication 8. Washington, DC: Government Printing Office.

———. 1980. *Infant Care*. 13th rev. ed. U.S. Department of Health and Human Services Publication 80-30015. Washington, DC: Government Printing Office.

Chira, Susan. 1996. Study Says Babies in Child Care Keep Secure Bonds to Mothers. *New York Times*, April 21, p. 18.

———. 1999. *A Mother's Place*. New York: HarperPerennial.

Choderow, Nancy. 1978. *The Reproduction of Mothering*. Berkeley: University of California Press.

Clark, Victor Selden. 1929. *History of Manufactures in the United States, 1860–1914.* Vol. 1. Washington, DC: Carnegie Institution.

Coale, Ansley J., and Melvin Zelnik. 1963. *New Estimates of Fertility and Population in the United States.* Princeton, NJ: Princeton University Press.

Collins, Gail. 1999. A Social Glacier Roars. The *New York Times Magazine,* May 16, pp. 77–80.

Coltrane, Scott. 1996. *Family Man.* New York: Oxford University Press.

Cook, Elizabeth. 1931. The Kitchen Sink Complex. *Ladies' Home Journal* 48 (September): 14, 148.

Cooley, Anna M. 1911. *Domestic Art in Woman's Education.* New York: Charles Scribner.

Coontz, Stephanie. 1997. *The Way We Really Are.* New York: Basic Books.

Cott, Nancy F. 1977. *The Bonds of Womanhood.* New Haven, CT: Yale University Press.

Cowan, Ruth Schwartz. 1974. A Case Study of Technological and Social Change: The Washing Machine and the Working Wife. In *Clio's Consciousness Raised,* ed. Mary Hartmann and Lois W. Banner, pp. 245–253. New York: Harper and Row.

———. 1976. Two Washes in the Morning and a Bridge Party at Night: The American Housewife Between the Wars. *Women's Studies* 3(2): 147–172.

———. 1983. *More Work for Mother.* New York: Basic Books.

Davies, Margery. 1975. Women's Place Is at the Typewriter: The Feminization of the Clerical Labor Force. In *Labor Market Segmentation,* ed. Richard C. Edwards, Michael Reich, and David M. Gordon, pp. 279–296. Lexington, MA: D. C. Heath.

Davis, Glenn. 1976. *Childhood and History in America.* New York: Psychohistory Press.

Davison, Jane. 1980. *The Fall of a Doll's House.* New York: Holt, Rinehart and Winston.

Degler, Carl N. 1967. Revolution Without Ideology. In *The Woman in America,* ed. Robert Jay Lifton, pp. 163–210. Boston: Beacon.

———. 1980. *At Odds.* New York: Oxford University Press.

Demos, John. 1970. *A Little Commonwealth.* New York: Oxford University Press.

De Rham, Edith. 1965. *The Love Fraud.* New York: Clarkson N. Potter.

Deutsch, Francine M. 1999. *Halving It All.* Cambridge, MA: Harvard University Press.

Deutsch, Helene. 1944. *The Psychology of Women.* New York: Grove and Stratton.

Dewees, William. 1847. *A Treatise on the Physical and Medical Treatment of Children.* 10th ed. Philadelphia: Blanchard and Lea.

Dobson, James, and Gary L. Bauer. 1990. *Children at Risk.* Dallas, TX: Word Publishing.

Earle, Alice Morse. 1898. *Homelife in Colonial Days.* New York: Macmillan.

Ehrenreich, Barbara, and Deirdre English. 1978. *For Her Own Good.* New York: Anchor.

Eisenstein, Zillah R. 1982. The Sexual Politics of the New Right: Understanding the Crisis of Liberalism for the 1980s. *Signs* 7 (Spring): 567–588.

Eliot, Martha M. 1929. *Infant Care.* 3d rev. ed. Children's Bureau Publication 8. Washington, DC: Government Printing Office.

Escalona, Sibylle. 1953. A Commentary upon Some Recent Changes in Child Rearing Practices. In *Selected Studies in Marriage and the Family,* ed. Robert F. Winch and Robert McGinnis, pp. 208–214. New York: Henry Holt.

Ewen, Stuart. 1976. *Captains of Consciousness.* New York: McGraw-Hill.

Fabrikant, Geraldine. 1999. Martha Stewart Sellling Stake in Her Company. *New York Times,* July 29, p. B1.

Faludi, Susan. 1991. *Backlash*. New York: Crown Publishers.

Farrar, Eliza. 1974. (Orig. 1836.) *The Young Lady's Friend*. New York: Arno Press.

Filene, Peter Gabriel. 1976. *Him/Her/Self*. New York: New American Library.

Fraiberg, Selma. 1977. *Every Child's Birthright*. New York: Basic Books.

Frederick, Christine. 1913. *The New Housekeeping*. Garden City, NY: Doubleday.

———. 1919. *Household Engineering*. Chicago: American School of Home Economics.

———. 1929. *Selling Mrs. Consumer*. New York: Business Bourse.

Friedan, Betty. 1974. (Orig. 1963.) *The Feminine Mystique*. New York: Dell.

Frost, J. William. 1973. *The Quaker Family in Colonial America*. New York: St. Martin's Press.

Gainesville [FL] *Sun*. 1999a. Working Fathers. February 5, p. 7B.

———. 1999b. Child Care Impact Undercut. August 22, p. 5.

Galbraith, John Kenneth. 1973. *Economics and the Public Purpose*. New York: New American Library.

Garrison, Dee. 1974. The Tender Technicians: The Feminization of Public Librarianship, 1876–1905. In *Clio's Consciousness Raised*, ed. Mary Hartmann and Lois W. Banner, pp. 158–178. New York: Harper and Row.

Giedion, Siegfried. 1948. *Mechanization Takes Command*. New York: Oxford University Press.

Gilbreth, Lillian M. 1928. *The Homemaker and Her Job*. New York: D. Appleton.

Gilman, Charlotte Perkins. 1898. *Women and Economics*. Boston: Small, Maynard.

Ginott, Haim G. 1965. *Between Parent and Child*. New York: Macmillan.

Glazer-Malbin, Nona. 1976. Housework. *Signs* I (Summer): 905–922.

Glickman, Beatrice Marden, and Nesha Bass Springer. 1978. *Who Cares for the Baby?* New York: Schocken.

Godey's Lady's Book. 1839. Learning vs. Housewifery. Vol. 28 (August): 95.

———. 1860. Children. 60 (January–June): 272.

Goldin, Claudia. 1990. *Understanding the Gender Gap*. New York: Oxford University Press.

Goode, William. 1963. *World Revolution and Family Patterns*. New York: Free Press.

Goodman, David. 1959. *A Parents' Guide to the Emotional Needs of Children*. New York: Hawthorne.

Goodrich, Henrietta I. 1900. Suggestions for a Professional School of Home and Social Economics. *Proceedings of the Second Lake Placid Conference on Home Economics*, pp. 26–40. Lake Placid, NY.

Goodstein, Laurie. 1999. After Killings at Church, Texans Look for Meaning. *New York Times*, September 18, pp. 1, 9.

Gordon, Ann D., Mari Jo Buhle, and Nancy E. Schrom. 1971. Women in American Society: An Historical Contribution. *Radical America* 5(4): 3–66.

Gordon, Ann D., Mari Jo Buhle, and Nancy Schrom Dye. 1976. The Problem of Women's History. In *Liberating Women's History*, ed. Berenice A. Carroll, pp. 75–92. Urbana: University of Illinois Press.

Gordon, Linda. 1977. *Woman's Body, Woman's Right*. New York: Penguin.

Gorer, Geoffrey. 1964. *The American People*. Rev. ed. New York: Norton.

Gornick, Vivian. 1975. Here's News: Fathers Mother as Much as Mothers. *Village Voice* (October 13): 10–11.

Graham, Billy. 1970. Jesus and the Liberated Woman. *Ladies' Home Journal* 87 (December): 40–44.

Graves Mrs. A. J. 1843. *Woman in America*. New York: Harper and Brothers.

Greenberg, Milton, and Norman Morris. 1974. Engrossment: The Newborn's Impact upon the Father. *American Journal of Orthopsychiatry* 44 (July): 520–531.

Greven, Philip J., Jr. 1970. *Four Generations*. Ithaca, NY: Cornell University Press.

———. 1972. The Average Size of Families and Households in the Province of Massachusetts in 1764 and in the United States in 1790: An Overview. In *Household and Family Life in Past Time*, ed. P. Laslett, pp. 545–560. London: Cambridge University Press.

———. 1973a. *Child Rearing Concepts, 1628–1861*. Itasca, IL: Peacock.

———. 1973b. Family Structure in Seventeenth Century Andover, Massachusetts. In *The American Family in Socio-Historical Perspective*, ed. Michael Gordon, pp. 77–99. New York: St. Martin's Press.

Gross, Jane. 1998. Women and Their Work: How Life Inundates Art. *New York Times*, August 23, section 3, pp. 1, 9.

Groves, Ernest R., and Gladys Hoagland Groves. 1928. *Parents and Children*. Philadelphia: J. B. Lippincott.

Gruenberg, Sidonie M., and Hilda S. Krech. 1957. *The Modern Mother's Dilemma*. Public Affairs Pamphlet 247. New York: Public Affairs Committee.

Hacker, Andrew. 1999. The Unmaking of Men. *New York Review of Books*, October 21.

Hale, Sarah Josepha. 1839. *The Good Housekeeper*. Boston: Weeks, Jordan.

Hall, Elizabeth S. 1849. A Mother's Influence. *The Mother's Assistant* 14 (February): 25–29.

Hall, G. Stanley. 1904. *Adolescence*. Vol. 2. New York: D. Appleton.

———. 1911. (Orig. 1904.) *Youth*. New York: D. Appleton.

Hambridge, Gove, and Dorothy Cooke Hambridge. 1930. Leisure to Live. *Ladies' Home Journal* 46 (May): 30, 141.

Hamilton, Marshall L. 1977. *Father's Influence on Children*. Chicago: Nelson-Hall.

Hardyment, Christina. 1983. *Dream Babies*. New York: Harper and Row.

Harris, Judith Rich. 1999. *The Nurture Assumption*. New York: Touchstone.

Harris, Marvin. 1979. *Cultural Materialism*. New York: Random House.

———. 1981. *America Now*. New York: Simon and Schuster.

———. 1999. *Theories of Culture in Postmodern Times*. Walnut Creek, CA: Alta Mira Press.

Hartmann, Heidi I. 1974. *Capitalism and Women's Work in the Home, 1900–1930*. Ph.D. diss., Yale University.

———. 1981. The Family as the Locus of Gender, Class, and Political Struggle: The Example of Housework. *Signs* (Spring): 366–394.

Harwell, H. I. 1816. *The Domestic Manual*. New London, CT: Samuel Green.

Hass, Nancy. 1999. We Are Family: Mom, Dad and Just Me. *New York Times*, October 25, p. B8.

Hayden, Dolores. 1982. *The Grand Domestic Revolution*. Cambridge, MA: MIT Press.

Heath, Mrs. Julian. 1915. The New Kind of Housekeeping. *Ladies' Home Journal* 32 (January): 2.

Heloise. 1967. *Heloise All Around the House*. New York: Pocket Books.

Heloise II. 1981. *Hints from Heloise*. New York: Avon.

Hochschild, Arlie. 1997. *The Second Shift*. New York: Avon Books.

Hoffman, Betty Hannah. 1963. I'm Going to Get a Job. *Ladies' Home Journal* 80 (July): 107.

Holcomb, Betty. 1998. *Not Guilty! The Good News About Working Mothers*. New York: Charles Scribner's Sons.

Honey, Maureen. 1976. Images of Women in the Saturday Evening Post, 1931–1936. *Journal of Popular Culture* 10(2): 352–358.

Horsfield, Margaret. 1998. *Biting the Dust*. New York: Picador.

Hoy, Suellen. 1996. *Chasing Dirt*. New York: Oxford University Press.

Hymowitz, Carol, and Michaele Weissman. 1978. *A History of Women in America*. New York: Bantam.

Jenkins, William D. 1979. Housewifery and Motherhood: The Question of Role Change in the Progressive Era. In *Woman's Being, Woman's Place*, ed. Mary Kelley, pp. 142–153. Boston: G. K. Hall.

Jhung, Paula. 1995. *How to Avoid Housework*. New York: Simon and Schuster.

Johnston, David Cay. 1999. Gap Between Rich and Poor Found Substantially Wider. *New York Times*, September 5, p. 16.

Kanner, Leo. 1941. *In Defense of Mothers*. Springfield, IL: Charles C. Thomas.

Kelly, Alice Lesch. 1999. For Employed Moms, the Pinnacle of Stress Comes After Work Ends. *New York Times*, June 13, sec. 15, p. 18.

Kenyon, Josephine. 1940a. Tired Mothers. *Good Housekeeping* 110 (January): 63, 77.

———. 1940b. Less Rigid Schedules for Babies. *Good Housekeeping* 110 (February): 92.

Kessler-Harris, Alice. 1975. Stratifying by Sex: Understanding the History of Working Women. In *Labor Market Segmentation*, ed. Richard C. Edwards, Michael Reich, and David M. Gordon, pp. 217–242. Lexington, MA: D. C. Heath.

———. 1981. *Women Have Always Worked*. Old Westbury, NY: Feminist Press.

Key, Ellen. 1909. *The Century of the Child*. New York: C. P. Putnam.

———. 1914. *The Renaissance of Motherhood*. New York: C. P. Putnam.

Kinne, Helen, and Anna M. Cooley. 1919. *The Home and the Family*. New York: Macmillan.

Komarovsky, Mirra. 1953. *Women in the Modern World*. Boston: Little, Brown.

Kotelchuck, Milton. 1972. *The Nature of a Child's Ties to His Father*. Ph.D. diss., Harvard University.

Kraditor, Aileen S., ed. 1968. *Up from the Pedestal*. Chicago: Quadrangle.

Kreps, Juanita M. 1971. *Sex in the Marketplace*. Baltimore, MD: Johns Hopkins University Press.

Kuhn Anne L. 1947. *The Mother's Role in Childhood Education*. New Haven, CT: Yale University Press.

Kutscher, Ronald E. 1991. New BLS Projections. *Monthly Labor Review* 114: 3–16.

Kyrk, Hazel. 1933. *Economic Problems of the Family*. New York: Harper and Row.

Ladd-Taylor, Molly, ed. 1986. *Raising Baby the Government Way*. New Brunswick, NJ: Rutgers University Press.

———. 1995. *Mother-Work*. Champaign: University of Illinois Press.

Ladies' Home Journal. 1905. Editorial, January, p. 2.

Ladies' Magazine. 1840. Influence of Women—Past and Present 13: 245–246.

The Ladies' Museum. 1825. Maternity. (September 17): 31.

Lane, Rose Wilder. 1936. Women's Place Is in the Home. *Ladies' Home Journal* 53 (October): 18.

Lawlor, Julia. 1998. For Many Blue-Collar Fathers, Child Care Is Shift Work, Too. *New York Times*, April 26, sec. 3, p. 11.

Lazarre, Jane. 1976. *The Mother Knot*. New York: McGraw-Hill.

LeMasters, E. E. 1970. *Parents in America*. Homewood, IL: Dorsey.

Lerner, Gerda. 1979. *The Majority Finds Its Past*. New York: Oxford University Press.

Leslie, Eliza. 1845. *The House Book*. 8th ed. Philadelphia: Carey and Hart.

Levine, James. 1976. *Who Will Raise the Children?* Philadelphia: J. B. Lippincott.

——. 1999. The Other Working Parent. *New York Times*, March 4, p. A25.

Levine, James, and Todd L. Pittinsky. 1998. *Working Fathers*. San Diego: Harvest Books.

Levy, David M. 1943. *Maternal Overprotection*. New York: Columbia University Press.

Lewin, Tamar. 1998. Men Assuming Bigger Share at Home, New Survey Shows. *New York Times*, April 15, p. 16.

——. 1999. Father Awarded $375,000 in a Parental Leave Case. *New York Times*, February 3, p. 11.

Linder, Staffan. 1970. *The Harried Leisure Class*. New York: Columbia University Press.

Lindquist, Ruth. 1931. *The Family in the Present Social Order*. Chapel Hill: University of North Carolina Press.

Lopate, Carol. 1974. Ironies of the Home Economics Movement. *Edcentric* 31–32 (November): 40–42, 56.

Luker, Kristin. 1985. *Abortion and the Politics of Motherhood*. Berkeley: University of California Press.

Lundberg, Ferdinand, and Marynia Farnham. 1947. *Modern Woman: The Lost Sex*. New York: Harper and Brothers.

Lynd, Robert, and Helen Merrill Lynd. 1929. *Middletown*. New York: Harcourt, Brace.

McCarthy, Mary. 1963. *The Group*. New York. Harcourt, Brace, and World.

McClellan, Pam. 1995. *Don't Be a Slave to Housework*. Cincinnati: Betterway Books.

McKenna, Elizabeth Perle. 1998. *When Work Doesn't Work Anymore*. New York: Delta.

Mandle, Joan D. 1979. *Women and Social Change in America*. Princeton, NJ: Princeton University Press.

Mansfield, Edward. 1845. *The Legal Rights, Liabilities, and Duties of Women*. Salem, MA: John P. Jewett.

Margolis, Maxine L. 1976. In Hartford, Hannibal, and (New) Hampshire, Heloise Is Hardly Helpful. *Ms. Magazine* 9 (June): 28–36.

——. 1995. Blaming the Victim: Ideology and Sexual Discrimination in the Contemporary United States. *Anthropology: Annual Editions, 1994–95*. Guilford, CT: Duskin Publishing.

Marin, Rick. 2000. At-Home Fathers Step Out to Find They Are Not Alone. *New York Times*, January 2, pp. 1, 18.

Martin, M. Kay, and Barbara Voorhies. 1975. *Female of the Species*. New York: Columbia University Press.

Marwedel, Emma. 1887. *Conscious Motherhood*. Boston: D. C. Heath.

Mason, Karen O., Maris A. Vinovskis, and Tamara K. Hareven. 1978. Women's Work and the Life Course in Essex County, Massachusetts, 1880. In *Transitions: The Family and the Life Course in Historical Perspective*, ed. Tamara K. Hareven, pp. 187–216. New York: Academic Press.

Mather, Cotton. 1978. (Orig. 1741.) *Ornaments for the Daughters of Zion*. 3d ed. Delmar, NY: Scholars Facsimiles and Reprints.

Matthews, Glenna. 1987. *Just a Housewife*. New York: Oxford University Press.

Mazerik, A. G. 1945. Getting Rid of the Women. *Atlantic Monthly* 176 (June): 79–83.

Mead, Margaret. 1955. *Male and Female*. New York: Mentor.

——. 1962. A Cultural Anthropologist's Approach to Maternal Deprivation. In *Deprivation of Maternal Care: A Reassessment of Its Effects*, ed. Mary D. Ainsworth, pp. 45–62. Geneva: World Health Organization.

Mechling, Jay. 1975. Advice to Historians on Advice to Mothers. *Journal of Social History* 9(1): 44–63.

Meissner, Martin, Elizabeth W. Humphreys, Scott M. Meis, and William J. Scheu. 1975. No Exit for Wives: Sexual Division of Labor and the Cumulation of Household Demands. *Canadian Journal of Sociology and Anthropology* 12 (November): 424–439.

Mendelson, Cheryl. 1999. *Home Comforts*. New York: Scribner.

Meyer, Agnes E. 1950. Women Aren't Men. *Atlantic Monthly* 186 (February): 28–29.

———. 1955. Children in Trouble. *Ladies' Home Journal* 72 (March): 68–69, 204–216.

Milkman, Ruth. 1976. Women's Work and Economic Crisis: Some Lessons of the Great Depression. *Review of Radical Political Economics* 8(1): 73–97.

Miller, Daniel R., and Guy E. Swanson. 1958. *The Changing American Parent*. New York: John Wiley.

Minturn, Leigh, and William W. Lambert. 1964. *Mothers of Six Cultures*. New York: John Wiley.

Mishel, Lawrence, Jared Bernstein, and John Schmitt. 1999. *The State of Working America, 1998–1999*. Economic Policy Institute. Ithaca, NY: Cornell University Press.

Mohr, James C. 1978. *Abortion in America*. New York: Oxford University Press.

Moore, Didi. 1981. The Only-Child Phenomenon. *New York Times Magazine*, January 18, pp. 26–27, 45–48.

Morgan, Marabel. 1975. *The Total Woman*. New York: Pocket Books.

Morris, Richard Brandon. 1930. *Studies in the History of American Law*. New York: Columbia University Press.

Mungean, Frank, and John Gray. 1994. *A Guy's Guide to Pregnancy*. Hillsboro, OR: Beyond Words Publishing Company.

Nelson, Kevin. 1998. *The Daddy Guide*. Lincolnwood, IL: NTC Contemporary Publishing.

New York Times. 1999. Till Dust Do Us Part. January 28, p. F3.

Norton, Mary Beth. 1980. *Liberty's Daughters*. Boston: Houghton Mifflin.

Norton, Mary Beth, and Carol Ruth Berkin. 1979. "Women and American History." In *Women of America: A History*, ed. Carol Ruth Berkin and Mary Beth Norton, pp. 3–15. Boston, 1979.

Nye, F. Ivan, and Lois Wladis Hoffman. 1963. *The Employed Mother in America*. Chicago: Rand McNally.

Oakley, Ann. 1974. *The Sociology of Housework*. New York: Pantheon.

———. 1976. *Woman's Work: The Housewife, Past and Present*. New York: Vintage.

Olds, Sally Werdkos. 1975. *The Mother Who Works Outside the Home*. New York: Child Study Press.

O'Neill, Molly. 1999. "What Would Martha Say?" The *New York Times Magazine*, May 16, pp. 145–146.

O'Neill, William J. 1971. *Everyone Was Brave*. Chicago: Quadrangle.

Oppenheimer, Valerie. 1970. *The Female Labor Force in the United States*. Population Monograph 5. Berkeley, Los Angeles, London: University of California Press.

Parents' Magazine. 1841. The Responsibility of Mothers. 1 (March): 156.

Parke, Ross D., and Armin A. Brot. 1999. *Throwaway Dads*. Boston: Houghton Mifflin.

Parkinson, C. Northcote. 1957. *Parkinson's Law and Other Studies in Administration*. Boston: Houghton Mifflin.

Parloa, Maria. 1905a. How I Plan a Week's Work Without a Servant. *Ladies' Home Journal* 22 (January): 31.

———. 1905b. How I Keep My House Clean and Sweet. *Ladies' Home Journal* 22 (February): 40.

Patterson, Alicia. 1962. Address to the Radcliffe Alumnae Association. Reprinted in *Harper's* 225 (October): 123.

Peters, Joan K. 1998. *When Mothers Work*. Reading, MA: Perseus Books.

Petersen, Melody. 1999. Working Mother Regains Custody of Two Children. *New York Times*, July 15, p. C10.

Pinkham, Mary Ellen, and Pearl Higginbotham. 1979. *Mary Ellen's Best of Helpful Hints*. New York: Warner.

Pittman, Joe, and David Blanchard. 1996. The Effects of Work History and Timing of Marriage on the Division of Household Labor. *Journal of Marriage and the Family* 58, p. 88.

Pogrebin, Letty Cottin. 1974. The Working Woman: Working Mothers. *Ladies' Home Journal* 91 (August): 60–62.

———. 1978. Rethinking Housework. In *Feminist Perspectives on Housework and Child Care*, ed. Amy Swerdlow, pp. 49–60.

———. 1980. A Partnership Plan for Parents Who Work (or: How to Bring Dad More into the Act and Give Mom a Break). *Ladies' Home Journal* 97 (October): 152–154.

Politt, Katha. 2000. Home Discomforts. *The Nation*, January 24.

Popenoe, David. 1996. *Life Without Father*. New York: Free Press.

Pruett, Kyle. 1987. *The Nurturing Father*. New York: Warner Books.

———. 2000. *Fatherneed*. New York: Free Press.

Pruette, Lorine. 1972. (Orig. 1924.) *Women and Leisure: A Study of Social Waste*. New York: Arno.

Radl, Shirley. 1973. *Mother's Day Is Over*. New York: Charterhouse.

Rainwater, Lee, Richard P. Coleman, and Gerald Handel. 1959. *Workingman's Wife*. New York: Oceana.

Reid, Margaret. 1934. *Economics of Household Production*. New York: John Wiley.

Ribble, Margaret A. 1943. *Rights of Infants*. New York: Columbia University Press.

———. 1965. *Rights of Infants*. Rev. ed. New York: Columbia University Press.

Richards, Ellen Swallow. 1914. *The Cost of Cleanness*. New York: John Wiley.

Richardson, Anne E. 1929. The Woman Administrator in the Modern Home. *Annals of the American Academy of Social Sciences* 143 (May): 21–32.

Robinson, John P. 1980. Housework Technology and Household Work. In *Women and Household Labor*, ed. Sarah Fenstermaker Berk, pp. 53–67. Beverly Hills, CA: Sage.

Roe, Constance. 1944. Can the Girls Hold Their Jobs in Peacetime? *Saturday Evening Post* 216 (September): 28–39.

Rollin, Betty. 1972. Motherhood: Who Needs It? In *The Future of the Family*, ed. Louise Kapp Howe, pp. 69–82. New York: Simon and Schuster.

Roosevelt, Theodore. 1905. The American Woman as Mother. Address before the National Congress of Mothers. Reprinted in the *Ladies' Home Journal* 22 (July): 34.

Rossi, Alice S. 1971. (Orig. 1964.) Equality Between the Sexes: An Immodest Proposal. In *Roles Women Play*, ed. Michele Hoffnung Garskof, pp. 145–164. Belmont, CA: Brooks/Cole.

Rothman, Sheila M. 1978. *Woman's Proper Place*. New York: Basic Books.

Rupp, Leila J. 1978. *Mobilizing Women for War*. Princeton, NJ: Princeton University Press.

Ryan, Mary P. 1975. *Womanhood in America*. New York: New Viewpoints.

———. 1979. Femininity and Capitalism in Antebellum America. In *Capitalist Patriarchy and the Case for Socialist Feminism*, ed. Zillah R. Eisenstein, pp. 151–168. New York: Monthly Review Press.

Schaffer, Rudolph. 1977. *Mothering*. Cambridge, MA: Harvard University Press.

Scharf, Lois. 1980. *To Work and to Wed*. Westport, CT: Greenwood.

Schroedel, Jean Ruth. 2000. *Is the Fetus a Person?* Ithaca, NY: Cornell University Press.

Schuler, Loring A. 1928. Homebuilders. *Ladies' Home Journal* 45 (January): 32.

———. 1929a. Experience. *Ladies' Home Journal* 46 (February): 30.

———. 1929b. Editorial. *Ladies' Home Journal* 46 (March): 34.

Scott-Maxwell, Florida. 1958a. Should Mothers of Young Children Work? *Ladies' Home Journal* 75 (November): 58–59, 158–160.

———. 1958b. Women Know They Are Not Men. *Ladies' Home Journal* 75 (November): 60–61, 166.

Sears, Robert R., Eleanor E. Maccoby, and Harry Levin. 1957. *Patterns of Child Rearing*. Evanston, IL: Row, Peterson.

Segal, Julius, and Herbert Yahraes. 1978. *A Child's Journey*. New York: McGraw-Hill.

Sharlet, Jeff. 1999. Martha Stewart Gives Scholars a Way to Discuss Class, Domestic Fantasy and Frosting. *Chronicle of Higher Education*, November 19, p. A22.

Sicherman, Barbara. 1975. *Signs* 1 (Winter): 461–485.

Sigourney, Lydia. 1838. *Letters to Mothers*. Hartford: Hudson and Skinner.

———. 1841. *Letters to Young Ladies*. 6th ed. New York: Harper and Brothers.

Sirageldin, Ismail. 1969. *Non-Market Components of National Income*. Survey Research Center. Ann Arbor: University of Michigan Press.

Skelsey, Alice. 1970. *The Working Mother's Guide to Her Home, Her Family and Herself*. New York: Random House.

Sklar, Kathryn Kish, ed. 1977. (Orig. 1841.) Introduction. In *A Treatise on Domestic Economy*, ed. Catherine E. Beecher, pp. v–xviii. New York: Schocken.

Skold, Karen Beck. 1980. The Job He Left Behind: American Women in the Shipyards during World War II. In *Women, War, and Revolution*, ed. Carol R. Berkin and Clara M. Lovert, pp. 55–75. New York: Holmes and Meier.

Slade, Margot. 1997. Have Pump, Will Travel: Combining Breast-feeding and a Career. *New York Times*, December 14, sec. 3, p. 12.

Slater, Peter Gregg. 1977. *Children in the New England Mind*. Hamden, CT: Archon.

Slater, Philip. 1974. *Earthwalk*. New York: Anchor.

———. 1976. *Pursuit of Loneliness*. Rev. ed. Boston: Beacon.

Smart, Mollie Stevens, and Russell Cook Smart. 1946. *It's a Wise Parent*. New York: Charles Scribner's Sons.

Smith, Daniel Scott. 1974. Family Limitation, Sexual Control, and Domestic Feminism in Victorian America. In *Clio's Consciousness Raised*, ed. Mary Hartmann and Lois W. Banner, pp. 119–136. New York: Harper and Row.

Smith, Hugh. 1796. *Letters to Married Women on Nursing and the Management of Children*. 2d ed. Philadelphia: Mathew Carey.

Smuts, Robert W. 1971. *Women and Work in America*. New York: Schocken.

Spangler, Doug. 1994. *Fatherhood: An Owner's Manual*. Richmond, VA: Fabus Publishing.

Spitz, René. 1965. *The First Year of Life*. New York: International Universities Press.

Spock, Benjamin. 1968. (Orig. 1946.) *Baby and Child Care*. Rev. and enlarged ed. New York: Pocket Books.

————. 1972. Women and Children: Male Chauvinist Spock Recants—Almost. In *The Future of the Family*, ed. Louise Kapp Howe, pp. 151–158. New York: Simon and Schuster.

————. 1976. *Baby and Child Care*. Rev. and updated ed. New York: Pocket Books.

Spruill, Julia C. 1938. *Women's Life and Work in the Southern Colonies*. Chapel Hill: University of North Carolina Press.

Stendler, Celia B. 1950. Sixty Years of Child Training Practices. *Journal of Pediatrics* 36: 122–134.

Stevenson, Mary. 1975. Women's Wages and Job Segregation. In *Labor Market Segmentation*, ed. Richard C. Edwards, Michael Reich, and David M. Gordon, pp. 243–255. Lexington, MA: D. C. Heath.

Strasser, Susan M. 1982. *Never Done: A History of American Housework*. New York: Pantheon.

Sunley, Robert. 1963. Early Nineteenth-Century American Literature on Child Rearing. In *Childhood in Contemporary Cultures*, ed. Margaret Mead and Martha Wolfenstein, pp. 150–167. Chicago: University of Chicago Press.

Sullivan, Andrew. 1998. Going Down Screaming. *New York Times Magazine*, October 11, pp. 46–91.

Talbot, Margaret. 1996. Les Très Riches Heures de Martha Stewart. *New Republic* 214 (May 13): 30.

————. 1999. The Little White Bombshell. *New York Times Magazine*, July 11, pp. 38–61.

Thom, D. A. 1925. *Child Management*. Children's Bureau Publication 143. Washington, DC: Government Printing Office.

Thompson, Dorothy. 1939. If I Had a Daughter. *Ladies' Home Journal* 56 (September): 4.

————. 1940. It's a Woman's World. *Ladies' Home Journal* 57 (July): 25.

Thompson, E. P. 1967. Time, Work Discipline, and Industrial Capitalism. *Past and Present* 38 (December): 56–97.

Thompson, Roger. 1974. *Women in Stuart England and America*. Boston: Routledge & Kegan Paul.

Thurow, Lester C. 1999. The Boom That Wasn't. *New York Times*, January 18, p. 19.

Toffler, Alvin. 1970. *Future Shock*. New York: Random House.

Trall, Russell Thacher. 1874. *The Mother's Hygienic Handbook*. New York: S. R. Wells.

Tryon, Milton Rolla. 1917. *Household Manufactures in the United States, 1640–1860*. Chicago: University of Chicago Press.

Uchitelle, Louis. 1999a. The American Middle Class, Just Getting By. *New York Times*, August 1, sec. 3, pp. 1, 13.

————. 1999b. As Labor Pool Shrinks, a New Supply is Tapped. *New York Times*, December 20, p. C4.

Ulrich, Laurel Thatcher. 1979. Vertuous Women Found: New England Ministerial Literature, 1668–1735. In *A Heritage of Her Own*, ed. Nancy F. Cott and Elizabeth H. Pleck, pp. 58–80. New York: Touchstone.

United States Department of Labor. 1975. *Handbook on Women Workers*. Washington, DC: Government Printing Office.

————. 1980. *Perspectives on Working Women*. Washington, DC: Government Printing Office.

————. 1998. *20 Leading Occupations of Employed Women (1997)*. Washington, DC: Women's Bureau.

References

71

———. 1999. *Facts on Working Women*. Washington, DC: Women's Bureau.

Vanek, Joann. 1974. Time Spent on Housework. *Scientific American* 231 (May): 116–120.

———. 1978. Housewives as Workers. In *Women Working*, ed. Ann H. Stromberg and Shirley Harkess, pp. 392–414. Palo Alto, CA: Mayfield.

Van Gelder, Lawrence. 1979. Time Spent on Housework Declines. *New York Times*, May 22, part 3, p. 10.

Wade, Mary L. 1901. Refined Life on Small Incomes; or, The Woman Who Does Her Own Work. *Proceedings of the Third Lake Placid Conference on Home Economics*, pp. 95–102. Lake Placid, NY.

Wadsworth, Benjamin. 1972. (Orig. 1712.) The Well-ordered Family, or, Relative Duties. In *The Colonial American Family: Collected Essays*, pp. 1–121. New York: Arno.

Walker, John Brisben. 1898. Motherhood as a Profession. *The Cosmopolitan* 25 (May): 89–93.

Walker, Katherine E., and Margaret F. Woods. 1976. *Time Use: A Measure of Household Production of Family Goods and Services*. Washington, DC: American Home Economics Association.

Watson, John B. 1927. The Weakness of Women. *The Nation* 125 (July 6): 9–10.

———. 1928. *Psychological Care of Infant and Child*. New York: Norton.

Weisner, Thomas, and Ronald Gallimore. 1977. My Brother's Keeper: Child and Sibling Caretaking. *Current Anthropology* 18(2): 169–190.

Weiss, Nancy Pottishman. 1977. Mother, the Invention of Necessity: Dr. Benjamin Spock's Baby and Child Care. *American Quarterly* 29 (Winter): 519–546.

Welter, Barbara. 1973. The Cult of True Womanhood: 1820–1860. In *The American Family in Sociohistorical Perspective*, ed. Michael Gordon, pp. 224–250. New York: St. Martin's.

West, Jane. 1974. (Orig. 1806.) *Letters to a Young Lady*. Vol. 3. New York: Garland.

West, Mrs. Max. 1971. (Orig. 1914.) *Infant Care*. Children's Bureau Bulletin 8. Reprinted in *Children and Youth in America: A Documentary History*. Vol. 2. 1866–1932, pp. 37–38. Cambridge, MA: Harvard University Press.

White, Burton L. 1975. *The First Three Years of Life*. Englewood Cliffs, NJ: Prentice-Hall.

Wiley, Bell. 1938. *So You're Going to Get Married!* Philadelphia: J. B. Lippincott.

Wilson, Margaret Gibbons. 1979. *The American Woman in Transition*. Westport, CT: Greenwood.

Wishy, Bernard. 1968. *The Child and the Republic*. Philadelphia: University of Pennsylvania Press.

Wolf, Anna W. M. 1941. *The Parents' Manual*. New York: Simon and Schuster.

Wortis, Rochelle. 1977. The Acceptance of the Concept of the Maternal Role by Behavioral Scientists: Its Effects on Women. In *Family in Transition*, ed. Arlene S. Skolnick and Jerome H. Skolnick, pp. 362–378. Boston: Little, Brown.

Wright, Erna. 1973. *Common Sense in Child Rearing*. New York: Hart.

Wylie, Philip. 1942. *Generation of Vipers*. New York: Farrar and Rinehart.

Yankelovich, Daniel. 1981. New Rules in American Life. *Psychology Today* 15 (April): 35–91.

Zillessen, Clara H. 1927. When Housework Is Not Drudgery. *Ladies' Home Journal* 44 (January): 127, 133.

Zuckerman, Michael. 1975. Dr. Spock: The Confidence Man. In *The Family in History*, ed. Charles E. Rosenberg, pp. 179–207. Philadelphia: University of Pennsylvania Press.

INDEX

DATE DUE